Humanity, you are so very precious in my eyes, and within my heart, and I love you.

It is my desire to do my part, no matter how large or however small, in the encouragement, and the positive upliftment, and advancement of humanity upon the earth. Although it isn't much, I hope that the donation I am able to offer, when my books are sold, will make a positive impact. I pray that it will always make a wonderful, life changing difference, within the lives of others, throughout countless nations.

It is my hope, that as long as I live, that I will be a positive, a giving, and an honorable human being upon the earth. I pray that I will be a light that shines in the darkness, and someone that is patient, that is kind, and loving to you.

I pray that my bloodline, will continue the work of suicide prevention, and that they will harness the passion and the determination that I will leave behind someday, in my fight against suicide and extreme mental stress, that can push humanity over the edge of life.

Let us all do our part to save someone's life. Let us **ALL** accept the fact; that suicide affects us all; and that no one, no nation is exempt from this horrific, this truly wretched disease, that is called suicide.

Dear LORD, it is truly, truly, truly, my sincere hope, it is my desire that is buried deep within my heart, that these words will never be spoken when I die,

"Victoria served no purpose upon the earth."

"I Am Going to Live"

I know very well that this book is a very small pebble, that is being thrown into the great oceans of the world. Nevertheless, it is my desire, it is my hope, that I will create a great and magnificent wave of change, in love, patience, and in hope and compassion, and in understanding, for humanity. Please never stop saying;

"I Will Not Cast My Precious Soul into the Grave"

"I Am Going to Live."

Sir or Madam, Young man or young lady, little boy or little girl, please know that you are loved. This stranger loves you; this stranger cares for you, far more than you could ever imagine, and wants you to live. Yes, I do love you, and GOD willing, if I am here twenty years from now, my love for you will still remain. I love you, and I beg of you, please hold on. Please do not give up on your precious life. Please be encouraged. Do not cast your precious soul into the grave. <u>"Do not commit suicide."</u>

I ENCOURAGE YOU

I ADMONISH YOU

AND I BEG OF YOU

PLEASE I BEG OF YOU

PRECIOUS SOUL THAT YOU ARE

"PLEASE LIVE"

About This Book

This humanities book was written to save countless lives throughout nations. It was written for your encouragement. It was written to encourage you, the individual that is going through mental stress, or mental health breakdowns. These words are here to also help you, who are thinking about committing suicide to stay alive. We are here to encourage your precious heart and mind. This book precious you, are an essential instrument in the fight against suicide To help accomplish our mission of suicide prevention. This book was created as a helpful tool for those who are battling depression, bipolar disorder, and any other circumstances or sicknesses, that could lead the individual to self-harm, to harm someone else, or to commit suicide. It will also help the family, friends, colleagues, and even the stranger, to understand, and to help those who are experiencing these emotions.

You will be taken on a journey of understanding and resolve. Suddenly the most difficult of circumstances will be made clear to you. Through your new found clarity, you will find much needed answers, solutions and workable options, that are for both you, who are experiencing the mental health breakdowns, you who are having suicidal thoughts and tendencies, and you the person that wants to help these individuals that are going through their struggles. This information inside this book, will help everyone that are involved, to come out on the other side, where you will feel encouraged, enlightened, and strengthened. You will understand the workings of suicidal thoughts and tendencies, and what to look for, and how to fight, and how to survive this season of life.

THIS READ IS NOT LIKE ANY OTHER

To my readers; please keep in mind that, this is not a normal read. This book was written as a weapon to fight against suicide. The words inside this book, are to counteract the influence of suicide. Simply put, we want to stop suicide in its track. There are times when doing something different is needed, to accomplish one's objective. There are those of us that are trying desperately to turn the tide against suicide, in our attempt to save as many lives as we can.

This book is not written like a normal novel. The aesthetic of this book is completely different also. There are bold words throughout this book, there are underlines throughout and constant repetitive words. All things to avoid when writing a book. Which is my point exactly. This is not your normal book, and so it will be very different in its writing, its aesthetic, and in its conversation also.

The bold letters, the words in uppercase, the repeated words, the underlined, all written to get your focus, your steadfast attention. The more often you and I sees something, is the more we will remember it. The more someone hears something, is the more they will hold on to it. The bold words, uppercase words, the repetitive words, the underlined words, that is the effort to ensure the information stays with you, and resonates also. Yes, this book is different, I agree.

About This Book, Continued

Even if your specific situation is not listed, you will find some form of reflection of yourself throughout this book, within many different pages. You will relate to the numerous circumstances that are listed, even if you have not experienced them yourself. You will find that the many different solutions that are listed, are enormously beneficial to your journey.

For the family members, the friends and the stranger, you will have this all-important tool, that will give you crucial insights, into your family member, your friend, your colleague, your neighbor and even the stranger's journey. You are desperate for answers, you are frantic for ways to help, but you are limited in ideas. This book will give you the solutions, to make a wonderful difference in someone's life, that is teetering on the edge, and they are in desperate need of help.

This book is the meaning of the word "oxymoron." Its simplicity, yet complexity at the same time, is a contradiction, but that is precisely what suicide is. Metaphorically speaking, how does a book that is about the military, about vacation spots, and about government, and about music, and travel, about day dreaming, about relationships, and about food, how can this very same book be about mental health, and suicide? The answer is simple; suicide affects the individuals in every area that is listed. Suicide is a very complex disease. These different individuals they are from different cultures, different intellect, diverse backgrounds, and different races, and varied financial position in life. They are from numerous nationalities, and various government rule. Whether that nation is a democracy, or a sovereign rule, or a totalitarian rule and all others, it makes no difference when it comes to suicide. The tentacles of suicide in its simplicity and complexity, affects them all.

About This Book, Continued

This book will reveal the ebbs and the flows of suicide. The ins and outs, the twist and the turns of suicide; and how you can untangle the emotional pitfalls, that could lead you, or the individual you are concerned about, towards suicide. This important blueprint, it outlines the actions that are needed, to untangle you, or the individual, and to get them far, far, far away, from the psychological minefield, that is suicide. This book will encourage you to live, implores you to live, begs you to live, and also shows you how to live.

There is extremely important information, for any nation's government, on how you can establish, or expand the strength of your Mental Health, and or, your nation's Suicide Prevention Program. There are also solutions/ideas, on what you can do, if there are limitations in funding. There are suggestions on how to acquire funding from within your nation, and from outside your nation also.

There is also encouragement for you, and your staff. The information here will resonate with you, and will help to reinforce your determination, to establish your nation's Suicide Prevention Program. Suddenly the impossible will seem possible; and the desperate need to create your nation's program, will ignite a fire within you, with a sense of purpose and urgency.

This book is the conduit, by which we will send help to you that are suicidal, or are going through mental stress, from afar. This book affords us the ability, to create changes within your heart and mind; and also ignite the determination within you, to fight for your life, knowing that you are being cheered on by us.

I Dedicate This Book To YOU

YOU are my GOD MOST HIGH, and I Love YOU, I adore YOU, I praise YOU O GOD.

I will never forget; YOU gave me the gizzada in the first grade. You knew I had no money Most High God. God Most High thank YOU. Everyone was in line with money in their hands, and I had none. I joined the line because I really, really wanted one.

I was in the middle of the line, and I just stared at the seller with a desperate hope that she would give me one. I did not want the other students to know that I had no money. Out of the blue, a teacher walked up to the line and gave me the money I needed, to pay for the gizzada. It was YOU Most High God. I know that it was YOU, and I will never forget YOU. Thank YOU God Most High, thank YOU. Heading towards fifty years since it happened, and I still remember as if it was yesterday. I will never forget YOU.

YOU Most High God have kept us; YOU have protected my Tony and I, and my bloodline; and I thank YOU, I thank YOU; I thank YOU Most High God; I thank YOU.

Laughter is mine; peace is mine, and hope is mine; and faith is mine also. Unknown strength has borne fruit, and the childish grin that left me long ago, has now returned back to me. The physical pain from my injury, that should have taken my mind is tolerable; and the fear of what is to come is no longer. Instead of fearing the unknown, I am instead very grateful for the here and now. Love, mercy, comfort, and kindness, and the unexplained wonderful joy that I feel, along with the quiet peace. They are all from YOU, God Most High. The ability to understand the time and the season, precious wisdom, I thank YOU, I Thank YOU, I thank YOU, and I am exceedingly, enormously, tremendously grateful. Yes repetitive, I know. Different words with the same meaning. I needed to emphasize how very grateful I am.

YOU are my best friend and my constant companion, and I would have it no other way. YOU are never far from me. YOU direct my path, and Most High God, the love, and the gratitude that I have for YOU, that I feel towards YOU, is so very intoxicating O GOD, and so very overwhelming.

YOU Most High God are my first love and my last. My first breath and my last breath belongs to YOU. Most High GOD, I love YOU, I love YOU, I love YOU God Most High Forever, for all eternity, I love YOU, I love YOU, I love YOU, and I appreciate YOU, and I thank YOU God Most High.

I THANK YOU

I THANK YOU

I THANK YOU

What would you do to stop someone from committing suicide?

What would you do to protect someone's mental health?

What would you do to save someone's life?

Would you lay it all on the line to save a precious soul?

Would you tell them it will not always be this difficult, and that they will overcome this very painful season in their lives?

Would you plead with them, would you beg them to hold on, and would you ask them to not give up on their precious life?

Would you tell them that they are not alone in their fight for their life, and that you are fighting for them also?

Would you shout? Would you speak softly?

Would you tell them they are precious beyond measure, whether they know it or not?

Would you repeat lifesaving information, over and over, and over again, to ensure that the information resonates within the person you are trying to save heart and mind?

Would you shower them with endearments, and admonish them about the importance of their precious life?

Would you be willing to step out of your comfort zone, your safe place, to save someone else's life?

Would you beg them, and would you plead with them to not remove their bloodline, and the bloodline of others from the earth?

To save someone's life from suicide, would you abandon the rules in writing, and instead, write in bold letters, underline sentences, and use quotation marks to emphasize the importance of your words? Or would you worry about the way it might look?

To prevent someone from committing suicide, would you write in a way that will grab their attention, even if it is unconventional, and means going against the norm?

What matters most to you, when it comes to suicide prevention? Does the norm matter the most? Or are you willing to swim upstream to save someone's life?

Would you share your personal anecdotes, to get them to understand that they are not alone?

Would you be willing to draw on analogies from your life, or someone else's life, to get your point across?

Would you encourage them? Would you get the individual to laugh, and would you cry with them also?

To save someone's life, would you be willing to take criticism from the crowd, because they do not agree with your way of encouraging someone?

Would you speak in metaphors, would you tell stories, and draw on ideas to ensure that this person will understand everything you are saying to them, in the hope that it will pull them back from the edge?

Would you call on the heavens to give you strength, and the know how, to not give up on this precious soul, but to instead, dig in with them for the long haul?

Would you do everything in your power, to help to restore their mental health, so as to prevent self-harm, and to save their precious life, so as to keep their precious soul upon the earth?

Some Nations, Suicide and Crisis Lifelines; Their Contact Information

UNITED STATES of AMERICA:
Call or text the **Suicide & Crisis Lifeline** at **988**, the 1-800-273-8255 has merged with **988** as of July 16, 2022. **Active-duty members and veterans, please press one** when the call is answered, or text to **838255**. Non-military, if you are unable to speak, or you are hearing impaired, you can send a text to the Crisis Text Line 24/7, at **741741**. You can also go to **988lifeline.org** website.

If Needed, Please Call the National Domestic Violence Hotline

The Hotline can be accessed via the nationwide number 1−800−799−SAFE (7233) or TTY 1−800−787−3224 or (206) 518-9361 (Video Phone Only for Deaf Callers). The Hotline provides service referrals to agencies **in all 50 states, Puerto Rico, Guam and the U.S. Virgin Islands.**

CANADA:
(1-833-456-4566) or, for residents of Quebec, 1 866 APPELLE (1-866-277-3553).

FRANCE:
SOS Help Boite Postale 43, Cedex 92101 Boulogne Contact by: - Phone Hotline: 01 46 21 46 46 Website: soshelpline.org Hours: Mon, Tues, Wed,

Thurs, Fri, Sat, Sun: 15:00 - 23:00
Suicide Ecoute Paris
Contact by: - Phone Hotline: 01 45 39 40 00
Website: suicide.ecoute.free.fr
Hours: Mon, Tues, Wed, Thurs, Fri, Sat, Sun:
E.P.E. idF. Fil Sante Jeunes
Paris Contact by: - Phone - E-mail:
Hotline: 0800 235 236
Website: filsantejeunes.com
Fédération S.O.S Amitié France
11, rue des Immeubles industriels
75011 Paris
(+33) (0)1 40 09 15 22,
Website: sos-amitie.com

GERMANY: 08001810771

UNITED KINGDOM:
Samaritans UK & ROI
National Contact by: Face to Face,
Phone, Letter and E-mail:
Hotline: +44 (0) 8457 90 90 90 (UK local
rate) Hotline: +44 (0) 8457 90 91 92
(UK minicom) Hotline: 1850 60 90 90 (ROl)
local rate Hotline: 1850 60 90 91 (ROl minicom)

Website: samaritans.org
E-mail Helpline: jo@samaritans.org,
Scotland, Breathing Space: Over the age of sixteen
0800 83 85 87 Scotland, Breathing Space: Under
the age of sixteen, 0800 1111

SAUDI ARABIA: 920033360

The psychological counseling call center. Or call the unified emergency number **(911).**

EGYPT: 7621602

JORDAN: 911

FINLAND:
040-5032199

SWEDEN: 031-711-2400

GREECE:
Suicide Intervention Line 1018

PHILIPPINES:
028969191

CYPRUS: 0-777-267

ESTONIA: 6-558-088

QATAR: Their Website Information

The free Helpline is accessed by calling 16000,

selecting Arabic or English and then by selecting option 4 for the Mental Health Helpline; all calls are treated in the strictest confidence

BAHRAIN: Their Website Information

999, covers all emergency services, i.e. fire, police, and ambulance

SPAIN: 914590050

ARGENTINA: 5402234930430

DENMARK: 4570201201

SWITZERLAND: 143

SOUTH KOREA:
Tel: +82 2 2203 0053 Korean Association for Suicide Protection (KASP)

SINGAPORE:
Toll Free1-800-221-4444

NORWAY: 4781533300

AUSTRIA: 017133374

JAMAICA:
1-888-NEW-LIFE (1-888-639-5433) The public awareness campaign,
'Speak Up, Speak Now."

CAYMAN ISLANDS:

The Mental Health Helpline 1-800-534-MIND (6463) operational from 9am until 5pm. The line will be available Monday to Friday.
Outside of these hours.

If you are contemplating suicide, or having a mental breakdown, please dial 911 or go to the Accident and Emergency Department immediately.

BARBADOS: 429-9999

HOLLAND: 09000767

UKRAINE:
0487-327715 / 0482 226565

NEW ZEALAND: 045861048

POLAND: 5270000

ITALY: 800860022

MEXICO: 5255102550

BRAZIL: 21-233-9191

ST. VINCENT: 809-456-1044

GUATEMALA: 502-254-1259

ARMENIA:
2-538-194 or 2-538-197

PORTUGAL: 239-72-10-10

UAE:
800-Hope/ 800-4673
Launched by the National Program for Happiness & Wellbeing in support of the National Campaign "volunteers.ae,"

Connect on WhatsApp also in Arabic, or in the English language.

JAPAN: 810352869090

MONACO:
112, For Medical Emergency

LITHUANIA: 8-800-2-8888

YUGOSLAVIA: 021-623-393

SRI LANKA: 1-692-909

CROATIA: 014833888

INDIA: 8888817666

If your nation is not listed within this book

It does not mean your nation does not have their mental health, and their suicide prevention assistance program. Perhaps in my search, I just could not find it. Please seek out the help that you are in need of from a hospital, or a mental health facility. These I believe, are your best options to get the help that you are desperately, desperately in need of, within your nation. Please speak with someone I beg of you; please tell them you are in need of help immediately, and when I say immediately, I mean immediately.

You are abroad, and you are facing a language barrier, and all else has failed

Please call your embassy, the staff I am certain will direct you to the much-needed help that you are desperately in need of.

You are out of time; you must get help now! And when I say now, I mean NOW!

I wholeheartedly beg of you, I plead with you, and I admonish you, precious soul that you are. You must do everything to keep the oxygen flowing inside your lungs, I encourage you, I beg of you. Your today is not your year from now, please hold on, **"PLEASE LIVE."** I implore you; you must live precious soul that you are. You must live, your help is on the way!

Please give me a moment, I will not forget about you I promise. I am going to have a short, but very, very important conversation with governments of nations. I am hoping to inspire them, into establishing their incredibly important, mental health, and their suicide prevention program also, for their citizens.

You precious soul that you are, are not the only one; there are countless others throughout many nations, that are suffering also. They too are in need of help, and are a part of this book. I pray that the effort within this book, will cross countless borders, and break through barriers; and create its own universal language, for all who are hurting, and are having mental breakdowns; including you, that are having suicidal thoughts and tendencies, and are in need of help. This book will encourage the hearts of those who are trying to help, or want to help also.

I pray that social media will grab hold and not let go of this book, in the most positive, the most uplifting and relentless way possible. I pray that my weakness of being a loner, will be helped by their tenacity, their desire to get these words out, to prevent someone from harming themselves, and to stop someone from committing suicide.

As the heart of men and women wax cold, I pray that this book will ignite the flames of patience, compassion, love and understanding, inside my readers hearts throughout nations. I pray that the embers of care for each other, that was dying out, will reignite, and burn bright like never before.

Why am I talking with nations and governments, instead of just talking with you?

If you are reading this book, and are asking, you are saying to yourselves, **"why is she talking to nations and governments, she should be talking to me if she is trying to save my life?"** My answer to you, precious souls that you are is this. Our goal, is to not only save you; we are attempting to save countless others throughout nations; who like you, are in danger of having a mental breakdown, or committing suicide.

For us to save you, and others; it takes a combined effort of many citizens throughout nations, and also governments both here and abroad; to prevent you and countless others from taking your lives, or having a mental breakdown, and causing great harm to yourselves and or others.

Without fail, there has to be an all-hands-on deck approach, to win the war against suicide and mental sickness. Our concerted effort is needed to keep you and others that are in danger of self-harm alive. We must **all** do our part, the government, citizens of nations, your family members, colleagues, friends, acquaintances, and the stranger. Everyone must do their part to save your precious life, and the lives of others; that are experiencing suicidal thoughts and wants to take their own lives, and perhaps the lives of others. We are **ALL** in this fight; to restore your mental health.

Here is an example for you. Although I, the author

wrote this book, you will notice I used **we,** many times over. To get the help that is within this book to you; it will take others like the printer, that will print this book, the publisher will get the words out, the distributor will get it to where it needs to go. There are countless agencies, and bookstores that are on and offline, and state and federal governments also.

(My hope springs eternal), that they too will use this blueprint, in their fight against suicide, both here and abroad. Yes, **we,** is correct, as in all of the above. we must combine our efforts to get you the help that you are in need of; so that we can keep you alive, and encouraged.

Within The United States of America, we have The Centers for Disease Control and Prevention, the (CDC). There is the very important, Department of Defense; for our active-duty Armed Forces. And The Department of Veterans Affairs. We also have The Veterans Health Administration for our Veterans.

We have the so very, very important, **988 Suicide & Crisis Lifeline;** for everyone. We also have the **24/7 Crisis Text Line, at 838255;** for our active-duty military, and the **741741 Text Line** for all others; including those who are unable to speak, or they are hearing impaired. **There is a dedicated staff, that is waiting to help you.**

There are Hospitals, and Mental Health Facilities that are both federal and local, and the covering that makes it all possible is the agency called **SAMHSA.**

The Substance Abuse and Mental Health Services Administration, also known as **(SAMHSA).**

The agency within the U.S. Department of Health and Human Services, that leads public health efforts to advance the behavioral health of the nation. "This abbreviated biography was taken from their website"

There is also **The Family Violence Prevention and Services Act, FVPSA.** Which is also within the U.S. Department of Health and Human Services.

All of the listed entities are a part of the shortened list of the **we,** that are in the fight to save your precious life; to ensure that you live out your years upon the earth. Some entities are connected, and some are not. There are those of us, that because of our personal experiences, **we** too have joined the fight to save your precious life.

One of those individuals just happens to be me, the author of this book. Sir or Madam, please know this, please believe this stranger when I say to you, **we** Sir or Madam, **we** young man or young woman, **we** are unwavering, and **we** are absolutely resolute inside this battle to save your precious life. Sir or Madam, you must hold on, please do not give up on your life, **"PLEASE LIVE."**

The Suicide Prevention hotline information, will be repeated, over, and over, and over again, throughout this book. The more you see it, is the more it will remain within your memory, and resonate with you.

Please everyone, never forget, that humanities mercy given, is humanities mercy received; and is the same exact precious mercy within humanity, that is continually passed on by the receivers

Translation? Mercy given to humanity, is mercy received by humanity, and is mercy passed on by humanity, once received. There are some of us that in gratitude, will ensure that this cycle never breaks.

LORD, please I pray, please let the words within this book soar high into the sky, please let these words swim oceans, and walk throughout valleys. Please cause these words inside this book to travel amongst men and women, and live within their hearts and their minds throughout nations I pray.

Please allow nations to embrace these words, and invite them over for breakfast, for tea, for lunch, and for brunch and dinner, and for supper I pray. Please allow these precious words to receive invitations from schools, from boardrooms, corporations and governments, from unions, and all others. I pray O GOD. Please allow these words to be invited on vacations, to parties, to get-togethers, and all else.

I pray O GOD, please cause these words to live with children, teens, young adults, adults and seniors alike throughout their journey. Please allow these words from this book, to comfort hearts and minds, long after I am no more. Please give these words life I pray, and I thank YOU O GOD. Forever grateful I am to YOU, and I will always be, I thank YOU.

For the nation that wishes to establish a suicide prevention program within their nation. For governments in foreign lands.

Please see the **W**orld **H**ealth **O**rganization website, for their suicide prevention program called, **"LIVE LIFE."** The **W.H.O.** also offers implementation instructions, for establishing the program within any nation. Here is their abbreviated biography taken from their website, **"We champion health and a better future for all:** Dedicated to the well-being of all people and guided by science, the World Health Organization leads and champions global efforts to give everyone, everywhere an equal chance to live a healthy life."

You can also go to The **U**nited **N**ations **C**hildren's **F**und, **UNICEF** website; for help in creating your suicide prevention program for your children, and for your adolescents within your nation. The abbreviated biography information below; was taken from their website, "**UNICEF** works in the world's toughest places to reach the most disadvantaged children and adolescents and to protect the rights of every child, everywhere. Across more than 190 countries and territories, we do whatever it takes to help children survive, thrive and fulfill their potential, from early childhood through adolescence. The world's largest provider of vaccines, we support child health and nutrition, safe water and sanitation, quality education and skill building, HIV prevention and treatment for mothers and babies, and the protection of children and adolescents from violence and exploitation."

The **WHO** and the **UNICEF** organization, both have a universal framework for any individual that wishes to establish their suicide prevention program. I am certain their information will help any nations' program; no matter the location of that nation or their structure. I, with an abundance of earnest desire, and also motivation; encourages every single nation's Ministry of Health, and all other departments of government that oversees its citizen's health and mental wellbeing, to take on this worthy cause. Please take on this extraordinarily noble endeavor of establishing your suicide prevention, and mental health program; with much passion and fervor.

Suicide and mental health affect every nation. There is not a nation that is exempt from its citizens trying to commit suicide. There is not a nation that exists upon this earth where their citizens have not experienced some form of mental health crisis, or mental stress. This is a bold statement, yes, I know. It takes bold, unwavering, determined statements to save and to restore lives. I address you, Mr. or Madam President, Mr. or Madam Prime Minister, Your Highnesses', Sirs and Madams, make no mistake, **"WE"** are all in this fight together.

If the funds to establish your programs are just not available, please do not hesitate, please ask your citizens for help in the establishment of your suicide prevention and mental health program. I encourage every nation, no matter the size of the country or the availability of funds. Please do not underestimate your citizens, and their patriotism. You should trust their willingness to make a difference within their homeland. Your citizens, if at all possible, will help.

Ask your corporations, and your business owners, your philanthropists and your conglomerates within your nation to do their part. Have a conversation with them about the action called, **"Noblesse Oblige." As in, those who are in lofty places; are to do their part to make a difference within society, for humanity.** Please ask them for help in establishing your Mental Health, and your Suicide Prevention Program; I believe you will be shocked at the outpouring of help that you will receive. Never underestimate the ability of any nation's citizen, when it comes to a noble cause, they will always rise to meet the moment without fail. Please give your citizens a chance to help.

If your nation's citizens and businesses are just not financially equipped to help, and enough funding is not within your nation. Please seek out help from wealthier nations. Please put together an envoy, whose sole responsibility, is to search for, or travel to wealthier nations; to get the help that is needed; to build your mental health, and also your suicide prevention program. In days of old, men and women sailed on ships for many weeks if not months to get to other nations; to bring back the desperately needed help for their citizens, for their homeland or to represent their nation's interest abroad. Your nation's help is a three, five, seven or nineteen-hours flight away. Some of you will not have to travel to get the help you need. some governments, or businesses and even the large conglomerates house their grants online; and allow you the ability to apply online. Please give attention to their rules. There is one particular rule that many may overlook. The rule states that you must be within a specific number of miles from their head office; to apply for help. Yes, I agree, their product (s) are on sale throughout your nation, but nevertheless; that rule could prevent you from getting funding, I totally get it.

Use your embassy as a facilitator also. Your embassy staff that is within that specific nation, more likely than not, may have the information on the individuals to contact when it comes to these subject matters, Mental Health and also Suicide Prevention. Ask them for help, these subject matters could create the much-needed partnership that your nation has been searching/hoping for with the host nation.

Your embassy staff would be overjoyed; that they assisted in bringing home funding to their homeland, for their mental health and their suicide prevention programs. Please keep this in mind as you go about your search for financial support for your programs for your nation. You Sir or Madam are not in search of help for something that is farfetched, unrealistic and unknown to the people you intend to meet when it comes to funding. At this juncture, every nation understands the extreme urgency; when it comes to mental health and suicide prevention. Citizens from every nation are having mental health breakdowns, and or, suicidal thoughts and or tendencies. This horrible epidemic of suicide, and also mental health breakdowns has crossed over borders, and it has jumped our lines of defenses, and it now involves an enormous cross-section of people, nations, races, backgrounds and also intellect, it runs the gamut. Before you Sir or Madam enters the room/meeting, whether through your in-person consultation, or through a meeting website online, the information as to why you are asking for help to establish your mental health, and your suicide prevention program, is unquestionably known to the representatives of the funding nation. They too you can be certain, are neck deep within the wretched fight; to save their citizens lives. They I am all but certain, will completely understand your need for help, in establishing this essential program within your homeland.

You can do this, this work is for your nation. Your success will be ground breaking, it will be history in the making; and you Sir and or Madam, will be recognized for this life changing work. Tell yourself, that this effort of yours, is for your nation's citizens. Please improvise, please overcome and get the job done, I believe in you. Your precious citizens' hope; of having dedicated treatment centers, that they can turn to for mental health treatment is up to you. Their hope of having suicide prevention help, is contingent on you/your team finding/getting the much-needed funding. You cannot fail them, and you must not fail them. I beg of you, whomever you are, please build your mental health, and your suicide prevention program. Your precious citizens and I, thank you in advance, you Sir and or Madam; are your nation's treasure. **"I thank you for your hard work, and for your selfless dedication to your nation's citizens."**

Table of Content

Humanity	PAGE 1
"I AM Going to Live"	PAGE 3
About This Book	PAGE 5
I dedicate this book to YOU	PAGE 11
What would you do to stop someone from committing suicide?	PAGE 13
The Suicide and Crisis Lifelines	PAGE 17
If your nation is not listed within this book	PAGE 25
Why am I talking with nations and governments, instead of just talking with you?	PAGE 27
For the nation that wishes to establish a suicide prevention program within their nation. For governments in foreign lands,	PAGE 31
Table of Content	PAGE 36
To you, our readers, I have a huge favor to ask of you.	PAGE 43
ATTENTION and VERY IMPORTANT	**Page 46**

Table of Content, Continued

PLEASE NOTE	**PAGE 47**
CHAPTER 1: The Urgency is Upon You	PAGE 49
CHAPTER 2: Your Bloodline	PAGE 55
CHAPTER 3: If you do not believe the information, here is your proof	PAGE 63
CHAPTER 4: "Your experiences are not my experiences," you are saying	PAGE 70
CHAPTER 5: Here are some solutions	PAGE 74
CHAPTER 6: Do not rely on others, whose intentions towards you; are destructive. Your hurt is their pleasure	PAGE 78
CHAPTER 7: You must protect your precious heart at all cost	PAGE 87
CHAPTER 8: You have lost your home, car, and or job, or your resources are less than half of what it was	PAGE 89
CHAPTER 9: You have lost in an enterprise of some kind, and you are unable to deal with the failure of your endeavor(s); and so, you want to die	PAGE 95

Table of Content, Continued

CHAPTER 10: You are going through circumstances that are not listed	**PAGE 100**
CHAPTER 11: You are under age, and you do not believe that you can find your way out of the situation that you are in	**PAGE 104**
CHAPTER 12: Someone caused you pain, please forgive them	**PAGE 109**
CHAPTER 13: You have been sentenced to incarceration; for violent or nonviolent crime(s)	**PAGE 114**
CHAPTER 14: You are growing older, and you hate it	**PAGE 118**
CHAPTER 15: The death of a loved one, they died without any warning	**PAGE 121**
CHAPTER 16: Suicide is contagious; yes, suicide can absolutely be passed on psychologically to others	**PAGE 126**
CHAPTER 17: If you feel yourself moving towards suicide, you must halt your forward momentum	**PAGE 129**
CHAPTER 18: You are going through postpartum depression	**PAGE 132**

Table of Content, Continued

CHAPTER 19: You are lonely without an intimate relationship, you want to take your life	PAGE 140
CHAPTER 20: You are a millionaire, you are a billionaire, and depression haunts you	PAGE 146
CHAPTER 21: You are stalking someone with the intended result being murder and suicide	PAGE 158
CHAPTER 22: Someone an ignoble human being, used the pretense of love, to take advantage of you	PAGE 162
CHAPTER 23: Addiction to drugs/addiction to death	PAGE 165
CHAPTER 24: To decent and honorable Protectors, from government and other agencies throughout	PAGE 182
CHAPTER 25: You are being abused by a partner, your life is in danger	PAGE 186
CHAPTER 26: Recovering from the damages you have done to others. Recovering from the damages you have done to yourself. forgive yourself	PAGE 191

Table of Content, Continued

Recovering from the embarrassment by yours or someone else's actions	PAGE 191
CHAPTER 27: You must not use the pain inflicted upon you by your victimizer; to find others innocent or guilty	PAGE 197
CHAPTER 28: You contemplating suicide; is because you lost an opportunity within your career/employment	PAGE 207
CHAPTER 29: Holding someone hostage, with threats of suicide if they leave	PAGE 230
CHAPTER 30: For the precious soul that is unable to read, they are illiterate.	PAGE 237
CHAPTER 31: To you the owner, the manager, or the human resource representative, or any other person that is doing the hiring	PAGE 241
CHAPTER 32: You are entrenched within the ghetto, or you live in a shantytown, or are without any form of resource. You hate and pity your life; you want to die.	PAGE 245
You cannot return, jealousy could kill you	PAGE 265

Table of Contents, Continued

<u>CHAPTER 33: Our Armed Forces and Their *********<u>Family Members.</u>*********	PAGE 271
CHAPTER 34: You must see and recognize suicide for what it is	PAGE 300
CHAPTER 35: The death that was caused by a recreational adventure, or a social media challenge	PAGE 306
Chapter 36: You want to commit suicide; you want to end your life, because of an internet, or a phone scammer	PAGE 317
CHAPTER 37: Do not underestimate the importance of taking time off for yourself	PAGE 323
CHAPTER 38: Do not stereotype suicide, this I promise, will be one of the biggest mistakes you will ever make	PAGE 326
CHAPTER 39: Sorrow is the spear that pierces deep within us all, and it creates mountains of fear, and silence some of us	PAGE 331
CHAPTER 40: Your life's journey, is not just about you, it involves many others also	PAGE 341
CHAPTER 41: A conversation and questionnaire about your journey to suicide	PAGE 349

Table of Contents, Continued

CHAPTER 42: The murderers that walks amongst us	PAGE 364
CHAPTER 43: Do not allow the numbers to influence you. It does not matter if it is one, or one thousand, do not join them in any suicide pact	PAGE 377
CHAPTER 44: Humanity, your kindness is medicine to someone's precious soul	PAGE 381
CHAPTER 45: My closing statement, along with my thank you, my heart-felt sincere apologies, and my request and acknowledgements also	PAGE 384
My final words to you: Did I forget anything	PAGE 406
Humanities mercy: Mercy given	PAGE 413
Please give me a smile: Before I go, please give me a smile	PAGE 414
Distributed by: Copyright Protected, ISBN, website, and contact information	PAGE 415
Humanity I say to you: Humanity, you must live	PAGE 416

To you, our readers, I have a huge favor to ask of you

Please do not choose a topic that relates to only your circumstance from the tables of contents to read. Instead, please start at the beginning and stay to the end. My request is a fundamental desire that you, Sir or Madam, young lady or you, young man, will take something from every circumstance that is listed, to help yourself.

The active-duty member, and the individual that is suffering from depression due to the loss of a loved one, the veteran or billionaire, and the individuals that are going through postpartum depression, along with the middle class, the rich, and the poor who have lost their possessions at the same time, could all have some form of symptoms in common. Our protective services members, of the CIA, or FBI or Police, could have someone that is struggling with mental health at the same time.

Devastation is devastation, regardless of the person or their status. I need my readers to read this book in its completeness, and please take something from every situation to help yourself, or someone else. Reading this book in its entirety, instead of you only reading the area that lists your circumstance; will not only equip you to help yourself, it will also give you a deep understanding, that you are not alone within your struggles.

This entire book is for the individual that is going

through a mental health breakdown, or stress. It is for you the individual that is now experiencing suicidal thoughts, and or tendencies, and also for the family members and other loved ones, or the stranger, that is trying to help this person.

Reading it in its entirety, will give you the family members, the loved ones, friends and acquaintances, or even the stranger; the information that is sorely needed; to identify, and to help the individual that is experiencing the mental breakdown, or mental stress, or those who are having suicidal thoughts and or tendencies. It will add to, or refine your ability, to help someone that is going through their struggles.

There is no specific order to the circumstances that are listed within this book. Life is the same way. The person who just lost a loved one, and the active-duty member returning home, or the veteran, is going through at the same exact time. Pain and heartache have no schedule, and there is no sense, there is no order to it. The same is in the way that I have written the circumstances. There is no order to it, and any situation can be located at any place within this book.

That is the same way that our struggles, and our sorrows can occur, it can overwhelm us at any place, at any juncture within our lives. The billionaire is incapable of buying a schedule that prevents them from suffering loss, that prevents he or she from suffering devastation. The fireman does not have the ability to ensure his house will never burn down. The farmer does not have the ability to prevent loss of crop at all times, and the postman is not capable of preventing the loss of his mails. A cardiologist who is a heart doctor, to the dismay of their family has suffered a heart attack. We will always have with us, some amount of unpredictability within our journey. Loss, sorrow, and disappointments have no schedule, it has no order to it, and none of us are exempt.

Pain, heartache, and sorrow or loss does not come with a schedule, there is no rationale, no structural order to it. Today you could have the world at your fingertips, and tomorrow make no mistake, it could be destroyed. Sorrow does not function within any precise order, as in today is the veteran and next it is the billionaire. NO! We are all struggling at the same time.

The order of this book emphasizes just that. Any circumstance can happen at any time, at any season within our lives, this book is a reflection of just that. It is a reflection of our daily life, throughout you and I everyday living. Sometimes winter arrives early, spring is late, and the summer is shorter than what we expected. Sometimes the harvest is less or much more than what we expected; and this is all about the unpredictability of life.

Things are not always in order, or where we expect it to be. The same is in this book. Your situation could be throughout this book, in the middle of this book, at the beginning or the end, or a little bit of you is in every circumstance that is listed. Please start at the beginning and read all the way through to the end.

Attention

If you are **outside** The United States of America, and are not a United States citizen, **please do not use** the helpline numbers that are listed throughout this book. Instead, please look at the international information I have listed on pages 17-23. If your nation is not listed, as I mentioned before, please seek out your local area assistance that is within your nation, for the much-needed help that you are so very, very desperately in need of immediately.

Please go to a mental health facility or a hospital, speak to the stranger if you must. You must get the help that you are in need of to save your precious life, and you must get it now! Please move with tremendous accelerated urgency!

Here is some very important information for you to know

We do not want to discourage you in any way, while you are going through your difficult season in life. During your struggles with mental stress, or mental breakdowns, or while you are contemplating suicide, we are well aware that any misinformation, or any form of unintended misunderstanding, could push you over the edge. We absolutely do not want this to happen to you. Please read the information in our, **"please note section, next."** We thank you, and we encourage your heart and mind, and we love you. Precious soul that you are please, **"You Must Live."**

Please Note

We are <u>not affiliated</u> with any of the Suicide & Crisis lifeline. We Sir or Madam, young man or young lady, are simply a part of humanity, and we care. We are doing our part in helping you to keep your soul upon this earth. We are not a member of any hospital staff, we are not a member of any mental health institution, or program, we are independent. We Sir or Madam, young man or young woman, we simply care for you. I the author is someone that was suicidal for many years, and have overcome the journey of suicidal thoughts and tendencies, after tremendous sorrow.

I survived the journey, I made it out alive. It is with my experiences and added blueprint, combined with others that care, that we have now stepped into the battle to help to save your precious life. I believe that this powerful, this priceless and revealing blueprint of my journey, will help you. I believe it will change your life, in a positive way. This book will help you to find your starting point. It will help you to plant your feet in the most steadfast way, and fight to save your precious life. No matter your age, whether you are child, a teen, or in your twenties, thirties, or older, you have a life to live, and this book is your restoration.

I want you to use this book, to help you to save your precious life. These words exist to pull you out of your dark places, and to encourage your heart and mind. Grab hold and take this journey of recovery, have this conversation with me, please save your precious life. You must survive this dark and deadly place. I beg of you. Please, the precious, precious soul that you truly are, I encourage you. I beg of you, I implore you, and I even admonish you, PLEASE SURVIVE.

"PLEASE LIVE I BEG OF YOU!"

Please Note: The reason we sell our books

If you are wondering, why do we charge for our books, why not give it away for free? My answer to you is this. The first batch printed <u>is self and family funded.</u> The money collected from the much-needed sales, of our suicide prevention books, will pay for more books to be printed. The profits will help those who are in need, it will help agencies that exist to fight against suicide both here and abroad. We will also assist in the fight against poverty alleviation and anything else that we see fit to do. This ability is contingent upon us being able to sell enough books, <u>(my hope springs eternal).</u>

The profits from this book, if enough are sold, will also allow my family, from one generation to another, through financial posterity, the ability to build on this worthy cause, and to pass it on through my bloodline perpetually. This fight cannot be a short-term fight, we must be in it for the long haul. We must be willing, and be prepared, to go the distance in our fight against Mental Health Sickness, and Suicide Prevention also.

This dark, horrific, this deadly disease called suicide, haunts humanity, from generation to generation. The help, the fight against it must exist from generation to generation also. We must build the awareness within our future bloodlines, to take up these worthy causes. It is our responsibility to do so. We must explain <u>"Noblesse Oblige,"</u> to our bloodline. Please tell them that "those of us who are in lofty places, are to do our part to make a positive difference within humanity." Please take the time to talk about these causes over and over again. The more they hear it, is the more it will resonate within them. They are the future fighters of tomorrow, that will champion <u>"Noblesse Oblige."</u>

CHAPTER 1

The Urgency is Upon You

If you feel that you are in serious trouble, and that you are crashing, and you are now at a place where you are entertaining suicidal thoughts. Please I beg of you with unrelenting love, encouragement, care and an abundance of compassion for you, please speak with someone. Please reach out to someone for the help that you are desperately in need of, you must do this with much urgency; you cannot delay.

Please call the **Suicide & Crisis Lifeline** at **988**, the 1-800-273-8255 has merged with **988** as of July 16, 2022. **Active-duty members and veterans, please press one** when the call is answered, or **text to 838255.** Non-military, if you are unable to speak, or you are hearing impaired, you can send a text to the **Crisis Text Line** 24/7 at **741741.** You can also go to **988lifeline.org,** precious soul, please live I beg you.

Please give us a chance to get you the help that you need. Please do not end your precious life. This book is a lifeline that is being offered to you, please grab hold of it, and allow my sincere words, and my care for you, along with my encouragement, and my insight into your painful, painful journey, to assist you in finding your way out of the darkness you are imprisoned in. Please fight to keep your soul upon the earth. I know that some of you are consumed with sorrow, relentless anger, and helplessness. Others of you, depression haunts you. Please hold on I beg you.

You are not alone, yes, your heart and mind believe that you are alone within the dreadful evil battle that pits your life against death. On most days I know that you feel as if death is winning, and is drawing closer and closer, but I say to you, **"It Is Not So."** You will live precious soul that you are, and you will conquer this season of darkness, and you will not give up.

Find your way out, find the light that will lead you out of your dark place, and run with tremendous urgency towards that light. Give me your hand, I will help you to find your way. This book is my hand, please grab hold, read this book and use it to build up your strength and your resistance, so that when the urge overshadows you to take your own life, you will resist the urge, you will fight, and you will live.

This book is my way of getting word to you that you are precious, you are one of a kind upon this earth and you are needed. You have yet to leave your mark upon this earth, or your work is not done, please stay! Pretty please with sugar on top, please fight to stay alive, I beg of you, I admonish you, please live, you must live for you, and live for those of your future!

If you are in middle school, you are in junior high or high school, or you are in your late teens or twenties, please I beg of you, do not end your life. You have many incredible years ahead of you, and you have yet to live out those wonderful years. If you are in your thirties, your forties, fifties, or older, please understand the importance of your life. You Sir or Madam are the guide to direct the way for others.

To every precious soul, please hear me when I say to you, your season of change will come. It will not always be this way, it will get better; your future awaits you, where you will grow and you will flourish, and you will be stronger than ever. You will laugh, you will love, and you will binge on ice cream and or pizza, poutine, curried chicken, kimchi, ramen, roti, fish and chips or whatever your favorite food is. You will shout for joy when your favorite team wins, and you will scream at the TV when they are losing. You will break hearts, you will make hearts glad, and every now and then, you will think back to these sorrowful days and say to yourself, "I am so very thankful that I did not kill myself, I am beyond grateful that I held on, and **I LIVED**." Please say these words with me,

"My beginning is not my middle, and my middle is not my ending. I will not kill my-self. I will not cast my precious soul into the grave. I will survive, I will make it through this sorrow." "I Am Going to Live."

The hidden instinct, and also the inner strength that we possess, is more often than not, not revealed to us in times of great joy; they are instead revealed to us in times of great disappointments, in times of great sorrow. It does not matter your age, or if you are male or female, it does not matter if you are rich or you are poor, you must find your inner strength, and instinct, you must fight for your precious life.

You Have Help

You have help; you are not alone in this battle. Reach

out, talk with someone, cry to someone, scream at someone and live. Whomever you are, please know that I know your pain firsthand, I know your thoughts as you move about your daily routine. You look at the faces of the people around you, and you say to yourself, "how can they not see my pain, how can they not know that I am about to kill myself?" My answer to you is I see it as clear as the noon sky. I know it, and I am here for you. I too spoke those same words to myself; I said, "how can they not know I am about to die." You are saying to yourself, "Today is the day I will end it all, tomorrow is the day I will end it all." Precious you, please hear me, precious you, please see me. Please consider this stranger that is fighting to save your precious life.

Please allow these words to course through your veins, and to give you a fighting chance at life, please live precious you, I beg of you, please live. Please do not throw in the towel; please do not cause the sun to set on your life. You can overcome this dark place of suicidal thoughts, and or tendencies if you just hold on, and fight for your precious life. This place will eventually become a place from where your strength, your determination was forged, but for this to take place, you must hold on, and precious, you must live.

Although it may not seem or feel this way now, I can assure you, you can, and you will triumph over this dark wretched place. This place of complete and utter heartache, where you are now, will someday become a magnificent blueprint, for others to follow, so as to overcome their dark and wretched places, that is within their own lives, and their own struggles.

Yes, Your Pain is Real

Your pain is real; the horrors of your dreadful experiences are real. For some of you the betrayal that humanity has poured out upon you was, and is enough to bring a thousand men to their knees. You are only one soul, how much greater the pain I imagine, you are feeling. Please accept my sincere apology, on behalf of the men and women that have caused you this horrific pain. They have positioned you within this horrific place of utter darkness, where you want to end your precious life. I scream out loud, I whisper it quietly, with tears filled eyes, and a heart that is filled with sorrow, I say to you, "I am truly, so very, very sorry for what you have gone through, and what you are going through right now." For your experiences, for your horrific pain, for the abuse inflicted upon you, I say to you with sincere heart and mind,

"I am so very, very, very sorry, and I ask of you, I plead with you, please do not die I beg of you, please live I encourage you. Precious soul that you are, please, please, please stay alive, precious, precious you; YOU MUST LIVE." Please let me in so that I can have this very, very important conversation with you. Please take my hand and walk with me, please hide behind me. Please allow me to face the wind that is blowing relentlessly upon you, and allow me to give you shade from the hot desert sunlight that constantly burns upon your face. Please allow me to lift Mount Everest off your back, and let me in so that I can have this all-important conversation with you. Allow me to walk you through the all-consuming, this wretched physiological landmine that has attached itself to your brain, and is marching you towards your death. This death will not be singular; this death if brought on by suicide will not just take your life; instead, this death could be in the abundance. This death could be a murderous rampage inflicted upon many, many souls. It could be far reaching, way beyond your lone existence. It could be an annihilation of countless bloodlines, for both yours and others. I give you my word, this does not only affect you. Your death should you commit suicide would be far reaching beyond anything you have imagined. There is a cause and effect, an avalanche of results that could affect nations whether you can believe it or not. You have help, please I beg of you with the sincerest of heart and mind, please listen to me, do not give up on your precious life. You precious soul, **"Must survive Suicide, You Must Live!"**

Do you know what a whirlpool is? In my layman's term, it is when ocean or river water currents of two opposite directions meet. They get tangled up, and a fight ensues for each current to be able to continue on their journey.

You are caught in the whirlpool of life, you are tangled up in death that is heading to the grave, and life that is heading towards your wonderful future. You must survive this whirlpool of life. Keep breathing, I beg of you. Keep your head above water, please do not allow your sorrows to drown you. You matter more than you could ever imagine. I beg of you I admonish you, and I Encourage You. Please precious you, do Not kill yourself. Do not commit suicide. Please Do Not Die! "PLEASE LIVE."

CHAPTER 2

Your Bloodline

Your ancestor's children, children and also their children, with personalities, with traits that matches yours.

The Survival of the Bloodline

Your **great-great-grandfather Richard had four sons,** Paul, Michael, John, and Robert.

One of Richard's four children is Michael; **Michael is your great-grandfather.** The four siblings had twenty-six children including your grandfather.

The twenty-six children **one of whom is your grandfather, are born of four brothers,** then reproduce and have one hundred and four children including your father.

The one hundred and four children **including your father,** reproduce and now have three hundred and twelve children, one of them is you.

The three hundred and twelve children **including you,** reproduced and they now have a total of one thousand, two hundred and forty-eight children.

Each of the three hundred and twelve children had four children of their own. Three hundred and twelve children times four is one thousand two hundred and forty-eight children all together.

The one thousand two hundred and forty-eight children each had three children, which comes to three thousand seven hundred and forty-four souls.

Now let us add up the total number of people that came from the bloodline of Richard your great-great-grandfather.

4+26 = 30 + 104 = 134 + 312 = 446 +1,248 = 1,694 + 3,744 = 5,438.00

Five thousand, four hundred and thirty-eight human beings are within this bloodline born of your great-great-grandfather Richard.

The Destruction of a Bloodline

Sir or Madam, I regret to inform you, and also the other five thousand, four hundred and thirty-seven blood related family members, descendants born of your great-great grandfather Richard.

Richard, your great-great grandfather committed suicide. He killed himself before his descendants were born; which means five thousand, four Hundred and thirty-eight souls did not make it to this earth. Not one of Richard's blood related descendants that came after him ever existed. Why? Because Richard committed suicide before his children were born. Not one person from his direct future bloodline made it to the earth. Your great grandmother that you love so dearly, sadly she did not make it. Your incredibly precious grandfather that you love so much did not make it. His precious smile that the world loved, and they are encouraged when they see it, never existed, suicide made it so. Your favorite uncle did not make it to the earth. Your precious mother or father did not make it. Your nephews and nieces did not make it. Your cousin that you cherish so very much did not make it to the earth. All because your great great-grandfather Richard committed suicide.

Suicide comes with very far-reaching destruction

Please replace Richard with you; if you take your life, it will bring about the destruction of many, many souls. This without a doubt includes their dreams, their abilities, and accomplishments, and will wipe out the survival of untold many. This suicide could very well prevent the restoration of countless souls; and prevent the betterment of humanity, because you gave in to death; you gave in to suicide and you took your precious life.

Please allow me to clarify to you the meaning of my statement. If you are able to have children, how do you know how many lives are meant to come through blood relations, your bloodline descendants? Your child/children could be future doctors, attorneys, or teachers, they could be a chef, or an athlete, or a maintenance person. They could be members of our precious Armed Forces, writers, a mathematician, or members of the clergy and on and on. Your bloodline could produce presidents, a scientist, an investment banker. It could produce community helper, and or charitable workers. They could be an ambassador representing his or her nation, and or a Rhodes Scholar. From your bloodline could descend farmers, firefighters, police officers, or fishermen, counselors, and on and on. Sir or Madam, young man or young lady, you are making an incredibly big mistake in believing that because you are having mental stress, you are consumed with depression, or you have made untold mistakes, or you are in a bad place, or you suffer from mental illness, everything ends with you, and you have no future.

You are mistaken, my son is having a better life than I. My limits are not my son's limits. My sorrows are not my son's sorrow, and my suicidal years have never crossed my son's path. How can you say who you are, will be the same in your future bloodline? Give your bloodline a chance to see daylight, give your bloodline a chance to laugh, to cry, to dance, to taste ice cream, to lose, to win, to face struggles and to overcome them.

Please allow Victoria, Paul, Albert, Adam, Mary, Levi, Alicio, Rosario, Sandra, Chris, Jackie, Jose, Carlos, Rammed, Knnada, Benedetto, Lee Min, Prilapat, or Zoe Zang and Alanis, please allow them to be born. For GOD sake please, please give them a chance to live! Please hold on for yours and their sake I beg of you, I implore you, "**PLEASE LIVE.**"

Your sorrow is not theirs. Please allow them to enter this world and to live out their precious lives. Where they will make mistakes, and will experience some sorrows, and some incredibly wonderful magnificent accomplishments; like being a wonderful mother or father to their children. Please allow them to enter the earth, where they could end up saving lives both here and abroad; through medicine, through military, and many other avenues including through governing, or through humanitarian work throughout nations.

Make no mistake, the only way this will happen is if you allow yourself to live. The only way is if you do not give in to suicidal thoughts or tendencies. Instead, you fight to get pass this season in your life, and you go and get the help that you desperately need; so that you can break free from this horrific sickness called suicide, that has a death grip upon you, and wants to destroy you and your bloodline and their remarkable accomplishments for the future.

You have no idea who you will be five years from today. Give yourself a chance to recover, to find peace. Your peace will make your precious heart glad. Your peace will save lives, it will move mountains. Please for heaven and earth's sake, please hold on and do not let go of your precious life. Please be the precious soul that you are, I beg of you, and I encourage you, **"YOU MUST LIVE."**

This sickness was brought on by bipolar, extreme trauma, medication or drug addiction. Perhaps it was brought on by extreme depression, or some other form of cross-linking illness(es) or experience(s). Whatever the cause, the effect is a deathtrap that is within your precious life, and it is now marching you steadfastly towards the wide-ranging destruction of you, along with every precious soul and action that will travel through your bloodline.

Even in your worst failures, you are significant to this earth

You are a precious soul upon this earth; it does not start or end with you. In your worst failure, yes, you still carry great accomplishments, some incredible individuals inside your bloodline, and I urgently, I desperately, need you to understand this. Your worth to humanity goes way beyond just you. You say you are broken, you are not a good person? Well, hello there family, I am pleased to meet you, I too am an imperfect being. I read this somewhere, and I will pass it on, to you. "He who is without sin, please cast the first stone." Wow, we have no takers. Is there no one with a stone in his or her hand, to throw at the imperfect you?

I guess we must have run out of stones, in Michigan, Florida, Texas, or Virginia. They ran out of stones in the Dakotas, Alaska, New York, California, and all other states, along with Canada, France, Jamaica and the rest of the world. Not one of these people have a stone in their hand, and do you know why?

The answer is simple, we are all imperfect beings. Whoever we are, and whatever title(s) we are born into, the fact is; we are all imperfect human beings.

Please listen to me my precious North Americans, my precious South Americans, and my precious Africans, my precious Asians, and also my precious Middle Easterners, yes, I do know that some Middle Easterners are a part of the African continent. my precious Europeans, and to sum it all up, "MY PRECIOUS WORLD," there cannot be any stones within our hands, and you are asking why? Because just like you who are suicidal, we too are also fighting our own battles of imperfections.

Oh, and by the way, please do not tell anyone my secret. I live in a glass house myself, and with all my faults, I would go bankrupt from spending on replacement windows. There are no stones in my hands, not one. Now, will you accept the fact that you are not alone? Will you allow us all who cares for you, to stop your march towards death? Do you now see that if you take your own life, it would bring about the total annihilation of not just you, but your blood relation bloodline that comes through you?

Here are some important facts for you to hold on to, which should make you think twice about taking your own life. Please remember this, there are many different bloodlines that can travel through your life while you are upon the earth. Please allow me to explain what I mean. There is your posterity, as in your blood relations, your descendants that are to come through you. There is the bloodline through adoption; there is also the bloodline of the person from the grocery store that you spoke with, they decided not to kill themselves; all because of your on-time word of encouragement. There is also the bloodline of the child that your future relative will adopt from foster care, and raise them within an environment that causes their positive turnaround. Your future relative did not adopt them.

Because of your suicide, your future relative will not be born. That child will instead remain in foster care, and although most foster children do not end up with this outcome. This child will mature into a bitter angry person, that will maim and kill others, out of their desire to revenge society, for their suffering throughout their youth.

Do I have your attention now? There is also the bloodline of the person you will meet one, two, five, ten, twelve, twenty or thirty years from now. They will be drowning in despair, and will have no answer, no way out of their horrific sorrow, and they will just want to die.

It is your precious encouragement, you overcoming the debilitating suicidal thoughts and or tendencies, that will show them the way out of the wretched despair that they are living in. Your personal journey, will prevent their personal journey from spiraling out of control. It is your very, very personal blueprint of overcoming, that will become their lifesaver, their life saving solution; that will bring them out of their very dark places of struggles and discouragement. Your victory over suicidal thoughts and tendencies, over depression, over mental health taking you to some very, very dark places, is not just for you.

CHAPTER 3

If you do not believe the information, here is your proof

Please allow me to give you the proof that you are desperately in need of, the tangible proof, the substantiated proof that you need to hold on to. My journey has been one of tremendous sorrow and incredible restoration. In my teens, my twenties and even in my thirties, I had extreme suicidal thoughts and tendencies. If you are wondering, how could I be suicidal for that many years and not die?

The answer is, I had to get my precious son across the finish line, and into adulthood where he could manage on his own, before I killed myself. I had to protect my Tony from society. I filled him with love, let him know he was cared for and wanted. I had to equip him with education, and world knowledge, of finance, proper work, society, and also relationship etiquette, including how he treated others and the importance of forgiveness.

I had to make certain he had an understanding of the importance of hard work, and to push through when things seem impossible. I built within him the desire for accomplishments in life, and the understanding of what it meant to be a productive member of society. He had to know the importance of good hygiene, having a clean home, and how to live. He needed to understand self-control, proper manners towards his fellow human beings and respect for his elders.

He always had one dollar in his pocket, for when his friends stopped at McDonalds; this was to ensure that he did not have to ask his friends for money, which would cause them to look-down on him, or treat him with a condescending attitude, (young people can be vicious at times). I was a loner; he knew that he could go it on his own without following the crowd. He had a disciplined life, I was his mother, respect always mattered and it went both ways. Most importantly, he had to understand the love of GOD, and what it meant to serve HIM. Before I died, I had to make certain my precious son, my Tony GOD willing, would have a good, a safe, and a prosperous, and an accomplished life without me.

My entire goal was to get him to the point where he could do it on his own. I was about seventeen when the suicidal tendencies started; and it lasted for over fourteen years. Now, for me to explain my journey I will need to mention church and hell, I hope you will not prevent this book from reaching those who are in need because of my needing to mention these two words. Here is your tangible proof that you can survive where you are, and come out victorious. I now give you your substantiated proof that will reveal to you, that there are many bloodlines that will come through you, by you not committing suicide and staying alive.

At seventeen years old, I was an angry, bitter and hurt teenager. I wanted to die, far more than I wanted to live. Death was a comfort to me, and it beckoned to me every second of every day. I would scream it out in anger to my mom that I was going to kill myself, but she could not wrap her head around such actions and did not believe me. I was filled with anger like you have never seen and will never see in your life. I would go from one to one thousand out of anger and despair. This came about from what people had done to me, when I was the most vulnerable.

At that time, I had experienced trauma, and that trauma had created the human being that I had become. I had lost hope in humanity; I was leaving the earth slowly but surely and no one understood it.

I was suffering from bronchial pneumonia during that time in the most extreme way. When I spoke, you could hear the mucus in my throat. Before going to bed one night, I went into the shower and washed my hair, I put a plastic bag over my hair and covered it with a scarf to make sure it stayed wet; this is while I am suffering from bronchial pneumonia. I then took a bottle of pills and swallowed every tablet. I curled up and went to sleep. No one was coming to save me, they would just assume I was still sleeping, or I was trying to avoid them. Now here are the important facts, so that you will have a clear understanding of how profound my statement was that I am about to mention to you. I grew up in church and understood hell as a place that burns with fire for all eternity.

While having bronchial pneumonia, after washing my hair and while placing a plastic bag over my hair, and covering it with a scarf to make certain it stayed wet. After taking a bottle of pills, I went to sleep. I awoke to pitch-blackness within my room and I said aloud in the most comforting, the most rested from war voice, the most grateful voice. **"I am in hell now; I am safe now praise GOD. I am in hell now; I am dead now; I am okay now, they cannot hurt me anymore." And then I went right back to peaceful sleep.** Do you have any idea of the horrific sorrow that was in my poor soul, that I would say to myself, **"I am in hell now; I am safe now praise GOD. I am in hell now, I am dead now?"**

Do you have any idea of how utterly lost I was? My soul had lost its hope, my mind and heart had no peace, sorrow was my breakfast, my lunch and my dinner, and I no longer wanted to live, I wanted to die a thousand deaths. My mom checked on me the following morning; she worked the late shift and usually slept until mid-morning, but this particular morning she awoke early and she checked on me. She knew something was wrong immediately. She took me to the hospital where they pumped my stomach.

I was then admitted to the psychiatric ward for three days. I want you to read my story over and over, and over again. Now try to tell yourself that I do not know what I speak of, try to tell yourself I do not know what pain you are going through, try to tell yourself, "She was only seventeen years old, she was a child, she was just young and weak." Fourteen years of being suicidal means, I was suicidal in my teens, in my twenties, and even in my early thirties.

I survived it, do you hear me? I, Victoria survived it!

I survived the horrible, the most horrific wretched, sorrowful journey, and you will also. My survival was birthed within me, and I am certain yours will also. For this to happen to you, to survive your journey, you must fight through the horrific unrelenting pain, the tremendous sorrow, and precious you, "<u>You Must Live.</u>"

Please listen to me

Listen to me, precious souls that you are, please I beg of you, please listen to me. You must hold on for dear life, and no matter the circumstance, **"<u>Do not let go!</u>"** During wrestling, when someone wants to give up, when they want to tap out, they tap, tap with their hand, letting their opponent know, that they are giving up. You must never tap out of life! Say it with me, "I will not tap out of life, I will not give up on my precious life."

I will hold on, "I am going to live!"

You must believe me when I say to you, your beginning is not your middle, and your middle is not your ending. You must live precious you, you must live. You must live on, and you must prosper for a lifetime. Your overcoming, will blaze the trail bright for others. It will show them the way out of the pain, the death maze that they are struggling to escape. What if I had taken my life? What if when I had tried to commit suicide, I had succeeded?

Every precious act of mine would never have existed. Every heart I have ministered to, every call to come to the emergency room, because a patient is asking me to come. Every smile in public, that draws my fellow human being in, and then they tell me, "You made my day." Every platform I have stood upon, every well I have stood in, and encouraged hearts and uttered life-changing words. Every admonishment I have given to my fellow human beings, none of it would have existed, because I ended my life.

The mistakes I made that hurt others, the mistakes I made that hurt me, yet brought about changes within me, and taught me to change for the better, and to become a better human being. None of it would have happened, if I had taken my life. Face the truth, you are precious, your life is far more than just who you are.

Your journey is not just your journey; but many, many, many others to follow. Please I beg of you, please live, you must live. Suicide brings about the annihilation of not just you, but also the lives that would have been saved; based on your future years of you telling others, "I suffered, I went through suicidal thoughts and tendencies and overcame them, and you will also." Live and say to others, "here is my blueprint, my encouragement for you; this is how to overcome mental stress. This is how to overcome mental health breakdowns; and this is how you will overcome suicidal thoughts and tendencies."

You must resist with all your might. You must survive, you must overcome this dark and murderous horrific place; that wants to wipe you off the face of the earth, by using your own hands against you. **"Precious you please live."**

Please live so that you can show others the way out of their dark places. Please give birth to your very own survival instincts. Please create your very own blueprint, of how to survive the journey, of suicidal thoughts and tendencies; and some day pass it on-to others, so that they can survive their journey also.

CHAPTER 4

"Your experiences are not my experiences," you are saying

Perhaps you are telling yourself, your experiences and mine are not the same. Or it does not matter my experiences, I cannot help you. You are saying to yourself, your experiences are different, and so you need to do something completely different. Here is my answer for you; the destination and the change in direction are exactly the same. You are heading towards suicide, we are trying to get you away from suicide. Is that not the same exact situation for hundreds of thousands of individuals upon the earth, that is going through utter despair?

Please allow me to use this analogy to make my point to you. Many of us throughout the world are heading to The United States, Switzerland, France, Rome, the Hague or Jamaica, Mexico, or Canada. Some of us are heading to South Korea, Australia, or some other place in Italy. Some are heading to The United Kingdom, Dubai, or numerous other destinations throughout the world. Many have visited before us, and they have mapped out the journey, the flights, the hotels, the restaurants and the places to visit.

We avoid or we replicate these same steps, because someone else did it before us, and said that it was a horrible, or it was a fantastic location, restaurant, hotel, flight or overall trip. In other words, they drew us a road map, a blueprint of their travel, so that we can avoid or replicate it. Please hear me when I say to you all, I have gone through extreme mental stress, I have come close to having mental breakdowns, and I have experienced suicidal thoughts and tendencies up close, and very, very, very personal.

I know the looks, and its smell, its weaknesses and its strengths and so much more. I encourage you and your loved ones, to use the review of my very, very personal trip, to help you with surviving the mental stress that you are experiencing.

This is your safety guide, that was written to help to guide you through the heartache, the gut-wrenching sorrowful journey, that has now rerouted your precious life straight towards suicide. This blueprint is to guide you away from mental stress, away from suicidal thoughts and or tendencies. Additionally, this blueprint was created to keep your precious soul alive, upon the earth.

Your fight starts with you finding your trigger:

You must find your trigger; your survival depends on it. What is the catalyst, what is the method that is being used to haunt you with suicidal thoughts and tendencies? Is it a lack of what you are in need of? Is it the loss of possessions, or the loss of your job? Is it you being abused, or is it post-traumatic stress disorder? Is it postpartum depression, or are you being bullied? What is your trigger? Find it now; your life absolutely depends on it! Is it extreme financial stress? Is it sickness, is it you have broken the law?

Face it, your recovery starts here. How do you solve your problem, if you do not know what your problem is? Come on now precious, do not be afraid, let us find the problem, and let us fix it. You are not alone; I am here with you on your journey of recovery.

Here are Some Possible Triggers:

You have lost in love: Someone broke your heart

Death: is it the death of a loved one?

Bipolar: If you take your medication, you keep your faculties. If you stop taking the medication, you lose yourself, where reality and the imaginary, the unreal rolls into one within your mind. Where those around you no longer recognize you, nor do they know how to function with you. Nevertheless, the discomfort of taking your medication, is the only fact that matters to you, nothing else does. You are willing to take the chance, and have discontinued taking your bipolar medication(s), that the doctor prescribed, with no thought for the consequences of your actions.

Panic Attacks: "If I take the medication, I will be able to function within my everyday living. If I do not take the medication(s) as prescribed, I will find myself being overrun, with debilitating panic attacks. When I stop in traffic, my heart starts racing, as if I am about to have a heart attack. If I get into a drive-through line and there is a vehicle in front of me or behind me, my heart starts racing, and I feel extreme pressure in my head, as if I am about to pass out. I have no choice, I must take the medication, even though it makes me extremely depress to the point of me wanting to commit suicide."

Other Illnesses: Any other illness that causes you to take medication(s), although their side effects are extreme at times, and makes you sick in other ways.

CHAPTER 5

Here are some solutions, some thoughts and ideas, and some actions for you to take, to help you to find your way out of the dark places.

What you say matters

Speak less about your pain, and more about your positive changes that you desire. Speak less about where you have been, and more about where you want to go. Look ahead towards your brand-new destination. Believe for your deliverance, and keep saying it, until you start believing it. The more you hear something, is the more it sets in. The longer you hear something, is the more likely it is, that you will take it into your heart and your mind.

Speak, "I will survive this chapter, this season of my life." Say to yourself, "the darkness of suicide will not overtake me." Speak, "I will recover from this sickness of wanting to take my life." Repeat to yourself, "I will recover, I will prosper, and I will be victorious." Speak life into your soul, life into your children, and into your marriage. Speak life into your job, and speak magnificent life into your journey.

Your words matter, your words are significant in your recovery/survival. Speak being victorious over suicidal thoughts and or tendencies. Please speak restoration of your mental health, and relief from mental stress and more. The words you say, believe it or not can sustain you in times of great difficulties, or your words can help to bring you to your knees.

Your words can help to catapult you to greatness, or put you into the grave. "Your words matter."

Always remember, there is hope within each day

Try to awake each morning with hope and patience within your heart, believing for your deliverance. Embrace the fact that you are in a new day, with new chances to get it right, or at least, you can try to get it right. This is a brand-new day, and this day brings incredible opportunities for breakthroughs. You will get through this pain, but to do so, you must do your part. You must encourage yourself.

Cry, and let the pain out. Unless you are truly fasting, as in, you are weakening your flesh to strengthen your spirit. Force yourself to eat; you need your strength. If your fast is not a spiritual fast but instead, you are not eating because you are discouraged, you must eat.

You need your energy. Lack of energy fuels your depression, and keeps you in bed. Get up, take a shower, and go for a walk. Do your part in the saving of your life! Do not allow what you are going through to overtake you. Fight! Fight, and then fight some more! stay alive! And keep on breathing!

Your belief will make a huge difference, when it comes to your survival

You must believe in your precious deliverance, say to yourself, "although I am going through heartache and pain, I will not give up on my life. Although I see no light at the end of the tunnel, I will not throw in the towel. Even though I see nothing to hope for, I will not cast my hope aside. Even though I have shed a river of tears, still, I will maintain my life upon this earth, believing in my heart, that my deliverance will come."

"Although, I have seen and felt pain and sorrow beyond reasoning, beyond the conceivable. In spite of it all, nonetheless, nevertheless, and nevertheless, I will not give up on my life, I will not quit on my GOD given destiny. I will maintain my journey upon the earth, and I will not give up."

Encourage your soul. Yes, it is beyond difficult, I agree. Nevertheless, I need you to do it. As I speak life into you, I also need you to speak life into your precious soul, and speak life into your precious journey also. You have a life to live, your providence yet unfulfilled, and is yet to be lived out. Keep your soul encouraged even when you see no reason to do so. Cry out loud, whisper in tears and let it out as you encourage yourself to keep going.

Believe me when I say, I get it. I know exactly what it feels like for you to be without hope, to be without answers, and the walls have already closed in and are crushing the life out of me. Yes precious, I totally, I completely understand what you are going through. Nevertheless, you must encourage yourself. Have faith in your deliverance. Tell yourself that your change will come, that yours is on the way, and build your strength from the faith you are holding on to.

Do not trust your mind, your mind wants to surrender to suicide, wants to surrender to death

Do not rely on your discouraged mind to give you understanding; trust the people around you, that are encouraging you instead. Your flesh is in give-up mode, it wants to call it quits. Open your heart, your mind, your spirit, and also your soul, and hear how much you are loved, and for some of you even in spite of all your mistakes. In spite of all your imperfections, yes precious you, you are loved way beyond measure. If not by your family, please know that this stranger loves you.

Please see and hear the encouragement that I am sending out to you. Please receive the comfort that I have packaged within this book for you, so as to save your precious life.

Please precious, call the **Suicide & Crisis Lifeline** at **988. Active-duty members and veterans press (1)** when the call is answered, or **text to 838255.** Non-military, if you are unable to speak, or hearing impaired, text to the **Crisis Text Line 24/7, at 741741,** or go to **988lifeline.org.**

They are waiting for you to call. I beg of you, please call. Please hold on! Please do not give up on your precious life! I beg of you precious soul that you are, **"Please Live!"** You can tell them what you are feeling, they will not judge you. The information you give, will help them to know how best to help you, to overcome your mental stress, or your breakdown.

CHAPTER 6

Do not rely on others, whose intentions towards you are destructive. Your hurt, is their pleasure

Some of these people near you, exist to drive you to your death. You need to let them go. Say your goodbyes to them, and get as far away from them as is possible. You need to remember this, when it comes to your journey in life. There are those who exist to bring you to destruction. It does not take a rocket scientist, to identify someone that means you no good. Every bell, every whistle is going off inside you. Your stress level rises when you are near them, and yet you still hold to that relationship. This individual, or these people, have driven you to the cliff, and are pushing you over. What is wrong with you, are you a glutton for punishment?

Why do you refuse to let them go? Their intention, is to cause your destruction. Your mother, your father, your brother, and your sister, some of you even your neighbor and your employer, have all warned you about this person, and still you have refused to listen, to the prudent advice that you have been given. **Let him, her, or them go. Walk away! Your precious life depends on it. Run for your life, and do not look back.** Mark my words, your destruction is staring you in the face, your destruction is telling you how much they love you, and will make you happy for the rest of your life.

If your survival means saying goodbye to family,

then as sad as it may be, you precious, must say your goodbyes, and leave their presence

I would not want this for my worst enemy. No human being should have to say goodbye to their mother, to their father, their sister or their brother, or any other relative, just so that they can survive. However, if this is what it takes to keep you alive upon this earth, then precious you, say your goodbyes to them, and live. How can you live without them you ask?

Precious you, my answer to you is a question back to you. How can you live with them? They have heaped great sorrows upon you, to the point of death. For you to live, you must leave. Survive today, forgive them tomorrow. Right now, all you can do is live. A year from now, when you are strong, and out of danger, you can let them back in. But for now, you must love them from a distance, and live. The only way you will live, is if you are willing to let them go for now, and allow only those who can help you, to be near you, while your heart and your mind heals from this great sorrow.

Keep it in the family you say:

'DISCLAIMER"
For Active Duty, and Veteran Military Members.

There will never be a moment, a time when it is okay to abandon your nation's Armed Forces. Make no mistake, undermining the Armed Forces, means you are undermining your nation. You can spin it, curse it, dance around it, and find every excuse in the entire universe, and still the unbreakable truth of the matter is this.

"You undermining your nation's Armed Forces, is you undermining your nation."

If you have a problem in the military, take it up the command chain. Yes, I am looking around while I am saying this, expecting someone to tar and feather me, or put a sign on my back that says, "make a circle with your knuckle in her forehead ten times, every time she passes by.

Listen, first give your immediate command the chance to fix it. Be fair about it, give them enough time to figure it out. Your complaint could ruin your command life, when all your command needed, was some time to get it done. If there is urgency, it is imperative that you express this over and over, and over again. If nothing is done, you must move up the chain of command. There are **NO** Circumstances, that gives you the okay to go outside of the military.

Do you know why? There are countless leaders, YES, countless leaders within the Armed Forces to turn to. For every one that does not care, there are ten times more that does care. Never allow your Armed Forces to look incompetent, weak, dishonest, or in any form of negative manner. If there is any mistake, any failure, voice it within the military enquiry, and always, always, always Sir or Madam leave it there.

When it comes to the Armed Forces, "It Stays Within the Family."

Now, let us talk about our non-military family, our relatives outside of military.

Keep it in the family you say:

Many of you have said, others should keep it in the family, when it comes to their family members, that are causing them harm. This is whether the family member is causing them physical, or it is psychological pain. There is much to be said about family members, that know that they have the power over you, through age, or status, or hierarchy. And uses it continually, to hurt their family members. They attack their loved ones year in and year out, with physical and psychological warfare, in the most detached and painful way.

It doesn't matter the care that is spouted from their lips, their actions towards you, have broken your spirit. Their actions have caused you to spend your life, finding ways, even if harmful, to survive their treatment of you. They know their power over you, and when no one is watching, or when they are with their wolfpack, they exert their mean-spirited actions towards you, as a reminder of who is in charge. You are at their mercy, and they know it.

You know that you can no longer let your guard down. Throughout your life, they have pounded you with brutal cruelty, or passive aggressive spite, when you least expect it; or when you are at a place where you are thinking, "he hasn't attacked me in a while, she hasn't attacked me in a while, thank GOD it is over." The next thing you know, their returned attack on you is like a sucker punch to the head and your gut. You say to yourself, "There is no getting away from them, they are family, they have access to me forever, for as long as I am upon the earth." The hopelessness inside you, has led you down some very, very dangerous paths, of self-destruction. This is in your never-ending pursuit, of trying to stay ahead of the extreme mental, or the physiological pounding, that you are continually taking from your family member(s).

You are depressed, and you are broken, and you are always nervous. Your mental stress is off the chart, and you are having a nervous breakdown. This is while you are pretending that you are doing great, and that all is well with you. While inside, you are having a complete mental breakdown, and you are giving up on life.

"Keep in in the family they say."

I say to you, young man or young woman, Sir or Madam, for your survival, along with the restoration of your mental health. For you not to breakdown in despair, or for you to avoid some form of self-harm, that could end your precious life. For you to keep yourself from reacting due to utter desperation. I say to you now, **"please tell someone, you must tell**

others, please let it out. Your silence gives them power, your silence will drive you to end your precious life.". Your family member is loving you with an exorbitant amount of malice, their mean spiritedness has created a ticking timebomb within you, and you must save yourself. Once it is out in the open, they will stop, so as to cover their tracks, and so that they can also feign innocence.

Let the people talk, let them say you betrayed your family, because mark my words, as long as you say nothing, that family member will keep coming. Their actions towards you are a drug they cannot resist, and they will keep coming until you stop them. You are trading one misery for another misery that will hound you for exposing your family member(s) you say?

Here is my answer to you, I will take the stranger outside of my circle attacking me for exposing my family, over a family member within my circle driving me to a mental and Physiological breakdown. You must shut that family member down once and for all.

Do you really believe, other family members have not seen their warfare on you? Have they done anything to help you? The answer is no. If there is no help within your family, then please, you must get help from outside of your family. They attack you in the dark, bring it into the light. The exposure will reduce their attack, and grant you some much needed relief.

Always keep this in mind, the individual that says to

you, **"keep it in the family,"** has not a clue of your suffering. If they were suffering the way that you are, they would change their tune in a heartbeat. Please attend to my words; hold onto these words and never forget them. They will help you to face reality.

"The stranger has saved many lives, that the family has all but cast into the grave." Family members have sent the laughter, the health, the dreams and aspirations of their very own family members into the grave. They have robbed their family members of their GOD given destiny, and left these poor souls broken in heart and mind.

Keep it in the family they say?

If only they knew precious, oh if only they knew, of the heartache, and the pain that you have been put through.

Keep it in the family they say?

Stay alive! Your journey is yet to be lived out.

This is about you staying alive upon this earth. This is about the fight in you coming alive, no matter how young or old you are. If you are ten, you must fight. If you are forty, you must fight. If you are eighty, you must fight. Come on now my love, come on now. Do not throw in the towel, and please do not put your pen down. Precious you, I promise you with all my heart, your life story is continuously being written. Please give it a chance to become a bestseller. I see joy in your future, I see peace. Precious you, I see laughter. I can see you someday telling your future generation, about your experiences of pain and sorrow, and how you manage to survive, and that they will also. Come on now precious, yes, I understand; you have no strength to look up. I say to you now, just do not look down. If you are not looking up or down, then the position of your head is level. This means whether you realize it or not, what you are doing is looking out ahead, and that is exactly where I need you to look.

You can do this; I believe in you. You can do it; you will overcome this. Yes, I know, the pain is beyond human imagination, and you do not have any answers. Yes, you feel as if the world has abandoned you. You feel as if your family, your friends, and society has failed you. But precious, you cannot, you must never give up. Keep on breathing; keep on allowing oxygen to enter your lungs. Do not take your life! Please seek out help for the mental breakdown you are experiencing, I beg of you.

Do not commit suicide! Do not end your precious, precious, precious life, I beg of you. I admonish you, and I plead with you, please I encourage you, you must hold on I beg you!

You are precious, you are a wonderful gem. You precious soul are a masterpiece. You are one of a kind, just one of you. The world needs you, you have so much to offer, and yes, I know you do not see it. My love, give it time, you must give your life time to develop. With all my heart, that is filled with love for you, I promise you, you will look back at this period of your life with gratitude; being thankful that you did not end your life. You can do this; you will overcome it all. My beloved, whomever you are, please know how much you are loved and cared for. So much so, that a stranger in your time of pain and sorrow, is giving you an on-time word of encouragement, to restore your heart and mind, and to help to preserve your life. Please do not close your eyes, do not close your ears! Instead, see my advice that I am giving to you, and hear me when I say to you, "you are not alone; I am in the battle, **NO**, correction, **WE** are in the battle with you.

"Young man or young lady, Sir or Madam; you are definitely not alone." A team at the Suicide & Crisis Lifeline is waiting for your call, and this book was written for you. Please resist the urge to take your life. Please do not allow yourself to suffer from the violence of your own hands! Fight for your precious life! Please, please precious you, please do not give up, please live! I promise you, your beginning is not your middle, nor is it your ending. Please Precious You, **PLEASE LIVE!** "**YOU MUST LIVE.**"

Please precious, contact the **Suicide & Crisis Lifeline** at **988**, the 1-800-273-8255 has merged with **988** as of July 16, 2022. **Active-duty members and veterans, please press (1)** when the call is answered or **text to 838255.** Non-military, if you are unable to speak or you are hearing impaired, you can send a text to the **Crisis Text Line** 24/7, at **741741**. You can also go to **988lifeline.org** website. Please live! Please give them a chance to help you, please give them a chance to restore you, precious I thank you.

CHAPTER 7

You must protect your precious heart at all cost

From your heart comes the desire to fight, or to give up. You must protect your heart. Allow your heart to be encouraged, and your precious mind and spirit will follow. Please allow this stranger's love for you, to fill your heart with the awareness, that you are far beyond precious. You are beyond precious to this stranger, I love you, I love you, I love you. Yes, this complete stranger loves you.

You are suffering from panic attacks

Please precious, you must fight to break free from this debilitating sickness. Listen to me my love, when you are driving, and the traffic backs up, and your heart starts racing, ask yourself why? "What is the reason for my panic, what is the problem? Am I such a diva that I cannot wait in traffic, are you kidding me?" Make it funny and real, and see the true reality of the situation. When we have an out-pouring of rain, and you panic, tell yourself that our reservoirs will now have enough water in them. Ask yourself, does the earth not need to replenish itself? Do we not need water for our crops, lots of snow so that when it melts it will replenish our lakes?

If there is a flood, or there is a bad snowstorm, or any other environmental disaster, you panicking could end your life. You must remain calm; do not panic, be strong. Help yourself, and seek help from others, and help them also. Helping them will keep you calm. What if you do not have help? You must talk yourself down from the ledge of panic, that you are standing on, or will stand on in the future. You must encourage yourself through it. Ask yourself, "Why am I panicking, the solution is right before me? I can do this, I can overcome; I will get through it, I will not panic." Speak slowly, & calmly to yourself; assure yourself that you will be okay, and you will get through it.

When you panic because you are stressed, tell Oscar, Paul, Aaron, Melissa, Soyfah, Lee Ming, Sharon, Andrew and whomever else you need to tell, but refuse to, tell them goodbye. Tell them to leave you alone. Destress your life, (deeee stress, not distress). Stress weakens you, and removes the ability to fight off panic when it approaches.

Find peace, the kind of peace that will build you up, and make you strong; so that when you feel the panic approaching, you will be able to say, "Oh no, not today, I am not having it. My mind, my heart and my spirit is at peace, and I refuse to have any form of panic attack." Stress heightens frustration, nervousness and panic within you. Those are all precursors to having a panic attack. Destress your life; and you will start on your road to recovery. You should not underestimate the powerful result of removing stress from your life. This is the beginning of you taking action to assist in your recovery. Many times the change needed within our lives, starts with us; not from outside. "NO," it starts with us needing to take the necessary actions for change on our own behalf.

CHAPTER 8

You have lost your home, your car, and or job, your resources are less than half of what it was.

You worked hard for everything you own/owned. Yes, I get it. You invested time, energy, money and then some, and now you are about to lose it all, or you have lost it all. Please hear me, please listen to me when I say to you, **"you will survive this."** Yes, you are confused beyond measure, the fear within your heart is real, the hopelessness that grips you is debilitating, and you have no answers. Precious you, let us start here. The hurricane, fire, flood, tornado, the divorce, or bankruptcy, does not have the power to take your life. Rebuild your life one hour at a time. Wood, paper, metal, cement or cloth does not make the man or woman. The condition of the heart is what makes the man or the woman.

The actions of your heart, your inner characteristics are what defines you, not material possession, as in house, car, or even furniture. For the wealthy, Gucci, a Ferrari, Prada, Louis Vuitton, Louboutin, Chanel, Dolce Gabbana, a Mercedes Benz, a Jaguar, a Rolls-Royce or Koenigsegg CCXR Trevita, a Lamborghini or any other expensive car or million-dollar home should not define you. **YES,** they are fabulous, there is absolutely no doubt about that. However, none of it makes you into a great human being. A serial killer can own all that I have listed. Now I ask you, what kind of human being is that serial killer? I will give you the chance to answer the question yourself.

For the poor, the middle class and the rich alike, yes, personal loss is devastating, I completely agree. But please hear me, starting over is not a death sentence. Cloth as in clothing does not make the person. Wood as in furniture does not make you who you are, and metal as in cars does not identify you. Cement as in housing does not make your character.

Yes, the devastation is real, you worked hard for your possessions, your job paid your bills, and kept a roof over your head, and now your job is gone, or both your job and your possessions are all gone. This is due to your financial, or environmental devastation, loss of employment, or through a divorce.

Unbeknownst to you, you are in a place of rebirth. The burden of continuity, although sometimes very heavy, will get you to a place of renewal. This place is a place of self-discovery, and a place where you will persevere and rebuild from. Please allow your precious heart to shine through, during these trying times, and show its brilliance, without being hidden, or influenced by material possessions.

I Promise you, a male or female shaped by noble sincere actions of the heart and mind, even without material possessions, you are an incredible child, or teenager, you are a great man or woman. You are a great human being. Be brave, be enduring in your time of great turmoil. Outlast your adversities and believe in yourself. You can do this, a loss of material possessions will not, must not, be the death of you. Please take courage, this is not the end of you. You will recover, and you will rediscover you. Tough it out, and get back into the fight. Yes, the possessions you owned were out of this world magnificent. Some items are irreplaceable. The value was not just in numbers, it was also in magnificent history, a part of ancestry, and a blueprint to the past, yes, I completely get it, I promise you, I do. But still precious you, you are not finished; there is much more in store for you, but to get to it, precious incredible you, **"YOU MUST SURVIVE THIS PLACE OF DEVASTATION, AND LIVE."**

You have lost everything, or your resources are cut in less than half, of what it used to be

Taking your life because you have to live with less must never happen. Precious you, please fight for your survival, there is help for you. If your loss is because of an environmental devastation, and the government has given you some form of help, take it and build from there. Add your wisdom, your life experiences, and the end result you desire, to what the government has given you, and fight for the restoration of your life. For you the wealthy, you have experienced opulence upon the earth. You more than anyone should want to stay alive. You more than anyone should be able to say, "I have already lived with a lot, I am willing to live with a little also." Please everyone, middle class poor and rich alike, do not give up. I know that you are in tremendous pain, fear of the unknown overwhelms you, and this is debilitating, and not like anything you have ever experienced before, or perhaps because you have experienced it before, it now makes it even harder.

You are worn out from the experiences of your financial and material loss. You do not have to go down the road of suicide, this I can absolutely promise you. Reinvent yourself, and improvise and overcome. Transfer from a ten bedroom, to a four. Change from a three bedroom to one or two, and buy a cheaper car. Live somewhere that allows you to live within your means, use clearance isles to help fit your budget, and start enjoying the things in life that cost less or are free, and are enjoyable. Wealth does not amount to happiness; we both know this. Precious you, please place great value to your entire life's journey as one. Not, you having possessions, equals happiness, and not having possessions, equals I am miserable and want to give up on life and die.

NO! Life in itself is not attached to wealth; life is life all by itself. Case in point, are you able to take your possessions with you when your life ends? Does a baby enter life carrying possessions with them? The value of your life supersedes any amount of wealth on earth. Your life is precious all by itself. You must live it, appreciate it, and hold on to it, and see it all the way to the very end.

For additional help please call the **Suicide & Crisis Lifeline** at **988**, the 1-800-273-8255 has merged with **988** as of July 16, 2022. **Active-duty members and veterans, please press (1)** when the call is answered or text **to 838255**. Non-military, if you are unable to speak, or you are hearing impaired, you can send a text to the **Crisis Text Line** 24/7, at **741741**. You can also go to **988lifeline.org**. They are waiting for you to call. Talk with them, please release your fears and your pain, they are waiting to encourage your heart and please I beg of you, please live.

We can all survive with less, I promise you. Live in a smaller home, own less in possessions, take the bus, (the environment thanks you). Drive a cheaper car, drive to the next city or two over to get a job, to rebuild your life. Whatever it takes to survive, as long as it is not illegal, please be prepared to do it.

For you the rich, poor and middle class, these are scary times, but you have help. Yes, your life is a struggle, but you will survive. There are charitable organizations that will bless you with clothing, food and shelter. Why are you giving up, why are you throwing in the towel? You want to end your life because you have lost your material possessions, and or your job? Your precious life is far, far more valuable than employment, wood, cloth, cement or metal, this I can wholeheartedly promise you.

To the wealthy, middle class, and poor individuals and families, yes, I get it. You are all tired, hurt, and perhaps a bit confused. The trauma of your loss has damaged you and weakened your resolve. Please rest, take a day, a week, a month off and build your strength and then get back into the fight. It is not over until the skinny, medium and big beautiful women sing together, and I promise you that will not happen. They are too busy hating each other's diet.

You have time to rest and rebuild. Come on now

precious you, go and wash your face, brush your teeth and take a shower, you are giving Pepe Le Pew a run for his money, hint, hint, hint. Eat something nourishing, and read something that will encourage your heart and mind, and please fight for your precious life. **You are a senior, or you are disabled, please pay attention to your health.** There are set aside help for seniors, the disabled and children. Yes, to everyone, it absolutely does hurt to lose what you have worked so very hard for. Yes, it is extremely painful, and I am so very, very sorry for your misfortunes. In spite of it all precious, you Sir or Madam, young lady or young man, "you must live."

My final words to you on this subject matter is this. Put a very vulgar, cantankerous, ill-mannered man or woman in Gucci, Louboutin, Prada, Louis Vuitton, Chanel, Balenciaga, Dolce Gabbana, and they are driving a Lamborghini, and what you now have, is an obnoxious, very-well-dressed, vulgar, cantankerous, ill-mannered man or woman, in the most fabulous, most magnificent clothing, driving a fabulous car.

Material possessions does not make you great; there are monstrous people in possession of untold wealth, but the human being that they are, leaves a lot to be desired. It is who you are that makes you great. Your heart is what makes you great. Please let the loss go; your precious soul is far more valuable than all of it. Please grieve, mourn your devastating loss, and let it all go, I beg of you precious soul that you are. And live out your precious life in peace and in harmony. Please I beg and I admonish you, **"PLEASE LIVE."**

CHAPTER 9

You have lost in an enterprise of some kind, and you are unable to deal with the failure of your endeavor(s), and so, you want to die.

You and I are imperfect human beings. At our worst we have our weaknesses; and even at our best it is the same. Our imperfections, our failures, even though we hate it, are our constant companions and our uninvited guest, and unwelcome friends throughout our lives. For the overachiever, well actually for anyone, this friendship is downright debilitating to say the least, and can be entirely destructive.

There are countless lives lost, many unfulfilled dreams cast along the wayside of life, because many individuals could not face their failures, and instead they committed suicide. Bloodlines of scholars, apprentices, blue blood aristocrats, blue collars, white collars, the lower class, and the middle class have all been lost. There are men and women of distinction within their particular field of study or studies. There are Rhodes Scholars representing their nation, scientists, landscapers, investors, custodians, mechanics, sanitation workers. There are also bakers, cooks, seamstresses, writers, mathematicians, actors, directors, nurses, and doctors, and dentists. All have been lost. We have lost students, musicians, business men and women, teachers, shopkeepers, technicians, technological experts, veterinarians and so much more. For every one that I have listed here, there are countless others, far more that are still not listed.

These souls either one, died too soon, or two, they were prevented from being born due to the darkness called suicide. For the unborn bloodline, none of these souls made it to the earth; these lives have all been lost. Someone in their bloodline suffered failure and could not deal with it, and due to their inability to deal with their failures, they committed suicide. They wiped out their bloodline and everyone in it, because their failure to them was insurmountable; to them their failure was just too great to overcome.

I want my words to have a long-lasting effect upon your heart and mind, and build within you the desire to be a stronger human being. I want to awaken the survivalist instincts within you, and help you to see past your failures. Please listen to me, instead of embracing your failures, pretty please with sugar on top, please appreciate the incredible effort that you did place into your endeavor(s) instead.

Please do not use that failure as a reason to harm yourself

Do not use that disappointment, that failure to harm yourself. Instead, you use that failure to motivate you to great success? Analyze it, what would you have done differently, where did you go wrong? Which part was a success, and which area failed? keep what you need, keep what you can reuse and discard the rest. Do not linger too long on it. Yes, your effort was great, and the loss earth shattering, and so you need to catch your breath. Grab some ice cream, have you figured out yet that I do not drink? Ice cream is my partner in crime, black cherry to be exact. Now back to what I was saying.

Take a week or two off and curse everybody out, including your goldfish or dog. Don't you dare put your hands on your dog, and do not flush your goldfish down the toilet. **Please note my challenge, "you can only curse with words you can say in church at the altar."** You can curse but no violence, heck curse me out too, get it all out. Failure can be very traumatic, deal with it, get it out, do not bury it.

Okay, now stand up, or sit up in your chair or bed, if you are laid out in bed and you are unable to sit up. This goes for you too, as long as you are able to. If you are physically unable to, then do it in your mind. Roll your shoulders forward, now roll them backwards, move your head side to side, now shake your hands, now stomp your feet. There you have it, we shook it off together. We cursed out your dog, your goldfish, and your pet lizard. We cursed out the loan officer at the bank, and even your best friend, with only words we can say in church, and now it is over. The pain remains but the negative influence on your psyche ends here, it is over.

Please embrace the effort you had put into your endeavor

I want you to embrace the effort you made, and not the negative end result. I want to assist you in your understanding that not every endeavor will have a win at the end. Nevertheless, your effort throughout the process is without a doubt valuable; and it is also something to be proud of.

Within your failure are your expertise, your valued ideas, and your dreams. Within your failed endeavor lies your great faith that you placed within it, and so much more. Grab a hold of the must keep, and use them for future success.

Why start from the beginning, when your first effort brought you halfway there. Where you see failure, I see you having a great head start, on the next chapter of your life. You Sir or Madam, have experienced, and have overcome failure. No longer will failure drive you to the edge of a cliff, but instead, it will be a very short diversion on the way to your success.

Failure is a part of our journey, whether we want to admit it or not. Whether we like it or not, and whether we think it is fair or not, failure is our unwanted guest throughout our journey in life. The cause-and-effect phenomenon burns bright, and is ever present within the result of failure. From the cause of failure, comes the effect of strength and determination. From the cause of failure, comes the effect of tenacity, the, "I will never quit," and the, "never say die effect." From the cause of failure, comes the effect of realizing, who is your true friend, and who is your enemy. From the cause of failure, the effect of you rethinking your direction, and your future strategies are born. No, everything is not destruction inside failure; great accomplishments have come alive from failure.

You have help to recover from this place, this I can promise you. This is not the end. Please give yourself the much-needed chance to recover. Please Call or text the **Suicide & Crisis Lifeline** at **988**, the 1-800-273-8255 has merged with **988** as of July 16, 2022. **Active-duty members and veterans, please press (1)** when the call is answered, or text to **838255**. Non-military, if you are unable to speak, or you are hearing impaired, you can send a text to the **Crisis Text Line** 24/7, at **741741**. You can also go to the **988lifeline.org** website. Whether by voice or text, please, tell them what you are feeling, they are there to help you. "PLEASE I BEG OF YOU, PLEASE LIVE."

Your blueprint, your compass

This precious you is your blueprint. This is your compass, your direction for you to find your way back to the land of the encouraged. Where your failed endeavor will no longer take you to the edge of the cliff, but instead, this information will be the catalyst, it will be the cause of your renewed mind, and your understanding, that failure is not the end result. You are now well aware instead, that within that failure, your effort deserves acknowledgement. Precious you please hear me when I say to you, failure is not the end result. Instead, failure is the obstacle that has to be conquered, on your way to success. These words are not empty words. Your intuition, together with your determination, that fortitude of yours, and hard work, will get you there. Do not give up on life. For you to gain success, the accomplishments that you so desperately desire, precious, **"YOU MUST LIVE."**

CHAPTER 10

You are going through circumstance(s), that are not listed.

In spite of the circumstances that have befallen you, in spite of what you are going through, you must live. Please, I beg of you, I encourage you to hold on, and to not give up. Please do not destroy your precious life. Please do not give in to the horrific, the vile wretched darkness that wants to steal your incredible life that is ahead of you. Listen to me, please hear me when I say to you, your beginning is not your middle, and your middle is not your ending.

Please be kind to yourself, please give yourself a chance to find your way, **"PLEASE LIVE."** In spite of your circumstances, that was brought on by tornado, earthquake, fire, tsunami, or flood, or even volcanic lava, and all else. Trust me when I say to you, we can absolutely survive them all, and you will also. To do so, you must dig in and fight for your precious life. What is it that makes you want to end it all? Find it, identify it, and declare an all-out war against it. If you need to move away from whatever it is that gives this darkness power over you, move now!

This is your precious life we are talking about, desperate time's call for desperate measures. Reach out to F. F. F., as in family, friends or a foreigner, which is someone not within your circle. Call the Suicide & Crisis Lifeline and fight for the saving of your soul. There is someone there every minute of the day with one purpose in mind, and that is to help you. They are professionals that are trained to talk you down from the ledge of life that you are standing on, please give them a chance to save you.

Please call or text the **Suicide & Crisis Lifeline** at **988**, the 1-800-273-8255 has merged with **988** as of July 16, 2022. **Active-duty members and veterans, please press (1)** when the call is answered, or text to **838255**. Non-military, if you are unable to speak, or you are hearing impaired, you can send a text to the **Crisis Text Line** 24/7, at **741741**. You can also go to **988lifeline.org**. Please live!

Please give them a chance to help you. You are precious, your life is before you, I encourage you, I beg of you, please live.

Please give us a chance to help you

Give us a chance please; give those of us who are upon the earth a chance to save your precious life. Precious you I beg of you, please give us, please give this foreigner, this stranger a chance to help you. Please do not allow the sun to set on your life.

There is rest up ahead, much laughter, joyful tears, apple pie a la mode, or your favorite dessert. The war will end, and your troubled mind will find hope and safe haven. First, it starts with you not giving up, with you not taking your life. Do not place suicide within your bloodline, and if someone or some others already did, then it is imperative that it stops at their actions. Do not allow it to take root through you. Do not place within your bloodline the saying, "suicide is a part of our family." No! you declare, "suicide is not and never will be a part of my family. Instead, it was a sickness that thankfully, we overcame." Yes, your pain is real; and your sorrow is real, but you can, and you will find your way from there, and **"LIVE."**

My medicine makes me groggy; it makes me lethargic

You have a preference to go without your bipolar or antidepressant medication(s), because you hate what it does to your mind and your body. However, going without it is far more harmful, and with far reaching consequences. You can choose to go without because of the unknown repercussions. You like the odds because you do not know what those repercussions are. You have not considered the potential damages you going without your medication(s), may cause you and others also.

Please allow me to spell them out for you. They are extreme anger that can lead to road rage, where you could run someone off the road. You could also lose control at a party or some form of gathering and beat someone to death. You might suffer an extremely bad psychosis that causes your judgment to become severely impaired. This could cause you to take a gun into an establishment and open fire, or cause you to use some form of weapon to cause bodily harm.

Do I have your attention now? Take your medicine precious you, it is far better than the alternative.

While you are taking your medicine, please work on a solution. Good communication is key in every situation including yours. There are a number of parts that make up that good communication, when it comes to your circumstance. You must be willing to listen; you must be willing to take action, and not just any action, but the correct one.

You must be willing to reach out to the correct person or to the correct organization that can help you. Or reach out to the individual, that can get you to the person or the organization that is able to help you. There is nothing to be ashamed of, when it comes to asking for help. I am beyond proud of you, that you are taking the initiative; you are taking control of the situation and seeking the help that you are in need of, by reading this book.

Ignorance is not bliss, what you do not know can kill you. Please research the medication(s) you are taking. Find out the positives, and the negatives. Ask your doctor or the manufacturer if there are any medication(s) that can soften or erase the side effects of the medication(s) you are taking all together.

If the information comes from the manufacturer or some other place, take the information to your doctor, and you both should discuss your best options, and how you should proceed from there. You can do this, precious, **"YOU MUST LIVE."**

CHAPTER 11

You are under age, and you do not believe that you can find your way out of the situation that you are in.

Precious you, please hold on, help is on the way, please do not give up. I know that you are tired, I know that you are heartbroken, but please hold on just a little bit longer. I have some very important information for you, and I believe it will make a huge difference within your life. Precious please hold on, and please listen to me, please know how much I love you and care for you. There are things that has to be done for your change to happen. Although you are underage, do not doubt yourself. You, I promise, can do what it takes to save your own life. Precious, be brave, and please do what it takes to get the help that you are so very desperately in need of.

You might not know it, but in the not so long ago, let us face it, many teenagers were husbands, wives and parents. They survived hurricanes, they made it through floods, famines, and bad crops, they crossed frontiers, helped to build railroads, prospected gold and fought wars, and led nations. You do not believe me? If you ask your teacher, or go through any royal genealogy book, for any nation, at your school or community library. Some day when you are better and all grown up, please visit some museums within your nation. If you can, travel to the Louvre Museum in Paris, and soak in the history. I promise you, many individuals under twenty years old and even younger have made their mark. They have left their positive impact throughout many nations, within countless societies. Make no mistake, you can do it also. You can do what it takes to save your life. Toughen up! find your inner strength, and get the job done!!! Resist, survive, and overcome the odds that are against you, regardless of your youth. If no one is offering you help, you must help yourself.

If you are being abused. Please precious, I beg of you, **you must call the child abuse Hotline at 1-800-422-4453**. You do not have to pay, and no one will know that you called. The hotline is available **always, day and night,** in more than 170 languages. Please call them precious, I beg of you, they will help you. or go to **www.childhelp.org** for information.

If you feel as if you want to harm yourself, if you feel as if you want to kill yourself. Please precious, please call or text the **Suicide & Crisis Lifeline** at **988**. If you are not able to speak, or your ears does not work, you can send a text to the **Crisis Text Line, day or night,** at **741741.** You can also go to **988lifeline.org**. Tell them what you are going through, and that you are thinking about harming yourself. Do not be afraid to tell them that you are having these overwhelming thoughts of killing yourself, if that is what you are feeling. Do not be afraid; it is okay to be honest with them about what you are feeling. They will help you; they will protect you.

My precious, if you have been a victim of sexual abuse. If a person has touched you where they should not. If a person has done bad things to your body. If a person has done things to your body and told you not to tell anyone. If a person has been saying things to you about yours, or their private body parts, and after doing any of this, they are telling you not to tell anyone, because they will be taken away. Or your mom or dad, or both will be harmed if you tell. <u>Precious please I beg of you, you must tell someone. Please be brave, you can do it.</u> Text **STRENGTH** to the Crisis Text Line at **741741.** Do not be afraid precious, and please do not feel ashamed, you did nothing wrong. Precious we love you and we want to protect you. **I Beg of you, <u>"Please Tell Someone."</u>**

If you feel that you need to be in a safe place right now, call 911. If you cannot do it from home, go next door, or to a nearby store; and tell them you need to call 911 for help. Yell and cry for help. If you do not know how to ask for help, please highlight, or underline the words below, and say it to the officers, or text the words to the **Crisis Text Line** at **<u>741741,</u>** or show the words below, to the police officer at the station, or when the officer arrives at your home. Once you show them these words, they will know what to do, and how to help you, I promise you.

"PLEASE HELP ME I DO NOT WANT TO DIE."

"PLEASE SAVE ME, I DO NOT WANT TO KILL MYSELF."

"PLEASE SAVE ME, I DO NOT WANT TO KILL ANYONE."

Speak clearly, and do not be afraid. **Tell them you are hurting, and you do not want to harm anyone, and you do not want to kill yourself.** <u>**Tell them you are asking them, you are begging them to please save your precious life.**</u>

Please do not use your young age as an excuse to not fight for your deliverance. Someone once shared this question from an unknown writer with me. "Why is youth wasted on the young?" Translation? When we are young, we have no clue, or our youth holds no value, and we have not a clue. I completely disagree with that writer. There are many young people whom in one-way or another, they are making a positive difference upon the earth, and you will do the same also.

Someday, you will talk about how you overcame your abuse, your suicidal thoughts and tendencies, your pain. You will be one of the heroes of your time that inspired those who are depressed, those who are hurting, and those who have lost their way. Before you can do for others, as young and as inexperienced as you are about life, you must do for yourself. What the adults refuses to do for you, you must do for yourself. Ask for help, tell them what is happening to you my precious, **"AND PLEASE, YOU MUST LIVE."**

Do not be afraid if they need to take you to safety, it is okay, please go with them.

Listen to me precious you, if they want to take you to some place safe overnight, please do not fight it. Do not be afraid, just go and get some much-needed rest. Go and sleep off the extreme feelings you are having right now. Due to the abuse, or the suicidal thoughts and tendencies you are having, you cannot, you should not be left alone, or you need a safe place. Allow the professionals to help you, so that you can get better. Hear me and hear me well, no matter your age, when it comes to your survival, you must scream for help, beg for help, run towards help, **"AND LIVE."**

The alternative is you breaking under the pressure of you being sick, of you being bullied, or being abused in some other way, and taking it out on your school, the members of your family, or a stranger. Moreover, when it is over you have injured or killed others, and is now in jail for life, you are on death row, or you have taken your own life. This precious you is not an option for your life, you will not travel down this road. Instead, no matter your age, you will take the courage I am sending to you, and you must fight for the saving of your life. You can do it, I have faith in you, go now and get the help that you are in need of, do not wait. **PLEASE PRECIOUS YOU, PLEASE LIVE.**

PLEASE NOTE: If you suspect child abuse, please call the Child help National Child Abuse Hotline at **1-800-422-4453,** or go to **www.childhelp.org**. All calls are toll-free and confidential. The hotline is available 24/7 in more than 170 languages.

If you or someone you know has been a victim of sexual abuse, **text "STRENGTH"** to the Crisis Text Line at **741741** to be connected to a certified crisis counselor. You have help, please be encouraged.

CHAPTER 12

Someone caused you pain, please forgive them, please let them go, please allow it to end.

Is this person still the same, or has this person regretted his or her actions? They have admitted their wrongdoing and they are very remorseful. It is thirty years later, they have lived a decent and honorable life. This person is a wonderful mother or father, and is an all-around good human being. I, please note the "I." Please note the, "me," as in speaking on myself. I am speaking on how I handled my pain and hurt. I will not erase thirty years, forty years of good from the person's life that caused my pain.

To the person or persons that is livid by my statement of forgiveness. Please do not try to talk me down, intimidate me, or look at me sideways, or try to insinuate. All with one goal in mind, and that is to get others to stop listening to me, or to stop reading my words. Instead, please accept the fact that my journey, my process has not only kept me alive, forgiveness has also given me much needed release from tremendous sorrow, heartache and destruction.

The forgiveness I have afforded others has not only kept me alive, it has also defined not only my life, but also my bloodline as well. Forgiveness causes you to let it all go. Forgiveness causes you to move on, which in turn creates room for bigger and better things. Forgiveness moves you from a dark, dark place, into a place of clarity, when it comes to you and your survival. Yes, I know some of you very well. You do not care about the fact that these words this book can save lives, all that matters to you is that victims continue to follow the hate and anger march. While never finding relief. Let's call a truce, and agree to disagree for the sake of those who are in pain and need release.

You continue trying to save lives your way, and I will continue trying to save lives my way. Now, to you that is in tremendous pain, please hear me out and then decide if you want to stay in the past five, ten, twenty, thirty, or forty years ago, or will you live your life anew, by letting go of the past, and living in the present, the now.

<u>If this person is a criminal that is a stain on society, and what they did was unspeakable, then one time is once enough. They should pay for their crime. They should be prosecuted, and they should be put behind bars.</u>

If this person's mistake was not extreme, there is no way in heaven, earth and the sea, I am going to wipe out twenty, thirty, forty years of this person's good living, to make them pay. Un-forgiveness is a prison that holds you hostage and grooms you for a suicide mission. It brainwashes you for twenty, thirty, forty years into thinking you can never recover from your wounds.

It tells you that everyone is against you, and all men are monsters, or that all women are monsters. Un-forgiveness causes you to ruin bloodlines; it causes you to throw a grenade into someone's forty years of good, just to appease your unforgiveness. Is forty years of good not enough to earn your forgiveness? Let it go, please let it go it is over. You are back in the fifties, sixties, seventies, eighties and nineties hating and plotting this human being's destruction. This human being during that entire time has lived with remorse for hurting you; they have been one of humanities best helper, and have lived an honorable exemplary life throughout the years.

Are they perfect? No, but they have done their best. While you stayed in the sixties, seventies, or nineties; they are in this current year, feeding the hungry, clothing the naked, and helping the sick. They are loving and taking care of their family, or they are single, and are a productive member of society, and is beyond considerate of others.

Now I ask you, this human being is the perfect candidate for what exactly? For hate, for disgrace, for destruction? They should lose their house, their car, their job, their family, because twenty, thirty, forty years ago they made a mistake? What about you, who have you hurt in those twenty, thirty, forty years? Should they come for your destruction in the middle of your struggle?

Precious you let it go! I beg of you; please let it all go and LIVE. Kick unforgiveness out of your life and start over. Divorce unforgiveness and run for your precious life. Do not ask for alimony. The only thing that is inside Mr. or Mrs. unforgiveness bank account is revenge. Please trust me when I say to you, you do not want anything from unforgiveness. The only thing unforgiveness has to give you are memories filled with sorrow and pain, and burdens the size of Mount Everest, that will sit on your chest daily.

Tell un-forgiveness to keep it all, and that you will find your way from here. You do not need un-forgiveness, trust me. You have an army of people including myself that is waiting to show you the way out. Hear me and hear me well, unforgiveness is a song that never stops playing, and a dance that never ends. It is up to you to stop listening, and it is up to you to stop dancing.

Quit that party, because precious you, trust me when I say to you, the unforgiveness gathering will never end. There will never be a day, when unforgiveness volunteers to leave your heart and mind, and to get out of your life. **OH NO, that will never happen.** It is all up to you to evict unforgiveness out of your precious life, once and for all, so that you can find your peace, your release, and your restoration.

Unforgiveness is the friend you had no idea you had, and the Tennant you never rented to. It just shows up uninvited, and it does everything it can to sweet talk you into keeping it around. It will remind you of so call enemies you never knew you had. Like that lady that stole your pacifier when you were one years old. That would be your mom. She "so called stole your pacifier to give you your bottle instead." That is how unforgiveness is at times, no reasoning, just hate.

Tell unforgiveness goodbye, pack up bitterness into unforgiveness suitcase and get rid of them both. Unforgiveness is quicksand from which there is no return, you only sink deeper and deeper into hate filled sorrow. Even after this person dies, you will still be holding a grudge against them. Precious you please, please with sugar on top, please let it all go for the sake of your precious sanity and overall health.

Please forgive them; you must rise to the occasion although it is hard to do so. Please let it all go, so that you can live out the rest of your precious life in peace, harmony and rest. Without you holding on-to destructive memories that cause debilitating pain and constant suffering.

Please let it all go and LIVE. If you need someone to talk to, please call or text the **Suicide & Crisis Lifeline** at **988**, the 1-800-273-8255 has merged with **988** as of July 16, 2022.

Active-duty members and veterans, please press (1) when your call is answered, or text to **838255**. Non-military, if you are unable to speak, or you are hearing impaired, you can send a text to the **Crisis Text Line** 24/7, at **741741.**

You can also go to the **988lifeline.org** website. **Please live!** Please give them a chance to help you. Yes, your pain is real, but in life we do not destroy every person that causes us pain, we instead forgive others, as others have forgiven us in our mistakes.

CHAPTER 13

You have been sentenced to incarceration for decades or for life, for a nonviolent crime

You want to die; you feel your crime does not fit your sentence and you have decided to take your life when no one is watching. First thing is first, please allow me to address your crime. I am certain we both agree that due to your actions, due to your crimes you are where you are. Being incarcerated is not the issue; the issue is the length of your sentence. You have no problem paying for your actions, your crime(s), the problem you have is that you do not believe your crime fits your sentence, your punishment. Due to your sentence, you now want to take your life, you want to end it all. Your despair is all-consuming and there is now a death march upon your life. You have it all wrong, your thoughts and your actions are going in the wrong direction and need to be redirected immediately.

Please do this instead, how about rebuilding your life while being incarcerated? By repaying humanity for your crime(s) against it, by being remorseful, and by making a positive difference. Through you being remorseful, make some changes within you and within your life. If you are already educated, put your plan of action together, when it comes to your desire for the betterment of your life in and out of prison.

You have a life sentence or you will not exit prison until you are in your seventies or eighties and I am talking to you about your exit, about you living your life outside of prison? Please allow me to give you a dose of reality. How do you know your life now will be your life years from now? Do you know what the future brings?

What if your name is sent to the Governor, the Prime Minister, or the President of your nation? What if the sovereign King or Queen of your nation pardons you? How do you know what lies ahead? The answer is you do not. You need to prepare for the best outcome. Do not prepare to die; instead, I say to you, you must do all that you can to live. Prepare yourself to go before them in the best possible way.

Build your resume, you already have a career? Then become a trainer/helper to others. You can no longer practice the career you have? Then reinvent yourself, train for a new career while you are incarcerated. Volunteer, try to keep up with what is happening on the outside, that way you will not be shell shocked if or when you are pardoned, and you will be able to survive the changing world.

A pardon is farfetched, impossible, intangible, and nowhere in sight? Yes, it is, but tell that to half the world that have worked towards what they do not see, suffered for the outcome they hoped for, although there was no guarantee, and not one hint of success. Nevertheless, some died trying and others are still in the battle. Start fighting for yours, suicide is not an option, the only option you have is to repay, restore, and work on the possibility that you might be released. If you are scared and not sure how to deal with those around you, ask your counselor for a mentor that can help you to navigate safely.

You have been sentenced to incarceration for decades or for life, for a violent crime

Due to your violent actions upon humanity, you are now incarcerated for life, or you are incarcerated for decades. Yes, perhaps someone, or some people, committed grievous horrendous, horrific crimes against you. And in return, you were shaped by their horrific actions. But nevertheless, your experiences, your afflictions are never an excuse, to harm your fellow human being. I am so very, very sorry for your pain, and for the evil, the wretched abuse that was inflicted upon you. Please forgive us that we did not reach you in time.

Please forgive me that I sat on my journey and refused to share it until now. Had someone reached you sooner, your life, your actions might have been completely different. Nevertheless, you are here now. You have caused great harm and sorrow, and judgment was placed upon you, due to your very own violent actions. Now you have decided that you would rather commit suicide, you would rather take your own life, than serve out your sentence. I beg of you, I plead with you, I admonish you, "Please Live."

Please reconsider, please stay alive and save some bloodlines. Perhaps you believe your bloodline stops because you are incarcerated for decades or for life?

For every bloodline that is saved, that is redirected to a new journey, through which positive changes, and successful achievements takes place, and this is because of your actions towards that individual that is also incarcerated. This person will be released in less time than you will, or not. That bloodline is now a part of yours. That family tree, that posterity was and will be birthed due to your honorable actions while being incarcerated, this you will achieve.

Please write to your prison director, and make an appointment to sit down with your guidance or your career counselor inside the prison, and tell them of your desire to stay alive and in your right mind. Express your desire to recompense for your actions, by making a positive difference while being inside the prison system. Look for the weak, the fearful, and the lost.

Encourage them, help them to avoid trouble and to survive inside those perilous walls, where death lurks around every corner. Stay alive so that you can keep others alive. That is your way of paying back your victim(s), and or their families, for the crime(s) you have committed against them. This is your honorable way by saving a precious life, or by helping to restore a bloodline. If you are scared, and you do not know how to function with those around you. Ask your counselor for a mentor that can help you to navigate inside those perilous walls. Join a group that is working to change their lives, even if they all have shorter sentences. Ask them to please write to you when they get out, and tell you how they are doing.

CHAPTER 14

You are growing older, and you hate it

We live in an era of great decadence, materialism, and outward appearances. To survive this place of doubt, fear and insecurities, you must be willing to cut your own path for your survival. You must understand that there is a natural process to life, and our seasons in life will come and they will go. The chapters of my thirties are behind me, and I am grateful. The chapters of my forties are also behind me, and for this, I am also grateful. Those years represent failures, and they also represent victories.

I made some really, really, really, did I say really? I made some really horrible decisions and I paid dearly for them. As those horrible decisions have aged, they have transformed into some incredible irreplaceable, beneficial, indispensable information. Believe me when I say to you, those horrible mistakes have now become worthwhile, unbelievably helpful, useful, important, and advantageous, constructive, and very, very precious information to not just me, but also for the younger generation that is in need of help, that is in need of advice for their journey ahead in life. Why did I write different words, but they all had the same meaning? It is because I wanted to place great emphasis on my statement.

Everyone is getting older right along with you. Your age represents triumph over your trials, and a life no matter how bad, someone on their deathbed wishes they had. Please do not cast your soul into the grave before its appointed time, **"PLEASE LIVE."** Imagine if you will, the older generation being removed from the earth. Do you have any idea of the sorrow, the confusion, and the emptiness that would be left behind?

We that are older, are the landmark for the younger generation

We are their landmark that points the way. It is our wisdom, our knowledge, and our very own precious understanding that they need to overcome, to survive in trying times, and to gain strength. It is our life experiences that will become their blueprint on how to avoid pitfalls, and how to dig in when life becomes unbearable for them.

How can we destroy their foundation, their roadmap, their safe harbor that they will turn to? All because of our insecurities, our doubt, or because of our fear. NO! You and I must live and get the job done. We have the significant responsibility of shoring up the younger generations that are coming after us, we must guide them, and we must show them the way. What are you thinking? Do you not realize that you are one out of one billion people in your age group that is getting older? What are you afraid of? Face your later years with grace and poise. Be the rock that those after you will want to reach out to for advice. Embrace the fact that you have lived thus far, and enjoy and embrace the years that are before you. Please enjoy your later years. There are many that went to their grave, that would have given all they had, to grow old upon the earth.

Here is important information for you, male and female **cougars** are no longer found only in the wild, or at the zoo; retirement living is overrun by them; and you will be happy to know that membership is available for your age group to join. The members I am certain will tear down your preconceived ideas, about ageing, and show you how to live to live, and not live to die. Please be encouraged precious you, live and enjoy your fabulous later years. These are your years of rest; be grateful you made it thus far.

Please call or text the **Suicide & Crisis Lifeline** at **988**, the 1-800-273-8255 has merged with **988** as of July 16, 2022. **Active-duty members and veterans, please press (1)** when the call is answered, or text to **838255**. Non-military, if you are unable to speak, or you are hearing impaired, you can send a text to the **Crisis Text Line** 24/7, at **741741**. You can also go to the **988lifeline.org** website. This information is "YES, Repetitive," I know. But you that are hurting needs to hear it, **"over, and over, and over again."**

To you who are hurting, you who are struggling in the debilitating circumstances that you are in, I say to you now, please express your fears; please do not be uncomfortable in expressing what you are feeling. Allow the wonderful **Suicide & Crisis Lifeline** staff to encourage your precious heart. Do not be afraid to say what is on your mind. PLEASE LIVE PRECIOUS YOU, PRECIOUS SOUL THAT YOU ARE, PLEASE LIVE.

CHAPTER 15

The death of a loved one, they died without any warning

You must scream out the pain, find some place private, and wail and cry with unending tears that could fill every lake and the five oceans of the world. If you do not release the grief that is inside you, you will implode in the most destructive manner, and will cause harm to yourself and others. Broken-hearted syndrome is real. You losing a love one is enough to shatter your precious heart, and stop your breath, and losing them without warning intensifies this result a thousand times more.

Do not think about how they died, those thoughts will break you into a thousand pieces. Fill your mind and heart with memories of who they were. Talk to them as if they are here with you. No, you have not lost your mind, does anyone own the market on how to remember our loved ones? You grieve in your own way, as long as it does not cause harm to you or anyone else. You need this, your life, and your sanity, your survival, your recovery depends on it.

Eventually you must wean yourself from talking to them constantly and instead; you must spend far more time talking with the living. In the beginning you were crashing fast and needed an immediate solution. You are stronger now, and time has passed, and you need to start embracing those who are still here with you amongst the living. Please do not accommodate any thoughts of suicide because you feel you are unable to live without them. I promise, you can. Many parents have buried their children and lived. Many spouses have buried their husbands or wives and lived. Many siblings have buried their sister or their brother and lived. Many men and women have buried their loved ones and have lived through the pain of it all and recovered, and you will also. Precious please live, please hold on; it will get better, you must live.

Your loved one is sick, and they are dying

Your movement have slowed down tremendously. it is summer, but you are always cold. You have no answer, you feel helpless. It feels as if you have been thrown into a bottomless pit of sorrow, the despair you feel is mountainous, and earth shattering to your very soul. Some of you spend most of your days at the hospital, and you have found ways to even sneak in at nights. Yes, I know, I did it also.

You make certain they are given pain medication even though they are unconscious, because you want to make certain they are not feeling any pain. You keep your head down at work, and avoid having your name called; out of fear that it will be the news you so desperately do not want to hear. They will only change for the worse; nevertheless, you refuse to leave your loved one side, in the hope for their recovery. They can no longer smile with sincerity; their smile is only for you, not for them, they are suffering and they need to rest from it all. You will take anything over them dying, and they are trying to hold on just for you, just for their family members. Precious you, I ask of you, I beg of you, **"Please Let Them Go."** The sun has set, the season of goodbye is here. Please I beg of you, please help them with their farewell journey. Please allow the end to their suffering. Let them know that it is okay for them to leave, and that they will always be in your heart.

Even in their unconscious state, talk to them, help them to prepare for their departure. The hearing is one of the last senses/organs to stop working. Tell them how much you love and appreciate them; tell them that their wisdom will always be with you and that they will never be forgotten. Most importantly, tell them that you will be okay, their children, their spouse, their parents will be okay and that they should not worry. Say your goodbye precious you, please say your goodbye and **"PLEASE LIVE."**

I earnestly give to you, the same advice also. Do not accommodate any thoughts of suicide because you feel you are unable to live without them. I promise you, you can, and you will. Many parents have buried their children and lived. Children have buried their parents and lived. Many spouses have buried their husbands or wives and lived. Many siblings have buried their sister or their brother and lived. Many men and women have buried their loved ones, and lived through the pain of it all, and recovered. You will survive this sorrowful season; you too will find your way out, **"PLEASE I BEG OF YOU, PLEASE LIVE."**

Grieve precious you, you must grieve and let it all out

My grief overtook me on the highway and I almost ran off the road. I called someone I knew within that area and was told not to go any farther, and that I should immediately stop on the side of the road. That was one of the best advices, I have ever been given.

I pulled over and I give you my word, not even two minutes later I started screaming out of control. The grief of losing my love one had over taken me in the most horrific way. I screamed until I lost my voice. My vision became blurred and I lost every sense of direction. It was bad and was getting worse by the minute. They had to bring someone to drive me home.

Can you imagine if I had kept on driving? It could have been catastrophic for not just me, but also for my fellow travelers who were traveling behind me, alongside me, or in front of me. Find a quiet place and just empty out the sorrow that is within you. Mourn your loss, reminisce on the seasons that you had them with you; and with solemn esteem, please precious, please say your goodbye.

Celebrate the times that you spent with your loved one, and be grateful for those times. Embrace what you learned from them, and hold on tightly to the information, as if it were diamonds, emeralds, and gold. After all, they are gone, they have left the earth. All you have of them now, are precious memories, their precious advice, and the essence of who they were. Treasure it all, use every bit of it that you can, for the betterment of your life and your journey, which is the best way to honor your loved ones. Their advice, their instructions, their guide remains. Hold fast to it and use it all in memory of your precious loved one. Good advice is fleeting, and replaced with the crowd, no matter how horrible the information is that comes from them. If it is popular it is good, that to the shame of us is all that matters.

Live a great life, they would want you to do so. They have gone the way of the dead, and you are amongst the living. Although it is hard, and waking up is the last thing you want to do, but at last, you must do so. Live a great life; live with passion and with much fervor, they would want you to do so. Live and laugh, and keep that grin on your face forever. Allow that light in your eyes to shine through to others, and embrace the precious gift called the earth.

Someday, I too will go the way of the dead, and with all my heart, I hope that those who I leave behind, will live a great life. You do the same for your loved ones that are no longer here in person, and this I promise you, is a wonderful, and treasured way, to honor their precious memory. Be encouraged by the love I am sending to you. Be strong in heart and in mind, you are not alone. Humanity is here with you. This complete stranger is praying for you. This human being that is a part of this vast earth, has written a book to encourage you. Precious soul I love you, yes, I do love you. **"PLEASE, YOU MUST LIVE."**

CHAPTER 16

Suicide is contagious; yes, suicide can absolutely be passed on psychologically to others

This is for every human being on the face of the earth. Teachers if your students, parents if your children, and spouses if your husband or wife, employers please note, if your employee, clergy if your member, boy or girl, Sir or Madam if your neighbor, and team if one of your team members, coaches if one of your players, students if one of your classmates, actors if one of your fellow actors, musicians if one of your fellow musicians.

If any human being upon this vast earth, within its seven, but six livable continents, loses anyone to suicide, you need to watch them like a hawk. Stalk them, harass them by checking on them constantly. Pour words of encouragement into their hearts and minds, and demonize suicide in every way that you can, because it is exactly that. It is a vile wretched monster to the wealthy, middle class and poor alike, and once it takes a life, make no mistake, it will go after the closest to that life.

For you who have lost someone to suicide, and is thinking, "if they did it I can too." Or, "it is not that bad because they did it." There is also the, "I wish I had done it with them." Suddenly what that person did is inspiring you to do the same, which is the very thing the person you lost would not have wanted. You are destroying this person's legacy even farther, by laying your death squarely on them, even if that was never your intention, that will be the end result. Not only is their death responsible for killing off their entire bloodline, or the rest of their bloodline that was to come through them. That bloodline could have included people, actions and solutions for other bloodlines, including wonderful breakthroughs in medicine, in technology, or within manufacturing. It could have included advancement in agriculture, in humanitarian achievements, climate improvement, education, and foreign relations. Your bloodline could have accomplished incredible achievements within the field of aeronautics, interplanetary travel, and so much more.

Now intentionally or not, you are adding the taking of your life, you are adding the killing off of your bloodline to this person's action, seriously? You are willing to tell the world that along with that person taking their own life, they also caused your death? Even if you do not say it, you taking your life would announce to the entire world that him or her taking their lives, caused you to take your life also. Please I beseech you, please I beg of you, please do for them what they could not do for themselves. Please I ask of you, **"PLEASE LIVE."**

Live through your early years, through your teenage years, your twenties, thirties and forties. Go off to college; join an organization that will help you to live out the next season of your life. Go ahead and visit museums, and historical sites. Imagine humanities gut-wrenching struggles, and the fact that we overcame our adversities. Read how difficult the journey was, but in spite of it all, we held the line and did not give in to the horrific sorrows, disappointments and much fear, that was in and before us. Instead, we dug deep within us, and we improvised, we overcame what could have destroyed us, and **"WE LIVED."**

You must also improvise, and you must overcome suicide before it destroys you. Precious please hear me when I say to you, **"You Must Live."** Please hold on and survive this season in your life. Please live through the horrific pain, and the dreadful, dreadful discouragement that you are now feeling. Please overcome this place of debilitating pain, and the relentless heartache. precious soul that you are I beg you, please precious, please stay alive, **Please Live**."

Please Call or text the **Suicide & Crisis Lifeline** at **988**. **Active-duty members and veterans, please press (1)** when the call is answered, or text to **838255**. Non-military, if you are unable to speak, or you are hearing impaired, you can send a text to the **Crisis Text Line** 24/7, at 741741. You can also go to **988lifeline.org**.

I know that breathing is hard to do right now, but I beg of you, please keep oxygen inside your lungs, please do not take your precious life. Although it does not appear this way now, it will get better, your strength will rebuild, and the pain will not be this intense always. Please dig in and fight for your precious life. Please keep your soul upon the earth I beg of you, and I admonish you, **"PLEASE LIVE."**

CHAPTER 17

If you feel yourself moving towards suicide, you must halt your forward momentum, and instead move to an emergency holding pattern, for as long as it takes

This miserable monster called suicide wants you to use your precious hands to take your own life. This monster wants you to kill yourself, wants you to finish the job of destroying what is left of your precious life. What trauma, what an illness, what an ignoble human being did not destroy, suicide now wants you to destroy. You must fight! You must fight for your precious life. The only thing I have for this monster is a GPS that takes this monster to the middle of the Indian Ocean, where it will sink more than six thousand six hundred meters deep, never to return.

STOP Everything and rush towards help!

Suicide is not my friend, please do not expect me to snuggle against a horrible monster that devours our children, our mothers and fathers, our brothers and sisters, devours our neighbors, strangers and lineages throughout many nations. **STOP!** If you are feeling overwhelmed by suicidal thoughts, you must close ranks. Close everything and run for help as if your life depended on it, because I give you my word, <u>PRECIOUS, YOUR LIFE DOES DEPEND ON IT.</u> Do not let your thoughts, do not allow your actions, and your instincts, to take you by any path that brings you closer to suicide. **STOP!** You must do everything in your power to turn everything off, block it all out except the help that you are in need of.

Please do not make bad decisions, because of the panic you are feeling

Whatever panic that is within you, that is pounding excess stress into your heart and mind is a short-circuit. It is not normal, it is a failure within your system that needs to be treated, and it has to be repaired. Mark time, do not move based on the panic within you. You move based on that panic, and what will come after is the revelation that there was much more panic to come, and it only became worse.

Panic also known as, "roach infestation." You will never see one roach traveling alone. If you should see one hurry up and fumigate, because there are hundreds if not thousands behind that one. That one is the lookout that is sent to spy out the land, and to give the coast is clear signal so that the attack, the infestation can begin. The real attack takes place when you give in to one. Block panic, make sure panic sends out the signal, "nope, it's a no go, he or she is holding and weighing all their options, and seeking out solutions. They even called the Suicide & Crisis Lifeline at **988**. They are in control, no regrettable decisions are going to be made here, and so on-to our next victim, we cannot win here. Let's go next door, I can smell lasagna, and apple pie."

All jokes aside, you must never forget that panic is the precursor to all things maddening. When panic sets in, it causes the mind and the heart to change its behavioral pattern, and act out of the ordinary; and to do things that at first will seem as if it will bring relief; but in reality, it will be the death of you. Many actions taken in panic both here and abroad have ended employment; it has ended marriages, ended friendships and destroyed great achievements. Panic has placed people in prison, and destroyed untold relationships; and worst of all, have even ended lives, whether you can believe this statement or not. If you were given the opportunity to go to any jail or prison both here or abroad, and you are allowed to have a conversation with any hit and run inmate, to ask them why they ran away or drove away? often the answer will be, **"I Panicked."**

Many crimes perpetrated by individuals, was based on them panicking. Something happened which was not their intention, and had they told the truth, the prosecutor, or the judge would have worked with them to figure it out. Instead, they panicked, and in reaction to that panic, they now perpetrate a cover up, which is the actual crime. Had they just stopped and done nothing except calling the police, and figuring it out with them; they would be home now instead of serving five, ten, twenty, thirty plus years in prison. Always remember; panic does not travel alone, **OH NO,** there are some despicable characters that are along for the ride. There is panic's best friend called **"I Will React Without Thinking"** and **"Do This Although It Will Make Things Worse For You."**

CHAPTER 18

You are experiencing postpartum depression

Your postpartum symptoms came about due to your body going through changes, to accommodate the baby you carried. These hormones have caused changes throughout your body. Your heart and mind have changed, your way of thinking, your reflexes, your emotions all changed due to your pregnancy. Here is my simple layman's term way of explaining postpartum depression.

There are some hormone changes that are only meant to happen during your pregnancy; once you have given birth, they are no longer needed. Now, you and I know that there are some friends and families that just love to overstay their welcome, and when they do, what was a happy visit is now an unwelcome visit. They stress your mind, upset your heart, and cause you to stay at work or locked in your room, to avoid them.

It is the same reaction with these hormones, they cause chemical imbalances that stresses your heart and mind, and cause you to lock yourself away, due to the stress of it all.

You stay in bed; you just do not have the strength to deal. You feel overwhelmed. You are thinking, but a brick wall is weighing heavily on your mind; and are blocking your much needed commons sense thought patterns. Your important limbic lobe, which is where your emotions reside is under serious, constant attack from every direction. You are desperately in need of help to function in your everyday living.

Out of all that I have explained, there is something that will be created from the storm that you are going through, and that is guilt. You feel guilty that you are not able to take care of your baby the way that you should. You feel guilty because you are out of answers, or the ability to give your family or the baby what they need from you.

The tears, the hopelessness haunts you, and instead of making the adjustments that is needed, by asking for help from your partner, or from your extended family and friends, you push ahead out of the guilt that you feel. This is where you are going wrong.

You desperately want to be there for your baby and for your family but I say to you, you must stop. Please stop, do not function in guilt just to remedy the situation. This is where you are going wrong, or this is where you will go wrong if you continue in this direction.

Your mind is being influenced, by your hormonal imbalances. these chemical imbalances within you, they are a significant part of your decision-making, and that is a huge red flag. Please STOP! Please give up the care of your baby to those around you that are able to be there for you.

Please make the adjustments that are needed

Please listen to me precious you; in life, you must always be ready to make adjustments. Things will not always work out the way you want or expect it to work out.

Here is an example for you. I often use a particular highway, entering any highway usually requires you speeding up to match the speed of the traffic that is already on the highway. The entrance ramp or lane is usually lengthy enough and allows you the ability to increase your speed before getting on-to the highway. On a particular entrance lane a few miles from my home, it is the opposite. The entrance lane is short in length and runs out very quickly. This specific lane requires far more adjustments. You are to speed up to enter the highway, but be prepared to come to a complete stop if the lane runs out, and you have not gotten onto the highway.

The same ability is needed in life at all times. Prepare yourself to get on the highway of life, and still be prepared to make the quick adjustments, that might be needed, in some situations in life. In some areas, the entrance to a particular situation or experience might take very little effort, and in other situations or experiences, it might take you having to make some large adjustments, along with other actions, as they are needed. The more prepared you are in the understanding, that this could take place in life, is the less strenuous the experiences will be for you.

Not only are these adjustments for your safety, for your wellbeing, these adjustments are also for your fellow human beings. Think about it; before you get onto the highway, someone or some others, in all probability has to change lanes to make room for you. Someone has to adjust their speed and or their lane, to accommodate you, and for your wellbeing. You too must also do the same while you journey through life.

As you are experiencing postpartum depression, you must make the adjustments that are needed; for not only you, but for the safety of your baby also. Instead of doing whatever comes to your mind, because of the guilt that you are feeling. If you continue, due to the guilt that you are feeling; you could cause great harm to you, to your baby, and to your entire family.

Do not be afraid or uncomfortable, to ask for help

Ask for help, seek out the help that you are in need of; you must do so before it is too late. You are not strong in mind, and the slightest frustration could cause you to snap. Your precious baby does not understand that their precious mommy is in trouble. They cry because that is the only way they can tell you they need help. That is their language to communicate, but to us it sounds like fingernail on a chalkboard after a while.

It takes a balanced mind to handle a nonstop crying baby. Your troubled mind will find it difficult to handle. You might snap in an instant and without meaning to, you could cause grave harm to your precious baby. A newborn is incredibly fragile, and needs to be handled with very gentle care. One shake and this precious, wonderful soul could die.

You must make the necessary adjustments. You must get the help you are in need of, and you must do it now. Listen to me; it is the perfect storm to push you to the edge of a cliff. You need to sound the alarm that you are in need of help. You are functioning on limited sleep, and your mind is going in many directions, your emotions have been placed in a blender and then given back to you.

Please hear me when I say, "You Must Cry Out." Reach out and get the help you are desperately in need of now, not tomorrow, NOW! Insulate your precious baby, with your family and also your friends. Tell them what you are going through, and that you need them to protect you and your baby, until you have overcome postpartum depression or until you have it under control, through medical treatment.

Yes, it means spending less time with your baby; but this is because you are not well. Get well today; give your baby all the love he or she deserves tomorrow. Please hear me; what you have today, are tons of frustration, confusion, and an abundance of other symptoms that comes with postpartum depression. Heal today, give your baby your all tomorrow.

See a specialist, and if you feel suicidal, please call or text the **Suicide & Crisis Lifeline** at **988**, the 1-

800-273-8255 has merged with **988** as of July 16, 2022. **Active-duty members and veterans, please press (1)** when the call is answered, or text to **838255.** Non-military, if you are unable to speak, or you are hearing impaired, you can send a text to the **Crisis Text Line** 24/7 at **741741.** You can also go to **988lifeline.org.** Please precious you, please get the help that you need to overcome postpartum, so that you and your baby can live a long and healthy life.

For your partner, your family members, your neighbors, your co-workers, friends and all others

Please do not tell yourselves that you are mistaken, and that what you are seeing is not real. NO! Acknowledge it and do something about it. Many times, we tend to gravitate towards unbelief. We do this by telling ourselves that what we are seeing is only our imagination.

Whether we understand it or not, this is our way out; this is our conscious or our unconscious exit strategy; that keeps many of us from having to deal with the situation. Who wants to take over the care of a nonstop crying baby? "Me, Me, Me," one hour later, you call in a false alarm to the fire station on your house, just so you can run back home and get away from the precious baby that has been crying for the past hour, and now they own your last nerve.

All jokes aside, whoever you are, please step in and help this mother. You could be saving both mother and her precious baby from harm. Please help them.

Call a family meeting, mom does not need to know until you make up the schedule, then find a way to tell her that you have a team on hand to help her get through these next few months. The reason you should not say anything before the schedule is made up is simple.

Please do not build up her hopes by telling her she has help, and then disappoint her when the meeting fails. This will cause even more harm to her already broken spirit. Once the schedule is ready to begin, that is when you should tell her, and ask her to make the adjustments that she wants to make. Mom still needs to know that she is still mom.

The helpers must all be trained, and they must understand that this is a precious newborn baby that is susceptible to every virus, and they will need to work together to have a germ-free environment as much as is possible.

Please have someone on hand to spend time with mom. Drive her to see the specialist and emphasize to her that there is no reason to feel guilty. Explain to her that for now she is sick, and that you will all work together to get her better. Create a blueprint for how to manage and pass it on-to others, you can do it, I know that you can. Encourage her heart, inspire her, motivate her into believing that she can do what needs to be done to get better, and saturate her mind with the information over and over and over again.

You are experiencing postpartum depression, and you have no family members near you.

You must be willing to do what it takes to get the help that you need. Speak with your doctor about needing assistance at home, due to your postpartum depression.

Find charitable organizations within your area; and tell them what you are going through, and that you do not want to harm yourself or your baby, and you are desperately in need of help.

Tell everyone that is willing to listen, about what you are going through. Tell them that you are fighting to keep you and your baby from being harmed by you.

Yes, it will take some effort, and you might need to be out there for a week or two, to get the help that you need; but that week or two will save you from a lifetime of utter psychosis, and complete devastation, and relentless pain.

PLEASE I BEG OF YOU, PLEASE PUSH THROUGH THE IMPULSE TO QUIT!

SAVE YOUR LIFE, SAVE YOUR BABY'S LIFE! YOU MUST BOTH LIVE!

The way to accomplish this is to get the help that you are in need of; from your doctor, from charitable organizations, churches and agencies, neighbors, and all else. You and your wonderful baby, you must all survive postpartum depression; **"YOU MUST LIVE."**

CHAPTER 19

You are lonely without an intimate relationship, and for that reason, you want to take your life

Because I am an extreme loner, your circumstance hits close to home for me, and I believe I can help you to overcome it. I know that I am about to burn every hall passes that was given to me. You have been holding strong with me, and taking in my words of encouragement and the admonishments I have been giving to you, with sincere acceptance.

However, in a few minutes that is probably going to change. You are going to tar and feather me, then take a break, and then tar and feather me some more. Hold on please; I need to put on my raincoat or my poncho, oh darn I almost forgot. Goggles too, before the tarring and feathering starts flying all around me. Okay here we go, precious you I hate to break this to you, but someone has to have the courage to do so. The only way you will overcome your loneliness, is by you starting from a place of true reality.

Precious you, please forgive me for saying this, but you might never find a companion. Your peace, your joy, your feelings of contentment must always come through you, and no one else. If no one enters your life, you must still be okay; you must still have joy and peace within your life. We are at a turning point upon the earth, whether we want to admit it or not.

Humanity is hurling at the speed of light towards a

place of utter selfishness. The syndrome, the disease that is called, **"me and my very own self and I,"** is spreading like wildfire with no end in sight. Being with one person, and being considerate of that human being, is becoming an anomaly instead of the norm.

Men and women alike, yes, a resounding yes; women too are brutal when it comes to the consideration of others. Men do not own the market, when it comes to using and abusing others, women do it too. You getting involved with someone right now, might be the thing that drives you over the edge, and destroys your precious life.

It is okay to go it alone, you will be okay

It is okay if you do not have a partner. Please find your happiness all by yourself and rebuild your strength, your joy and your peace of heart and mind. Reinvent yourself, and change your outlook on life. Change the way you see you, and the space around you.

First thing is first, clean your space, remove and add the necessary things that are needed for your recovery, and for you to go it alone. Remove anyone or anything that causes you unnecessary stress. There are some stresses that are unavoidable, and are simply a part of life, like someone that takes the credit while you do all the work.

Build an alone life filled with comforts for you. Start reading more if you were not already doing so. Have a great collection of books and movies on hand, and contrary to popular beliefs watch the same movie a thousand times, if that is your favorite movie. You must streamline your life in a way that will keep loneliness at bay, and keep suicidal thoughts and tendencies in the landfill where they belong.

Have within your home the comforts of home, including a hobby or project that will help to keep you busy. Take up knitting, knit some hats for the newborns at your local hospital(s) or elsewhere.

Volunteer at your local pantry, soup kitchen, schools or missions. The people you help will become a part of your routine. You will also realize that you are in a far better situation compared to many others. If it were not for the thoughts of suicide, you would not be doing so badly after all.

Travel, go on trips, get to know your nation more, and travel abroad if you can also

Travel if you can afford it. Support the tourism industry within your nation, and abroad also. Visit the Metropolitan Museum and other places within the United States, and visit Canada also. If you have a larger budget, travel, and experience the different foods and culture upon the earth. Head to Paris and visit the Louvre Museum, or the UAE Abu Dhabi Louvre also. Visit Saudi Arabia and see its culture. Bahrain and Qatar is right there, visit them all before heading back north, west, or the south. **(Disclaimer).**

Please do not enter any nation, if you cannot abide by their laws. "THAT IS THE UNIVERSAL RULE TO FOLLOW, WHEN VISITING ANY FOREIGN NATION." Visit Dunn's River Falls and Park, on the Island of Jamaica. Visit Great Britain, including Scotland, where Edinburg will beckon to your soul, from its ancient history.

This world that we live in is vast. There is much to love, discover and also appreciate about our different nations. Visit Italy, where you can experience places like Rome, Vatican City and Florence. Visit places within your nation, where you have never been before. These trips will reinvigorate you, and give you renewed focus, away from what use to be.

Visit the Middle East some more; go to more places within the United Arab Emirates, like Dubai, and Sharjah. Head to Africa, the Serengeti awaits, in all its wonders. **Just remember,** while you are thinking; "wow, that lion looks so very handsomely majestic," that same lion is gazing back at you, and is thinking, **"I LOVE THE CHANEL MY LUNCH IS WEARING."**

Do not give in to wallowing and feeling sorry for yourself. Visit Singapore, and South Korea awaits your visit, and so does Australia, along with other places you are led to visit. **Your life is yours to live.**

Please everyone I beg of you, Please be certain to check The State Department Travel Advisory Notices, or the Travel Advisory Notices within your nation, before planning your trip. You need to know the volatility within any nation, so that

you know where to avoid and where is safe to visit. Please plan ahead for unexpected emergencies.

Happiness was never based on companionship

Being in a relationship is not, and was never a true measure for any person to be happy. An intimate relationship exists so that certain things could happen within the boundaries of that relationship between you both, happiness is one of those things. Happiness is also one of those things that comes with you being single. Do not wait for someone joining your life before you find happiness. Move happiness from the back of the line while you are single, to the very front of the line.

Place happiness ahead of relationships. Happiness has always stood by itself. And contrary to popular beliefs; happiness was never married to relationship, or to any form of companionship. This ensures that if companionship leaves happiness will remain. They did not enter together, and will not leave together. Yes, if companionship leave's, more times than not it will hurt. However, due to the fact that you did such a remarkable job strengthening and positioning your happiness independently of, not tied to any form of companionship, you will recover far more easily.

Your routine will come back to you, your hobby and projects will come back to you, and your mission work will return. How do I know this? The answer is simple, these habits all existed before any form of companionship. Metaphorically speaking, this took place when your happiness saw your companionship leaving, and companionship beckoned to happiness to leave also. Happiness said, "sorry, but you are on your own, I was here long before you and I am not going anywhere." Companionship had to leave by itself. Yes, you are definitely hurt, but in spite of it all, you are holding strong. You had a foundation of happiness long before companionship showed up.

The reason for this outcome is simple. It is because everything you built before companionship arrived, is still inside your heart and your mind. Draw on those memory cells and allow them to lead you in a new direction, a healthy direction. Please keep this in mind, your happiness when it is tied to others, are like shifting sand; or it is like the ocean waves that are never steady, and are always rolling in and out.

After all that is said and done, if the pain becomes unbearable in-spite of it all, and you feel like harming yourself, please remember you have help. Please Call or text the **Suicide & Crisis Lifeline** at **988**, the 1-800-273-8255 has merged with **988** as of July 16, 2022.

Active-duty members and veterans, please press (1) when the call is answered, or text to **838255.** Non-military, if you are unable to speak, or you are hearing impaired, you can send a text to the **Crisis Text Line** 24/7, at **741741.** You can also go to **988lifeline.org** website. They will be there for you, and they will help you to overcome this very painful season in life. Please do not end your life because of a breakup, or loneliness precious, **PLEASE LIVE.**

CHAPTER 20

You are a millionaire, you are a billionaire, and depression haunts you

You are wealthy beyond measure, no matter how many lifetimes there are, you or your bloodline will never be able to spend it all. You are able to have just about everything that you desire, from this earth. Nevertheless, you feel empty. You feel a tightness around your heart that never leaves. Your doctor says you are healthy, your heart is fine, and that you have nothing to worry about. You feel lifeless, or you feel lifeless one day, and euphoric the next day, and these emotions are never ending. Some of you have days when you wish for the season when you had far less in material possessions, but you were happy. Others of you want nothing to do with those days.

If I were to place you all in a room together, I would find that your debilitating or functioning emotions with some of you are the same, and the rest of you have absolutely nothing in common. You may think I am rambling, but my statement above is the key to your problems. What you are experiencing is wide ranged, and you are unable to pin down the cause of your oppressive state. Many times, this causes you to surrender to these emotions as your destiny in life.

Please hear my warning, you are making the gravest mistake you can make for the survival of your life. Your suicidal thoughts and tendencies are not to be ignored, they are not to be pushed aside until you can deal with them. Suicide has to be dealt with NOW, not later, not tomorrow, NOW! You must find the solution, and heal from this sickness NOW. You ignoring suicide is like you having a murderer next to you, and telling them to hang out, have breakfast, lunch and dinner, go to spin class with you, sit next to you during the shareholders meeting or the press junket, or other corporate meetings, and them murder you the next day. That is exactly how suicide works; you must deal with it **NOW!**

The same way there are **"functioning alcoholics,"** please believe me when I say to you, there are also, **"functioning suicidal human beings."** You awake each day to your responsibilities of leading some of the largest companies, largest conglomerates in the world, and you make some of the world's leading decisions, that will reverberate throughout the earth. To the shock of many were they to find out, you are suicidal. You are holding on for dear life because you feel a noble responsibility towards your family and your employees.

You must be willing to shed the outer layers, that was built up as a defensive mechanism, but now these layers no longer work to protect you.

To survive this murderous monster, you must start with stripping down and shedding your many outer layers. Metaphorically speaking, visit the person you have not seen in years. The you from many, many years ago. The person you will have to visit is the person who has no experience of your lofty ideals.

This person has not met arrogance, nor have they decided to live together. The former you have not experienced the grandeur of who you are now, and in all probability, have yet to take the road that leads to suicide. It is that person, believe it or not, that can bring you out of the suicidal prison that you are in. The person you are now is in very serious trouble. The you now are in league with suicide. Bring back the desperate human being that starved them self of a normal life, cried, begged, and lived through sleep deprivation and ate humble pie to get you to where you are now. Bring back that person, the scrapper.

Draw on his or her days of old fighting spirit, and declare, "you want a piece of me? Come and get me, I will kick your butt." Bring back that person for this fight, and send the person you are now on vacation. Place the person that you are now into a holding pattern. Allow the former you to fight this battle. The former you fought for your legacy, and will not stand by while suicide destroys everything. We need that person and we need them NOW! Please, do not worry about what the world will think of the former you, their opinion is one of the reasons you are in the situation you are in now, and is having to fight for your precious life.

Hire a watcher. That person "MUST BE WILLING TO SIGN AN IRONCLAD CONTRACT," Their job is to stay very close to you, and to make certain you do not harm yourself. You should not be left alone; you could be a danger to yourself. Your vulnerability due to suicide is real, the possibility of self-harm is real.

Let's dig deep within you, and find the much-needed answers

Now that you have allowed the former you into the fight. Please allow me to ask some questions. Please tell me, when exactly did suicide enter your journey? Was it with you, when you were younger, and you fought through it and won? As you grew older, did the urge to commit suicide come back even stronger than before? Did you start thinking about suicide within your later years, after you went through those insurmountable harmful experiences, that pressured your heart and boggled your mind, and broke your spirit? During which times you just kept on living the perfect life, this is while you are dying inside. The former you saw the evolution of you, and knows how to unravel the suicidal maze you are in now.

Take a break and enter a space away from watchful eyes, where the former you can come alive. Live in that moment and breathe, cry, mourn and deal with your journey and its failures and victories. Curse at it, laugh at it and cry at it, and be grateful. For the moment you do not belong to the world; you are just one of a billion vulnerable people walking the earth; this is what the former you allows' you to do. That release is what your heart and mind need to survive suicide. Give yourself the release it needs please, or you will die under the pressure.

Please precious you, you need to place far more consideration into your physical wellbeing; your very own actions are now destroying your health.

There are many, many souls that have left the earth, and if they could, they would admonish you when it comes to your health. There is a misconception that working eighteen hours a day, seven days a week, year in and year out is special. Actually, you are correct; it is special in that it carries the title of the most wretched choice you could make for your life. **"Note the emphasis,"** It is, unquestionably, it is absolutely one of the most ungrateful ways to live. It is one thing to put in long hours because of a deadline or a short-term project; it is another to abuse the one body that you have to live upon this precious earth. When our body becomes extremely worn out on a continuous cycle, it causes a breakdown within our immune system. Numerous illnesses have, or will materialize after our body has been put through these rigorous experiences.

People are suddenly diagnosed with lupus, kidney failures, insomnia, or reoccurring migraines, or panic attacks and other illnesses. A worn-out body is a body that is susceptible to all manner of illnesses, all manner of very, very negative emotional reactions. We will suddenly become short tempered, we lose patience with others, and we have these angry loud outbursts, even when it was not our intention. Your precious heart, your kidneys, lungs, bones muscles and senses, are being driven over the edge without mercy, by your actions.

One of the reasons why you are experiencing this emotional turmoil which for some of you includes panic attacks, is because your mind is having a hard time coping with the tremendous workload you are unleashing on it day in and day out relentlessly. You constantly feel lightheaded, and still, you ignore your brain when it is telling you, **"Enough, please rest."** Your digestive system is in turmoil, your eyes are going dim and you are ignoring every warning sign that is being given to you. You have been given one of the loftiest of positions in aptitude, in financial gain, and in the incredible distant that you are able to travel, whilst you are upon the earth, and you are throwing it all away, by destroying your precious health. You thumb your nose at the universe, with the most arrogant of gestures, not knowing that your body will not last much longer; and it is because of this breakdown why you are having a flood of suicidal thoughts, and or tendencies, or you are an emotional wreck.

PLEASE STOP! Please take this moment to reflect on who you truly are, and what you are experiencing from within

PLEASE STOP! You are a rare gem to your family, to your friends and to humanity. **PLEASE STOP,** and give attention to the warning signs that are going off within you and through your friends, and your family. Please forget all that you have, and have accomplished, **PLEASE STOP and look at yourself for a moment.** No person can see you the way that you can. Please tell me, what do you see? Please answer me within your quiet space. Do you see heartache, disappointments, and the fear of failing?

Do you see the fear of giving your enemies, the satisfaction of their wretched desire to see you fail in your endeavors? Do you see the distance you want to go, and the oh so daunting, the backbreaking, mind-breaking journey ahead? Do you think to yourself, that you are just too far in to stop or to turn back? Do you see precious sleep that evades you, and the comforts of home that is out of reach? Do you think to yourself that it is no longer as enjoyable as when you started on this incredible journey? How am I doing, am I seeing through you?

You are in control; you can take the much-needed break

The incredible truth is, you are in control of how you will spend your time in the morning, noon, or in the evening. Leaving for seven days or fourteen days and going to a luxurious hotel where no one knows who you are. Where the bed you are laying in is so comfortable, it makes you not want to get out of bed. The quiet feels like a gift from the heavens, and the incredible food makes you smile for no apparent reason, other than you feel great while eating.

Please tell me, what is stopping you from taking time off for your peace of mind, and for your overall health? Are you afraid that if you take some time off you will fire yourself from your job? Are you afraid that you will reduce your benefits or take them away all together? Sir or Madam, are you afraid that when you return to your job, you would have already instructed the human resource department of your company that you created, to fire you?

Okay I get it, your boss is ruthless, and you do not want to cross him or her. I totally understand now, if you cut back your hours, or take some time off from the company, you might fire yourself, because you are just that ruthless. I completely understand your predicament, as to why you refuse to slow down, and give your body the precious healing rest that it needs to recover.

It does not matter if you are wealthy, but you are not the head of any organization, or you are wealthy, and the head of an organization. This same solution is for all of you. If you hate where you are now, admit it. Here, hold my hand, place it over your precious heart and weep for the journey of sorrow that has haunted your journey. Wealth at times will make it harder for you to let go, but I am encouraging you to do just that. Let go of the environment that you are in, and do things differently. If winter causes your bones to ache, you need to get out of winter and head towards warmer climate.

If the environment you are in now, causes you to be unrelentingly depressed, to the point of you having extreme mental stress, or you are wanting to take your precious life. You need to immediately distance yourself from that destructive environment. Please relocate to an environment that is healthy for you to live in. Yes, I know, "opulence is a nightmare from which many do not want to awake. Opulence is also the prison that most people want to stay in." Believe me, I completely understand.

Do not be afraid to let people, places, and things go. Do not be afraid to close this chapter, this season of your life, if this is what you want to do. Do not kill yourself, because you hate where you are, and you are desperate for change, but you believe change is impossible. **<u>You will be okay.</u>** In life, there are many seasons, there are many chapters in our lives, and there are times when it is best to leave and come back when that season, that chapter has ended. You do not believe me? Ask your Michiganders, Bostonians, Philadelphians, your New Yorkers and all others, who head south or west for the winter.

Perhaps your winter has arrived, and you need to head south, or west for a more suitable environment, until that season passes. Perhaps you want to remain in the cold for the winter. If that is your decision, you must protect yourself from the extremely harsh experiences of your winter environment.

Metaphorically speaking, if you wear a t-shirt in zero degree weather, with no protective clothing, you will die. Have you equipped yourself for the environment to fight off suicide, or have you been too busy, and have left it up to chance? Now winter has arrived, and you only have t-shirts and shorts for the outdoors environment, that is minus zero-degree weather.

If you are going to stay and live through this brutal season in life, you must be prepared. One of your protections is the **Suicide & Crisis Lifeline** at **988**, the 1-800-273-8255 has merged with **988** as of July 16, 2022. **Active-duty members and veterans, please press (1)** when the call is answered, or text to **838255.** Non-military, if you are unable to speak, or you are hearing impaired, you can send a text to the **Crisis Text Line** 24/7, at **741741.** You can also go to **988lifeline.org.** They will protect you from the dead of winter, and get you to spring. The same goes for you, as it goes for others. You must all find your triggers that take you to this dark wretched place of suicidal thoughts and or tendencies; and you must repair, or remove them.

The weight of moral and ethical responsibility is upon you

For you who are wealthy, and you are the head of a corporation/conglomerate. You have a moral and an ethical responsibility to you, and to every member of your company and also to your family, both here and abroad; to do all that is in your power to stay healthy and strong.

Your decisions, your input can make or break your organization and your family. There are generations within your care, both professionally and personally, and you must honor not only you, you must also honor them, by overcoming suicide and staying alive. Let us face the truth together, stocks rise and fall at the slightest negative rumor. You taking your life could bring your organization and your family to their knees. Your competitors would have a field day, they would spread rumors and innuendoes about you; all with the intention of destroying what you built and left behind. There would be dinner parties where suddenly innuendoes of you would be the cocktail of the hour, and dessert would be the rumors of the slush fund you created, that was discovered by the FBI, Scotland Yard, CSIS, or la Sûreté. You need to stay alive for not just you, but for all the blood sweat and tears, that has been given in honor of you, your family, and your organization. You must always fight to protect your achievements, and also those of your organization, your employees without fail.

This is not the form of relief that you are used to. It lacks splendor, the grandeur is missing

For you that are wealthy, and you are accustomed to all things that are grandeur in size. Perhaps you expected intellectual ideas of great magnitude, that are the equivalent, or close to the height of Chogori Mountain, or even higher.

That Sir or Madam is your mistake. If you want to live and overcome suicide, you must be prepared to use everything that is available to you, both simple and complex, to survive this wretched monster, that wants to take your life. I am not a genius; I am simply a human being who lived with the wretched monster called suicide for a long time. I am someone that had suicide's hands wrapped around my neck, and was able to pry them off me and live, and to the heavens I am beyond grateful. Your help is here, **ACCEPT IT.**

I have lived through the most debilitating panic attacks you could ever imagine, and I overcame them, and no longer have them. I am sorry, there is no grandeur here, I am simply a human being that has the ability to encourage my fellow human being's heart and mind, with the best of intentions. Please keep this information on you at all times, and do not hesitate to use it.

Please call the **Suicide & Crisis Lifeline** at **988**, the 1-800-273-8255 has merged with **988** as of July 16, 2022. **Active-duty members and veterans, please press (1)** when the call is answered, or text to **838255**.

Non-military, if you are unable to speak or you are hearing impaired, you can send a text to the **Crisis Text Line** 24/7, at **741741**. You can also go to the **988lifeline.org** website.

Whether it is night or day, or if it is before or after a board meeting, or shareholders meeting, please reach out to them. Call them if you are on vacation in Napa Valley, Italy, The Hague, in Rome or on the island of Jamaica. Call them from the Maldives, from the Riviera, UAE, Paris, or Prince Edward Island. I have made my point, and I have removed all excuses. It does not matter the day or the night, or the location, the **"Suicide & Crisis Lifeline staff will help you."**

PLEASE DO NOT KILL YOURSELF, PLEASE LIVE, PLEASE HOLD ON; IT WILL GET BETTER, BUT FOR THIS TO HAPPEN, **"YOU MUST HOLD ON, YOU MUST LIVE."**

CHAPTER 21

You are stalking someone with the intended result being murder and suicide

Please do not destroy your life! Every human being has the right to choose his or her partner. If they did not choose you, or no longer wants to be with you, precious you I beg of you, please let them go. Why stalk, why harass any human being to stay or return to you? Please let them go. For some individuals, your actions will not change, it does not matter what I or someone else say to you.

These individuals are dangerous, and the only thing that can stop them is prison or death, nothing more. You decide, is that who you truly are? Are you an individual that is dangerous, that is out of control, and only prison or death can stop you? If you are that person, I am here wasting my time, my thoughts, and my words in reaching out to you, because you want nothing to do with my useless book, or anything to do with me. Did I get it right, do I understand you correctly?

Well, you know what, I refuse to give up on you?

For you that are choosing prison, I am going to give you a taste of your own medicine. I am going to stalk you until you come to your senses. I will not stand by while you a human being, a soul, march your way to prison, or to death. Please look, please listen, and please act on my advice. How many people are upon the face of the earth? As of now, I believe there are approximately eight billion people upon the earth. How many countless people will cross your path in a lifetime? Amongst them all, do you truly believe that this is the only person for you? The person that you beat, you abuse in the most horrible way, that is your one and only? This human being was born upon the earth to be battered and be abused by you, in the most sorrowful, in the vilest most villainous of manner?

Please read the words you just read over, and over, and over again, let them soak into your soul, and please do one more thing for me. Please replace that human being you abused, with the most precious male or female within your family or someone that is dear to your heart. Now replace you with any man or woman. Someone else is doing everything you have done, and is doing to your victim, to the person that is dear to you.

Please advise your love one; please tell them what to do. Please save your love one's life. Please get them away from their abuser. They are your sister, your brother, your mother, your father, your aunt, or uncle, your child, your cousin, your neighbor or your friend, and you know they are suffering greatly.

Please tell them what to do, please save their life. They are drowning, and you can see it. They are so very precious to you, and they need your help to get out. Please help your love one that is dear to your heart, please help them to find their way out from the horrible situation that they are in, as death looms large upon them and an abundance of sorrow is their breakfast, lunch and their dinner. I am so sorry, I know I should be talking to you about the person you love and you are abusing. Instead, I ended up talking to you about the one you love, that is dear to your heart, and how to save them, and how to get them to safety. I ran out of time, maybe in my next book I will talk to you about your love one that is being abused by you, please take care, "**PLEASE LIVE.**"

There is help for you

No human being is perfect, we all make mistakes. How we deal with our mistakes, and how we recover from them, is what sets us apart. Please save your life, please turn things around, **"Please Live."**

Please Call or text the **Suicide & Crisis Lifeline** at **988,** the 1-800-273-8255 has merged with **988** as of July 16, 2022. **Active-duty members and veterans, please press (1)** when the call is answered, or text to **838255.** Non-military, if you are unable to speak, or you are hearing impaired, you can send a text to the **Crisis Text Line** 24/7, at **741741.** You can also go to the **988lifeline.org** website, and allow them to pull you back from prison, and from death.

<u>**Please check yourself into treatment, for your anger, and to stop your march towards murder and suicide I beg of you, I plead with you, and I encourage you. Please find your way back I beg of you. PLEASE LIVE, please allow yourself the opportunity to change I beg**</u>

of you! Please allow yourself the opportunity to heal, and to be restored. Please allow your victim to live. Give yourself a fighting chance to survive suicide, and to not become a murderer, I beg of you please.

Your bloodline is begging you to hold on, and to not give up. Your bloodline is begging you to please allow them to be born. Your precious bloodline is saying to you,

"it will get better, all we are asking of you, all we are begging of you, is that you please, please, please hold on for dear life; and allow yourself to change for the better. Please allow us to be born, please allow us to breathe, to laugh, to cry, to fail, to succeed and to hope. Please we beg of you, please precious soul that you are, even with all your mistakes, "PLEASE LIVE."

For some of you, those who you will meet up ahead is living in hope of that day. It is you that will save their lives through your testimony of survival, of change. It is you that will help their pain to lessen, when you tell them of your failures, and how you overcame, how you became a better human being.

THIS PLACE IS NOT THE SUM OF WHO YOU ARE, PLEASE HEAR ME, "YOU CAN STILL TURN IT AROUND. DIG IN AND FIND THE COURAGE FROM DEEP WITHIN, TO FIGHT FOR THE SAVING OF NOT JUST YOUR LIFE, BUT THOSE YOU ARE PLANNING TO MURDER ALSO. STAND BEFORE THAT MIRROR AND PLEASE LOOK YOURSELF IN THE EYES AND DECLARE OUT LOUD, "I WILL NOT MURDER MYSELF, I WILL NOT MURDER OTHERS, I WILL FIGHT TO SURVIVE; I MUST SURVIVE; I AM GOING TO LIVE."

CHAPTER 22

Someone, an ignoble human being, used the pretense of love, to take advantage of you

You are heartbroken beyond measure, and you feel taken advantage of. You gave so very much of you, and you receive nothing in return, except pain and heartache. You feel as if you are unable to go on without this person, but you will not stop them, because they have made their choice. In your pain, you want to kill them and then commit suicide, or you just want to kill yourself.

Precious you please hear me when I say to you, I am so very sorry for your pain, but here is your light bulb moment, here is clarity for you. Precious you, you were handed a gift, say "thank you." Hold up a finger from your right hand and one from your left hand above your head, make a cross with them and scream out loud, **"VAMPIRERRRRRRR,"** and run for your precious long-lasting life.

They are out of your life, "say thank you."

Sir or Madam, young man or young woman, that bloodsucker is gone, why in heavens name would you want that parasite back, or want anything from them? Do you really want a human being that has caused you so much harm, to still be in your life, to wreak more havoc? This is your opportunity to start over, to leave the madness behind and to get a fresh start. We can always replace material things. Please listen to me I beg of you, if it goes beyond material things, please let the heavens deal with him or her. You keep your hands clean. They have taken enough from you; do not allow them to take anymore. Why would you give up your life to someone that has done you so very, very wrong? Shut the door, nail the door shut to prevent them from returning, and if you have to move away, move away.

Take some time away if you can

If you own your home, take a vacation; or go and stay with someone, until you have broken the connection between you and him, or her. Buy a slingshot and some strawberries, for when they show up, or a big ripe mango, **(Jamaican in me).** I hope you have a good quarterback aim. and if they call the police because you slung strawberries at them, or threw the mango. Tell the police officer they looked hungry, and you felt very sorry for them, and so you slung strawberries or you threw mango for them to eat.

Trust me, the judge will believe you, when he or she notice the picture of the nice ripe mango turned in as evidence, but the actual evidence in the bag is only a mango seed. Explanation from the vampire, "I do not know what happened to that **"delicious"** mango Your Honor, he or she threw it at me. I was knocked out, and when I came to an hour later, it was a mango seed." **"Liar,"** note the word **"delicious,"** How did he or she know that the mango was **"delicious,"** unless they ate it? He or she ate your mango and then sued you for damages. **Okay, here is my disclaimer:** Forget the slinging mango and strawberries at them. For the last plundering they might try to sue you, for slinging strawberries and throwing mangoes at them.

Let us just call the **Suicide & Crisis Lifeline** at **988**, the 1-800-273-8255 has merged with **988** as of July 16, 2022. **Active-duty members and veterans, please press (1)** when the call is answered, or text to **838255**. Non-military, if you are unable to speak, or you are hearing impaired, you can send a text to the **Crisis Text Line** 24/7, at **741741**. You can also go to **988lifeline.org**. Tell them about your pain and sorrow, at how horrible this person was.

Precious you listen to me, all jokes aside; yes, you needed to take a moment to laugh, however now we need to be serious. Please do not allow this experience to drive you to the brink, and cause you to take your life. Do not allow this person, this situation to cause you to commit suicide. In life there are countless joys, laughter, sorrows and funny moments, and some heartaches throughout our journey, this is why it is called life. As we live, we experience them all, and we learn from them.

We learn what to embrace, and what to avoid, what to appreciate, and what to disdain, we learn what we can reuse and what we must discard, and we learn even more. Please live out your journey, place this experience within your rearview mirror; it is over, please let it go and live. There are some wonderful things up ahead, march forward and live your life.

CHAPTER 23

Addiction to drugs/Addiction to death

Yes, I agree, the heading above is precisely right. addiction to death. Addiction if not destroyed, will kill the relationship you have with your parents, and it will also kill the relationship with your precious children. Addiction will destroy any form of decent relationship you had with your girlfriend, or your boyfriend, your husband or your wife. Addiction will kill your future earnings, and it will also kill the relationships you have with your business partners, and with most of your friends that are decent. Addiction will kill your bank account. Addiction will kill the relationship you had with your neighbors. Addiction will kill your education, your dream job, your inventions, your health, your favorite food, your laughter, your conscience. Addiction intends to kill your ability to be a decent and honorable citizen, and will send you to the filthy underbelly of life.

Addiction will cause you to do and say things that only monsters or the depraved will do and say, and will leave you disgraced and broken into a thousand pieces. Addiction will give your wretched enemies the ammunition they need to rage against you in the vilest of manner, with the sole intention of pushing you over the cliff's edge, that you are standing on.

Addiction, make no mistake, will kill your future bloodline, and addiction will draw thieves, rapist and murderers to your life, and will turn them into your best friend and closest confidant. When all is said and done, this addiction will then move to finish its job so that it can move on-to its other victims. Addiction will plant people that was never meant to be in your bloodline into your bloodline. Addiction will plant generational sicknesses into your bloodline and then kill you through the drug of your choice, or by you taking your own life, which amounts to the same.

Please use my experience to help you to recover from your addiction

Here is some encouragement for you. I was in a horrific accident where I suffered over seventeen broken bones to my left leg, ankle and foot, yes seventeen. This does not include my five toes that broke towards my toenail and broke in the direction of my ankle. Chunks of bone fell out of my leg and left a hole.

The doctors placed a large screw in the middle of the bone where the chunk of bone fell out; to somehow keep it from collapsing in, I guess. Your ankle is a ball and a socket, please make your fist into a ball, and use your other hand to hold your fist. The fist/ball dissolved into fine splinter and powder, and only left the other hand/socket.

My instep broke into multiple pieces, and my foot bottom cracked in pieces and fell off. Not the skin but flesh, and left only a thin layer to my foot bottom. The bones inside my foot collapsed; and so, when I walk my bone is right there at the bottom of my foot.

I have multiple screws and plates within my foot, and to this day; my leg, ankle, and foot looks like Swiss cheese on any x-ray. I spent close to three weeks on morphine in the hospital, and was sent home with a prescription for Percocet. I took only one tablet, and became incapacitated, I called my doctor and they prescribed Vicodin instead, it was the same result.

I did my research, and found out these medications were narcotics, and they were highly addictive. I refused to take any of them from that point onwards. In my medical charts it is written/flagged, **"allergic to narcotics."**

In other words, from twenty plus years ago until now, I have not taken one narcotics medication, believe it or not. The strongest I took/take is Ibuprofen 800 milligram, and when I found out long term usage could damage my heart, I limit myself in taking it. Any doctor will also tell you, my injury is extreme, and many have never dealt with such extreme. The pain that comes with it will end when I die.

My doctor would tell you that I suffer from extreme swelling to my left leg, foot and ankle. They will tell you this injury ends any normal future this person was to have, they will not be able to walk even a mile, and running is now a thing of the past. They will tell you that long-term amputation is my diagnosis and the mental stress of it all is probably debilitating.

Please be honest, from reading this book, did you have any idea I carried this burden? Did you have any idea I still live with not just mental pain but physical pain also? My point is you can deal with what you are going through I promise you. For you who are not an addict, you must not go down that road; you will lose everything. You must survive, and if possible, recover from what you are going through, in the healthiest way possible. This is for the sake of you, your bloodline, and all that is dear to you. Find alternatives and figure it out, and yes, some of you your injury is from the battlefield and you need stronger medication. Have the tough conversations with your physician, a counselor, your pharmacist, and please fight to not become an addict. Do not allow anyone to influence you into taking drugs so as to have a good time, you will die, even while you are still living. That good time while taking drugs, will end the best of you; and the very worst will enter in.

Here are your options

For you who are an addict already, yes, I know, the process of becoming clean is worse than death. Well, you know what? There are two doors, if you open the first door it says, **"Recover or Die Trying."** Open second door and it says, **"Recover or Die Trying."**

You have no other options. Admit it, death has a murderous grip on you and wants your soul, and it is using addiction to lead you to either suicide or to the drugs killing you. One way or another, this vile monster called addiction wants you dead. Your recovery is all on you. You must let go of everyone and leave everything behind and run for your precious life. You must let go of everything or everyone that is a facilitator to your drug habits, including those who are not willing facilitators. It does not matter if they are your mother, your father, your husband, wife or your child. Yes, I know, it is the worst possible scenario to distance yourself from your child or parents, your husband or wife. But what choice do you have, if you stay you will die?

Enter a treatment center and stay as long as you can afford to. Whether through your finances, insurance coverage, or through charitable agencies. Tell them you are willing to volunteer while being there, if that will help you to stay longer. You need to stay in a holding pattern until the murderer has broken contact with you, through taste, through smell, muscle or cell memory, and also through your friends, family, and acquaintances, through your job, through partying and all else.

If you are in jail, please do not fight to be released too soon; please stay there and dry out. Yes, crazy, I know it is crazy; nevertheless, it makes sense given your circumstances. You must be willing to do whatever it takes to save your life. If they are unable to keep you long term; while in one treatment center apply to another; that way when you leave one you can transfer to another.

Say your goodbyes

Please precious, you must avoid going back to your old familiar party places. Please bury the thoughts of,

"I am going to have fun when I get there." That is over, the creek has risen and you can no longer crossover, say farewell to the other side. American law term, **"fruit of the poisonous tree."** "If the origin of the evidence is bad, the evidence is bad also." Addiction is bad; and almost everything that comes from it is bad also. Please **<u>I beg of you, please let it all go and please fight to stay alive; precious you, you must fight for your recovery.</u>**

If your family members are not enablers, tell them you need to go dark. In other words, you are no longer in existence for friends. Close rank and circle the wagons, let no one in, except those who belong inside your recovery. This is your precious life, your existence, the survival of your bloodline. You must climb Chogori Mountain and battle death, so that you can come out on the other side alive and well. You are going to have to become a jerk for your sobriety, and abandon people for your sobriety, relocate for your sobriety, divorce for your sobriety, and all else.

Face it, if you stay in these situations that enables you, you will die. **GET UP NOW!** Make the phone calls, and go to the recovery center, and live precious you. Please, please, please I implore you, I ask of you, I beg you, I admonish you, please I encourage you, please live, please survive, **"YOU MUST LIVE!"**

Addiction from the loss of a loved one, or loved ones

Your pain is unbearable I know, yes, I promise you,

"I DO KNOW." The sorrow that grips your soul is real; you have suffered loss that is unimaginable to the human mind. They died and you lived, you are still here. Unbeknownst to most, they have no idea, you died right along with them.

The life you were to have with them is dead. The dream and aspirations that would have come through them to you is dead. Your sanity is dead, and your strength is dead. Your ability to dream for the future is wiped out, and to your horror, to your sorrow humanity has shown you no mercy. Yes, yes and yes, I get it, I know exactly what you are going through. The drugs you take are not for recreational purposes, it is not for feel good purposes. You take drugs, you took drugs to numb your mind, to keep your sorrow at bay, and to keep your mind in a fog. You do this, you did this to keep yourself from thinking about your tremendous loss, and the sorrow that drenches it. The billows of despair rolls over your heart and mind, death haunts you nonstop, and the pressure on your heart and mind is crippling.

Your weakness, has revealed their wretchedness

Your so call friends and your family, the stranger, monsters within humanity, uses your addiction, the addiction brought on by horrific sorrows, which led to your mistakes to mock you, to vilify you, to drive you back to addiction or to keep you in addiction, and to push you over a cliff. The worse you look is the better they look, is their thinking. The reality is no matter how bad you look they look far worst in their nefarious actions. Any human being that uses a person's sorrow, a person's weaknesses to elevate himself or herself is in need of help.

The shame that has been poured out upon you is your saving grace. Ask any Pastor, any Priest, what the LORD does for the weak, for those who have made their mistakes, and those who are constantly under attack and mocked, by their enemies because of their mistakes. Mercy is yours, redeeming grace is yours, please grab hold of it to overcome and to live.

Your loved ones have gone the way of the dead, remember them, but please let them go

You, young lady or young man, you, Sir or Madam, must live. Those you have lost, they are gone, but you are still here upon this earth. They would not want you to be in this state, and would mourn for you. It is okay to mourn, yet still have laughter. It is okay to mourn, and still have joy. Yes, you have suffered great loss; but the rerouting of your life will still give you tremendous joy; if only you will allow it to happen.

Let them go, let him, let her, please let them go. You are still here for reasons that are obvious and not. What if you had died, tell me would your child, your children make it to the earth? What about the people around you that needs you? If you had died, would they have made it? Please shed the addiction precious you, please have the courage to live a drug free life. Cast off the fears that haunts you and **LIVE.**

No More Excuses

You must get away from addiction, and if you have gotten away from it, Sir or Madam, young man or young lady, you must never go back to addiction. Let it go please precious, and live. Live precious you; please I beg of you, you must live. No more excuses, no more wallowing, **YES,** yes, your sorrow is valid, it is justifiable, it is understandable, "same meaning, I know." This is my way of making a strong point.

Your sorrow is the type of sorrow, that would cause someone to go to sleep, without ever wanting to awake ever again. The sorrow you carry is deafening, it is boisterous, and it beats the living daylight out of you. Did you think I was lying when I said, "I know?" Yes precious, I know the sorrow that haunts you, because I too have sorrows that haunts me also, but in spite of it all precious, **"YOU MUST LIVE."**

PLEASE PRECIOUS YOU, NO MORE FROM THIS DAY FORWARD. YOU MUST LIVE IN JOY, YOU MUST LIVE IN PEACE, AND PRECIOUS YOU, YOU MUST LIVE FREE OF DRUGS. YOU PRECIOUS SOUL THAT YOU ARE MUST LIVE IN HOPE. I BEG OF YOU, PLEASE LIVE.

PLEASE DO NOT CAST YOUR PRECIOUS SOUL INTO THE GRAVE I BEG OF YOU. PLEASE HEAR ME WHEN I SAY TO YOU, YOU ARE A PRECIOUS, PRECIOUS, PRECIOUS SOUL UPON THIS EARTH, AND I ENCOURAGE YOUR SOUL. PLEASE GIVE YOURSELF A CHANCE TO SURVIVE THIS WRETCHED, HORRIFIC, ALL-CONSUMING SEASON OF LIFE, I BEG OF YOU, I IMPLORE YOU, I ADMONISH YOU. YOU MUST SURVIVE THIS MURDEROUS SEASON OF LIFE. DIG DEEP, FIGHT, SURVIVE, OVERCOME, AND LIVE.

If your precious heart is discouraged, and your mental stress is breaking you down. If you are being drawn to suicidal thoughts, and or tendencies. You must reach out to the **Suicide & Crisis Lifeline** at **988**, the 1-800-273-8255 has merged with **988** as of July 16, 2022.

Active-duty members and veterans, please press (1) when the call is answered, or text to **838255**. Non-military, if you are unable to speak, or you are hearing impaired, you can send a text to the **Crisis Text Line** 24/7, at **741741**. You can also go to the **988lifeline.org** website. Whether by voice or text, tell them what you are feeling, tell them about your pain, your heartache, and be honest about your desire to harm yourself if that is what you are feeling and thinking. They will not judge you; they are selfless in their desire to help you to overcome; they are there to help you.

PLEASE HEAR ME WHEN I SAY TO YOU ONCE MORE, "THEY WILL NOT JUDGE YOU, THEY WILL HELP YOU." PLEASE I BEG OF YOU, PLEASE LIVE. YOU MUST LIVE, PRECIOUS SOUL THAT YOU ARE, YOUR FUTURE AWAITS YOU. YOUR RESTORATION IS UP AHEAD, PLEASE PRESS FORWARD. SURVIVE THIS HORRIFIC SEASON IN YOUR PRECIOUS LIFE. PLEASE PRECIOUS, "PLEASE LIVE."

YOU MUST BEAT BACK ADDICTION WITH ALL YOUR MIGHT. FIGHT WITH EVERYTHING THAT YOU HAVE, AND DO NOT HAVE ALSO. AS IN, CALL ON OTHERS TO FIGHT FOR YOU ALSO. BORROW THEIR STRENGTH, THEIR IDEALS, THEIR DETERMINATION, BECAUSE YOU HAVE LOST YOURS. PRECIOUS SOUL THAT YOU ARE, GIVE IT YOUR ALL, AND THEN SOME, "YOU MUST LIVE."

My injury, my fight against addiction

As I said before, I suffered a horrific injury that left me with over seventeen broken areas to my left leg, ankle and foot. Splinters of bone fell out, and was replaced, with screws, and metal plates. My foot broke, and became straight as your hand, and was reshaped back into a foot. The flesh beneath my foot-bottom/plantar fell off, and now I only have a thin layer beneath my foot. The front of my foot, right behind my big toe fell lower than my heel and my toes, which means only that one spot touches the ground.

The area behind my big toe is the only area that touches the ground, and the bone hangs low. This means when I walk, I am walking on bone, because the soft cushion, the fleshy area is all but gone. I no longer have an ankle, screws replaced my ankle, and when I walk, it is bone grinding on bone, because the cartilage in my ankle area is also gone. My tibia and fibula look like Swiss cheese, there are fracture lines and mass injury throughout.

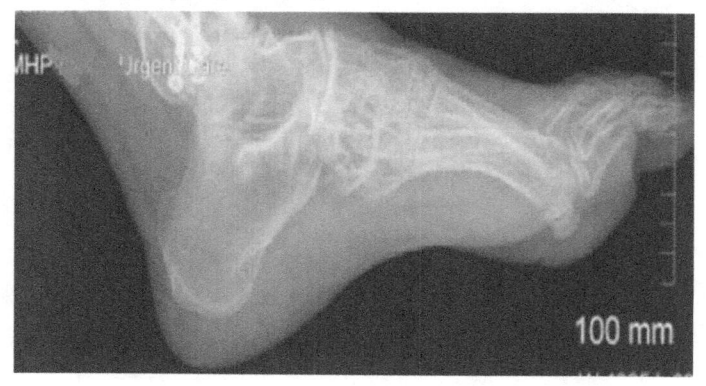

The five toes on my left foot broke towards my toenails, and also towards my ankle, and my instep shattered into pieces. A ball and socket is our ankle. The ball dissolved into splinters, and had to be washed out of my foot. The doctors had to harvest bone from my hip to patch some areas of my left foot. I have a scar that runs from my mid leg area all the way down to my instep.

Please hear me, three weeks into this horrific injury, and one day after being removed from morphine, I STOPPED taking any form of narcotics. My choice was addiction or life, and I chose life. Take this page to your doctor, and ask them how they think I am doing, when it comes to pain. Yes, yes, yes, and yes, and some more yes, yes you are suffering, but to live you must find a way, if possible, to not succumb to taking narcotics continually, or even at all. Again, if possible, because it will eventually kill you. please precious, please hear me, you must live.

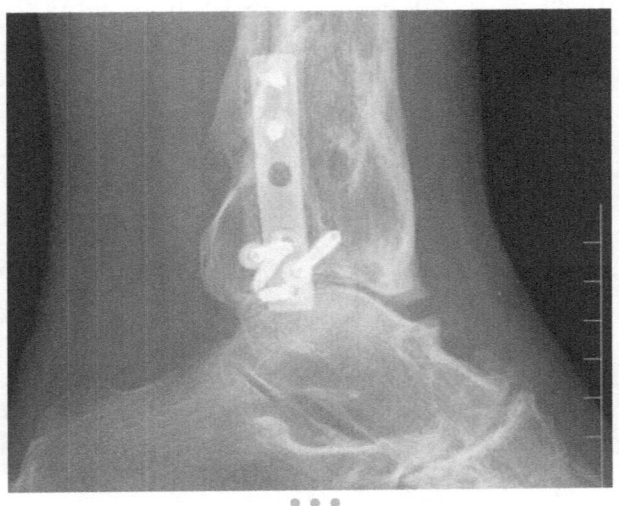

This is for your encouragement, and to inspire you into fighting through your hardship, and to save your precious life. Test yourself, find out what you can endure, and push yourself to the limit. This is to save your life; this is to keep addiction at bay. Please give yourself a fighting chance to make it, I beg of you. This is your precious life, and your precious future you are fighting for. Please dig in, and draw on every resolve that is within you, and LIVE.

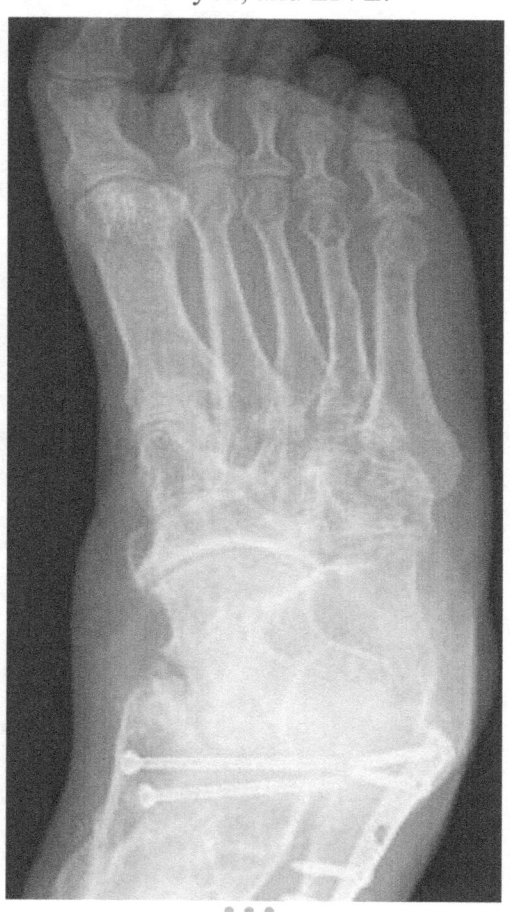

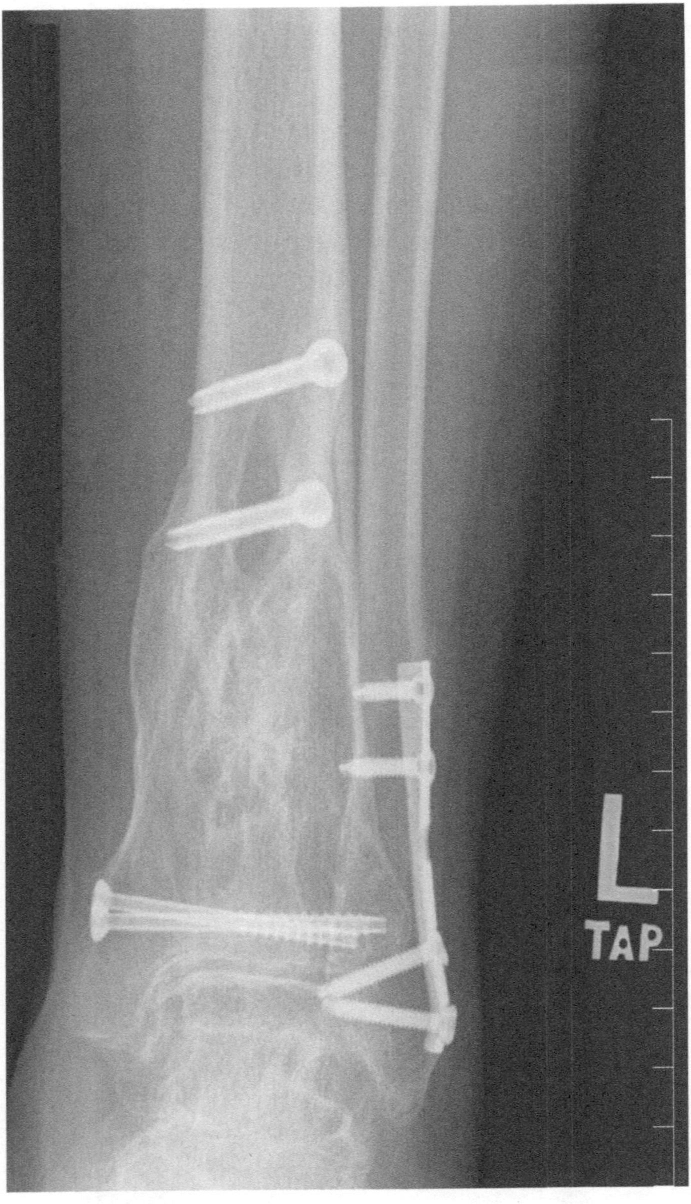
L
TAP

179

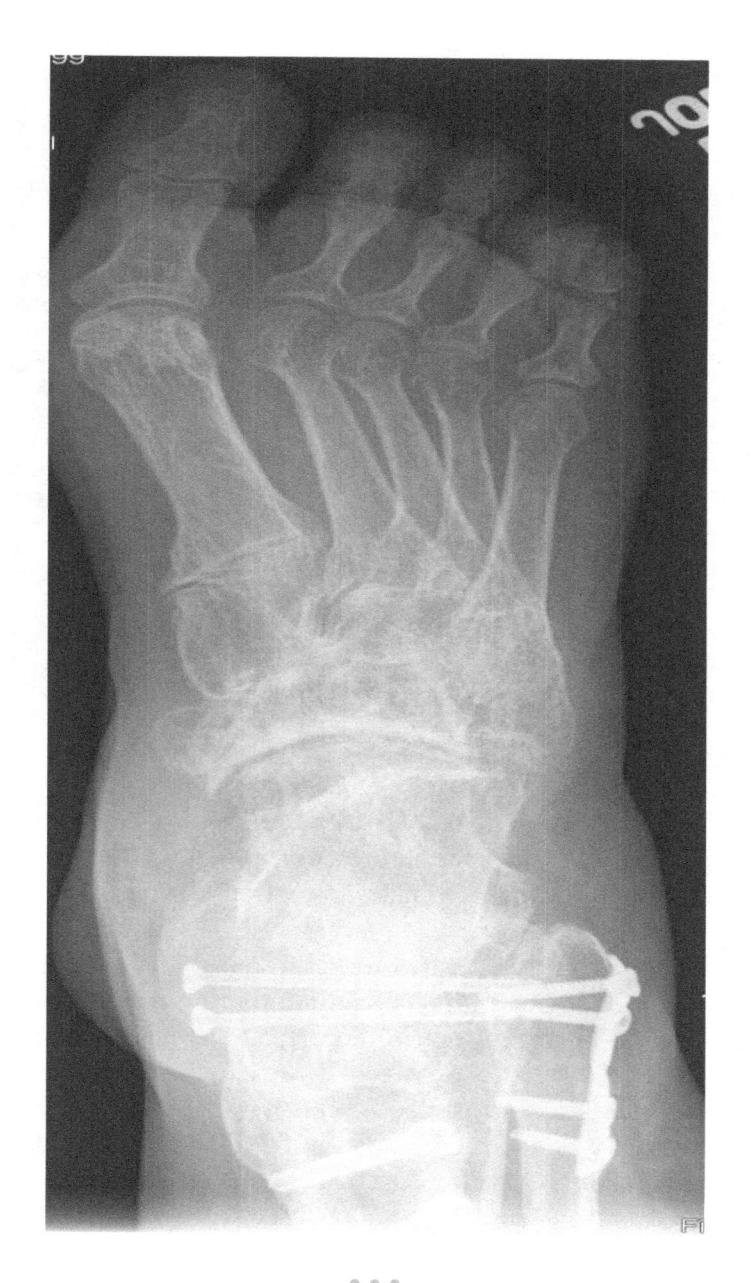

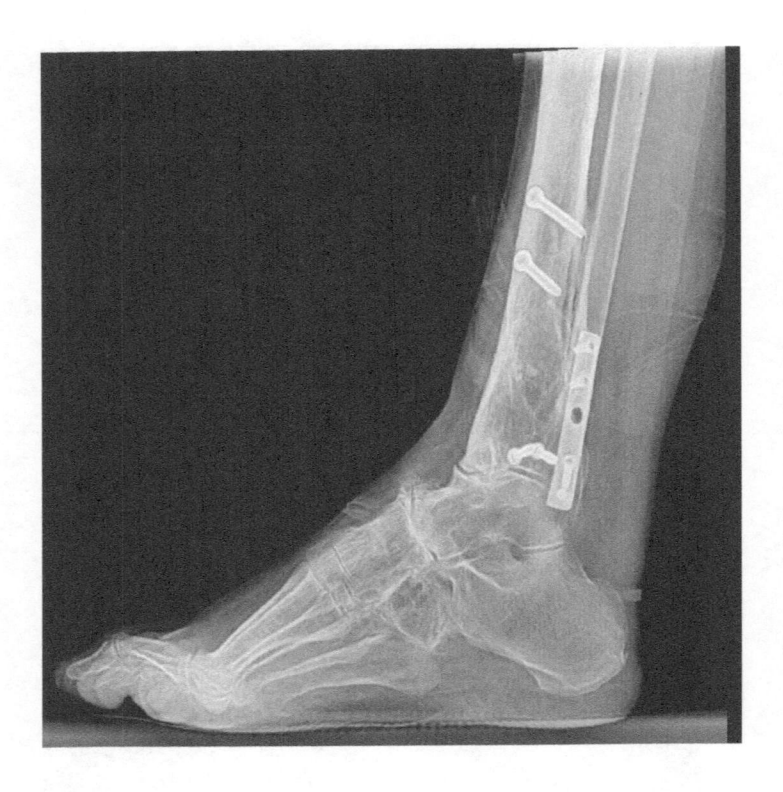

Like some of you, I too have extreme injuries; yet the last day I took narcotics, was on the day I left the hospital. I refused to take any narcotics thereafter. My choice was to keep my sobriety. I could not become an addict. I had to get my Tony across the finish line. I had to make certain that no matter the circumstances, my son could manage it, and my son could survive it. I knew what sorrows had befallen me, that broke my heart into pieces. I had to ensure my son was educated, strong in mind and body, and understood what it meant to be a good citizen within society. I needed to be sober to get the job done. I intended to stay alive long enough to get my son to his adult years. Then it would be over. The LORD used that goal to keep me alive. Find your goal and stay alive and sober, you can do it, I believe in you.

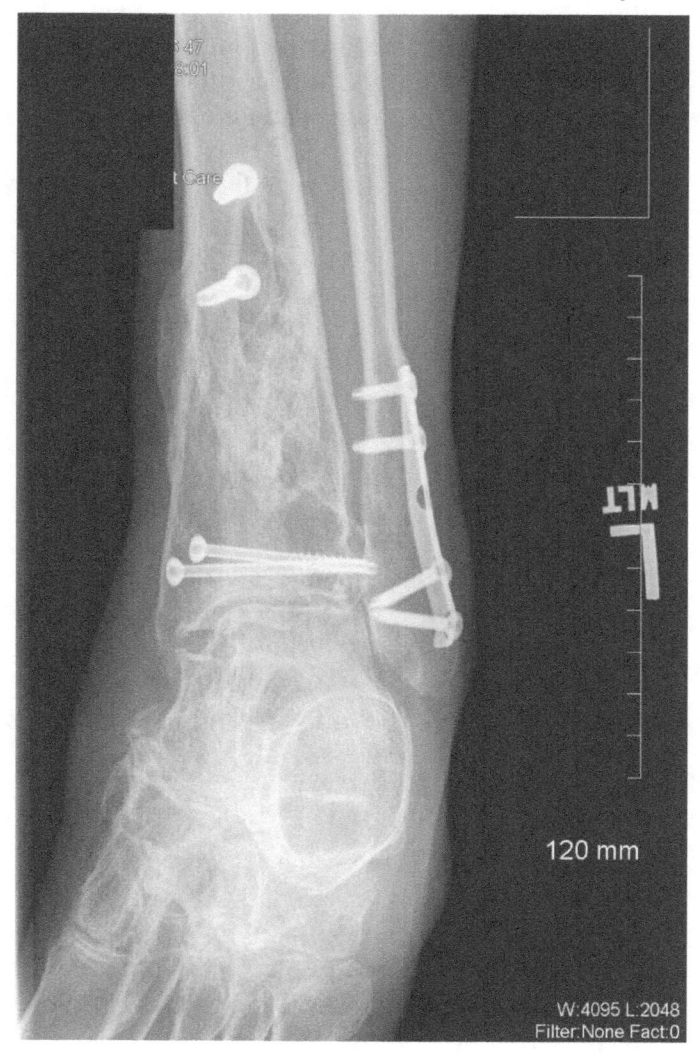

CHAPTER 24

To every decent and honorable Protector, from government agencies throughout, that protects their nation, through intelligence, justice, and protective services, along with all first responders, including paramedics, fire fighters, police officers, doctors, veterinarians, dentist, nurses and all else.

Your jobs are amongst the hardest within any career field. Your professions are some of the most grueling professions on the heart, the mind, and the spirit, and on the human psyche. From day to day, your life is uncertain. Many of you are prepared to give up your life to save those you serve. The responsibility, the stress that comes with your profession is tremendous. Doctor, Sir or Madam, I thank you for your service.

Pain and sorrow are your breakfast, your lunch and your dinner. Your job entails you experiencing heartbreak, and you having to see gruesome injuries like most have never seen. You experience the death of babies and children who did not get to live out their precious lives. You have had to watch as parents and grandparents die without being able to say goodbye to their love one's, and you have watched as dreams disappeared into the wind.

Some veterinarians have watched farmers lose their livestock; or their farms failed, and they could do nothing to save the animals. The family pet needs to be euthanized; and the family is going to be broken once you tell them. Their sorrows are yours; some of them only had that pet for a family. The despair in their eyes haunts you nonstop. The sorrow of it all is enough to drive any human being mad. But to you the precious gem, the selfless; you are humanity's precious diamonds. You have been shouldering it all. You live through it day-by-day, week by week, year by year, and from decade to decade without fail.

To all of you, Sirs or Madams or Doctors, I say with tremendous gratitude, again I thank you for your service, and I am beyond grateful. You have been driven to the edge by your experiences, or you are being driven to the edge and you are in desperate need of assistance. Your co-workers, some of you the First Responders you work amongst, have no idea that you are in need of their help. You are staring at deaths door, and you need immediate help to save your life, or to restore your health, but here you are, suffering in silence.

Please I beg of you, please ask for the help that you are in need of

Please precious you, incredible you, selfless you, brave you, loyal you, please ask for the help that you are in need of. Please have the conversation with your family, your employer, and your friends, your neighbors, and even the stranger, I beg of you. Please fight to save your life. Please get counseling, and allow a psychiatrist to give you the help that you are so very desperately in need of. Allow someone to help you find the way out of the death spiral you are in, or about to enter into. You are worn-out by the experiences of it all; and you need to take time away from the stress of it all, to heal. Please do not be afraid to ask for help, I believe with all my heart, that if you tell your employer what you are going through, they will do everything within their power to help you, they will not abandon you. Please do not worry about not being employed should you disclose what you are going through. Here is a reality check for you, if you continue down this road and lose your life, you having or not having a job will not matter.

Please release the fear of what you will lose, and instead, run towards the help that you desperately need. Please do not suffer in silence, you opening up to others to get the help that you are in need of, will bring you tremendous gain, and the only thing you will lose is the baggage filled with despair, and suicidal thoughts. It is okay, here, take my hand, trust me; and let us go in for help together.

Make the calls please; and speak with your family members, your employers, and a counselor. They all have their role to play within your recovery. You have options; if you do not want to go through your employer, please start with the **Suicide & Crisis Lifeline** at **988**, the 1-800-273-8255 has merged with 988 as of July 16, 2022.

 Active-duty members and veterans, please press (1) when the call is answered or text to **838255.** Non-military, if you are unable to speak, or you are hearing impaired, you can send a text to the **Crisis Text Line** 24/7, at **741741.** You can also go to **988lifeline.org.** Please live! Please give them a chance to help you. Please I beg of you, please fight to save your precious life.

Sir, Madam, Doctor, how can you who have given so much to humanity, fall along the wayside? **NO!** This cannot happen! It must never happen! you are loved, and you are appreciated beyond measure. On behalf of humanity, I thank you, I bless you, I encourage you. Please give us a chance to show you that,

"WE CARE FOR YOU"

"YOU MATTER TO US"

"WE ARE FOREVER GRATEFUL TOWARDS YOU"

"WE THANK YOU"

"YOU ARE LOVED"

"PLEASE HOLD ON"

"PLEASE DO NOT GIVE UP"

"PLEASE, YOU MUST LIVE"

CHAPTER 25

You are being abused by a partner, you are being beaten, stalked and cursed at, your life is in danger

Precious, please listen to me; please hear me, please understand me. **"IT WILL NOT GET ANY BETTER! YOU MUST GET OUT NOW! NOT TOMORROW, GET OUT NOW! YOU WILL DIE! YOUR CHILD/CHILDREN WILL DIE! YOU MUST GET OUT NOW! NOW I TELL YOU, YOU MUST GET OUT NOW! SAVE YOUR LIFE NOW!!!!**

There is no calming down, there is no, "a week from now it will get better." **NO,** for your partner to get better, he or she has to let go of their victim, and go it alone in a journey of recovery, through extensive treatment. The temptation of a partner living with them has to be removed. They have a trigger in their brain, that needs zero reason to go off. You will die by your partner's hand if you stay, you must get out now! Kindness will not help you, care towards that person will not help you and the next blow could take your life. Please get out. Please allow me to explain what I mean about kindness will not help you.

This happened to me in my twenties, and it still causes my heart to quake. My ex needed surgery and had no insurance. The cost of my insurance at that time was over half of my paycheck for both of us. I did not care, I added him. Yes, it was not an emergency, and I could let him wait until he found a job with insurance coverage, but I was worried that it could get worst over time. I took the day off and drove him to the hospital. I made certain I said or did nothing to set him off in the car, the last time I did he drove the car at 115 miles an hour and said he would crash it. While he was in surgery, I went to the pharmacy to buy a walking stick for him. He came out of out-patient surgery and I drove him home. I helped him unto the sofa and turn to get his pill, I was too slow. He took the walking stick I had just bought for him, and with full force whack me dead on my hip, the extreme blow caused my leg to give out from under me as if my hip was broken. My son heard me fall and came out and helped me to drag myself to his room.

Please muster the courage you need, and get out

Please think long and very hard about this, if I went through horrific years in my teens, that led me to become suicidal. What was the effect of the horrible additional abuse inflicted upon me during marriage? Still, I found the strength to get out. My poor baby had to live, He had to live, do you not feel sorry for yourself, for your child or children? How can you give yourself and them this wretched, this heinous life?

Let it all go, and run for you and your children lives

"Master your destiny for GOD sake, and live," I beg of you. Leave everything behind; grab yourself, your child or children and run for your life. You will have nothing you say if you leave? I have news for you; **"YOU ALREADY HAVE NOTHING." You have NO joy, NO peace; you have NO comfort; NO laughter, and NO safety, and NO rest; "YOU HAVE NOTHING!" GET OUT NOW! Please use the information below to get to safety I beg of you. You leaving with nothing, will make room for all things new.** Even if they are secondhand, they are new for you, because you have never used them. Leave it all behind, and gain your newness of life I beg of you. Here is the information that you need to get out and to make your way to safety. I bless you; I encourage you; and I implore you, please precious, please get out and live. Save your life, save your child/children lives if there are any. Please I beg of you precious, **"GET OUT NOW!"**

This information was taken from their website.

The Family Violence Prevention and Services Act (FVPSA) provides funding for the on-going operation of a 24-hour, national, toll-free telephone hotline. The Hotline is your immediate link to lifesaving help for victims. It provides information and assistance to adults, and youth victims, of family violence, domestic violence, or dating violence, family and household members, and other persons such as domestic violence advocates, government officials, law enforcement agencies and the public.

The Hotline can be accessed via the nationwide number 1-800-799-SAFE (7233) or TTY 800-787 3224 **or** (206) 518-9361 (Video Phone Only for Deaf Callers). The Hotline provides service referrals to agencies in all 50 states, Puerto Rico, Guam and the U.S. Virgin Islands.

Services are provided without regard to race, color, national origin, religion, gender, age, or disability (including deaf and hard of hearing). Assistance is available in English and Spanish with access to more than 170 languages through telephonic interpreter services.

Services

The Hotline provides the following services.
- Crisis intervention.
- Domestic violence education.
- Safety planning.
- Directly connecting callers to Service Providers such as local shelters.
- Referrals to agencies that provide legal, economic self-sufficiency, sexual assault, elder abuse, children's and other related services.

End of website information.

You have help, please accept the help that is being given to you

Please precious, please know that you have help, you are not alone. I beg you, please call the hotline, and save yourself and your child or children if there are any involved. They are waiting for your call, and will help you to find your way out of the abuse, out of the danger you are in. If you feel that your mental health is failing, or you are contemplating suicide, please call the **Suicide & Crisis Lifeline** at **988**, the 1-800-273-8255 has merged with **988** as of July 16, 2022. **Active-duty members and veterans, please press (1)** when the call is answered, or text to **838255**. Non-military, if you are unable to speak or you are hearing impaired, you can send a text to the **Crisis Text Line** 24/7, at **741741**.

You can also go to the **988lifeline.org** website; to talk with the **Suicide & Crisis Lifeline staff**. They are selfless in their care towards you, and they will help you to stay alive, and in your right mind. Please precious, please do your part to save your precious life, and the life of your child or children if there are any. This I promise you, is one of the best decisions you will ever make bar none. Please make the call.

CHAPTER 26

Recovering from the damages you have done to others. Recovering from the damages you have done to yourself. Learning to forgive yourself

Recovering from the embarrassment, that was caused by your own actions, or by someone else

Guilt and or shame has sent many men and women to their grave. The burdens of one's own actions are the heaviest of all burdens, and they are the hardest burdens to put down. Embarrassment is the monster that breaks the human spirit, and stops the heart from beating. Metaphorically speaking, its best friends are hyenas and wolfpacks, who will move in for the kill once embarrassment shows up. When you are embarrassed, when shame is upon you, you must place yourself into treatment.

Do not run away from this season of your life. You must face it head on, and do what needs to be done to make things right. If your mistakes brought you to this place, you must do what you can to correct the situation, and release yourself from the guilt of it all. If others are at fault, please work to forgive them, and if needs be, please remove yourself from these people and the situation immediately.

The guilt and the embarrassment that you feel are not because of your actions

I am so very, very sorry for your pain, please be

encouraged, it will not always be this way. Please do not kill yourself because of the shame, the wretched embarrassment that you feel, due to someone else's actions. Please hold on and do not give up, please do not commit suicide. If this is taking place at your school, please tell your parents or guardian, you must also tell your teacher, and the principal.

Step away if you can, and please inform your employer, your teacher, or your professors, or the leader within your organization about what is happening

If you are at work, you must file a complaint with your supervisor and your human resource, if there is one within your organization. In as much as you are able to, please go dark. Remove yourself from situations that might cause the feelings you have to worsen. If you are online, disconnect. Stop using your phone for a period of time. Take a break, stop-watching television and listening to radio. Watch movies and listen to your personal music instead.

You must create a space that is appropriate for your recovery. Fill your space with the things that brings you comfort and joy. Do not allow anyone to make you feel less than. Their actions are a reflection of who they are, not who you are. Do not be ashamed due to someone else's cruelty towards you, hold your head up high and live your precious life to its fullest. You will face difficult times in life, and you will become stronger with each experience lived through.

Please I beg of you, please do not take your precious life, tell others what you are going through, and call the **Suicide & Crisis Lifeline** at **988**, the 1-800-273-8255 has merged with **988** as of July 16, 2022. **Active-duty members and veterans, please press (1)** when the call is answered, or text to **838255**. Non-military, if you are unable to speak, or you are hearing impaired, you can send a text to the **Crisis Text Line** 24/7, at **741741**. You can also go to the **988lifeline.org** website, and talk with them, they will help you. You precious are an incredible human being all by yourself, and no one can take that away from you, by making you feel embarrass.

The guilt and the embarrassment that you feel are because of your own actions

Please, you cannot, you must never ever, take this place lightly. Embarrassment and or guilt have been known to take people down some very, very dark and debilitating roads, from which there are no return. Shame has caused people from all nations, races, pedigrees and financial backgrounds to commit suicide. Please listen to me, owning your mistake, even if you cannot recover from it takes inner strength and tremendous courage. It takes character of the heart and mind, it takes humility and it takes honor.

The day you own your mistakes, even if you are unable to recover from them, is the day you will start your journey of healing, even if your past life is no more. If your past life is no more, if the damage is beyond repair, accept it. Do all that is necessary, to show your remorse to your victim or victims. You can now start over, knowing that you have done your best to show your victim(s) that you acknowledge the hurt you have caused, and are sorry for your actions. Listen to me please, do not get angry or depress because others treat you as if you are the same person that caused them pain. In their eyes, for now you are the same person. Give it time, allow them one, two, three years or more to see the new you. Your change will not happen overnight, and theirs will take time also. Give them space; every time they see you, they relive your mistakes.

Forgiving does not mean forgetting

There is something very, very, important that you must understand. Them forgiving you does not mean that they have forgotten the trauma inflicted upon them. There is trauma that follows us for life. It does not prevent us from forgiving others, but the pain of that trauma is at times so very horrific, that it will haunt us for life.

For me the grace and mercy and miracle of GOD has allowed me to survive the horrific, horrific trauma that was inflicted upon me. I have forgiven all but the memory lives on. What you must hold onto is, you have been forgiven, or in time, you will be forgiven. This does not mean the pain you inflicted is no longer. If your situation does require it, please be prepared to relocate. Let everything go and start over.

You must do everything in your power to be a much better human being than you were before.

It is okay, you can talk about your mistakes, and the fact that you are working to do better

Do not be afraid to talk about the fact that you are not proud of whom you are, but you are working to change for the better. Being honest with yourself and others is the medicine you need for the wounds you carry. Yes, you are ashamed of yourself and you do not want to face yourself in the mirror, but you must. You still have a life to live, and a journey ahead. Release yourself from your torturous mind, heart and soul, and allow yourself to recover from your all-consuming, regrettable actions. Face the shame of it all, but do not break under the load. You must survive this all-consuming mistake filled season of your life.

Believe me when I say to you, it is only a human being without conscience, that will not face his or her wrongdoings. Face your actions, mourn and let it go. You will someday help someone that will travel the same road that you are on right now. Please become a great human being, and that way when you meet someone and speak with them, they will find hope from within you.

Please forgive yourself, release your mistakes, let it all go and live. contact the **Suicide & Crisis Lifeline** at **988**, the 1-800-273-8255 has merged with **988** as of July 16, 2022. **Active-duty members and also**

veterans, please press (1) when the call is answered or text to **838255.** Non-military, if you are unable to speak, or you are hearing impaired, you can send a text to the **Crisis Text Line** 24/7 at **741741.** You can also go to the **988lifeline.org** website. Please live! Please give the incredible staff at the **988 Suicide & Crisis Lifeline,** a chance to help you.

CHAPTER 27

You must not use the pain inflicted upon you by your victimizer, to find others innocent or guilty. Please allow the true facts within their situation, to decide their innocence or guilt.

Please allow me to say this, I do not want to lose any of my readers because of any misunderstanding caused by this chapter. This chapter is for not only you, it is for me also. We must be careful when anyone is accused of any wrongdoing. Our trajectory seems to be heading in the direction of, **"never considering the other person's experiences,"** we instead draw our conclusions based on our very own pain.

Yes, you experienced abuse, or someone close to you did. It does not mean that everyone that says they were abused is telling the truth. **Our experiences cannot be the trigger that causes us to believe that everyone that is accused of abusing someone is guilty.**

"NOT EVERY SITUATION IS THE SAME."

The accuser could have done this with nefarious reasons. The accused could have broken off the relationship and the ex-partner, their accuser is now implementing the scorched earth formula; where they hurl a bunch of accusations at their ex with the purpose of burning their life to the ground. Someone could be trying to ruin a life because that person walked away from them, or they could be doing it for financial gain, to inflict notoriety or because of an old grudge, or to get custody of their child/children.

I need you to please separate your circumstances, where the person you accused was guilty, compared to circumstances where the accused is innocent, and they are being accused for Nefarious reasons, that is aimed at destroying that person's life. In reality these people leaving these relationships, are going through circumstances that is already weighing on them.

These innocent individuals are already burdened way, way down, some are broken and are terrified of what their ex will do to them, and yes, them meaning both women and men also. For some, the exit is just as brutal as living with their abuser. They are leaving with absolutely nothing so has to save their lives. The weight or their responsibilities in life has them at a breaking point.

Imagine the world turning on you in the middle of these painful season in your life. You are fighting to keep your head above water, fighting to survive the pressures of life; you are fighting to go on with your precious life; after being in a horrific relationship, and now you are being accused of being the abuser. Imagine you the victim watching as the world sides with the monster, while you the innocent man or woman are vilified.

Why? Because your ex, the abuser hurled out claims

that you the victim abused them; and we all believed the lies and took the abuser's side. In other words, we buried you the person that suffered the abuse, and strengthened the abuser. How truly horrific this must be, to you the victim.

We believe the accusations, because of our past experience and not because the accused was actually guilty. We believe the allegations because the person making the allegations is rich. In other words, the rich are innocent and the poor is guilty. We believe because a woman is the accuser. In other words, the woman is always innocent, and the man is always guilty. Do you see where I am going with this. Guilt must always come from the fact that the man or woman is guilty. Not from their a-lot or a little in life. Not from pedigree, or from our past experiences, or gossip.

This mark my words could be very egregious, in the worst possible way

The moment we go against this, we could send many innocent souls to the grave. The same way women have been abused by men, men also, believe it or not, have been victimized, have been abused by women. Our pain must not cause us to gravitate towards believing based on who victimized us, and bury the other person based on the makeup of our past victimizer. This mistake could cause someone to go to jail, to be locked away for something they did not do. This mistake could cause someone to take their life out of their sorrow and desperation. If this is happening to you right now, please do not cast your soul into the grave. Instead, fight to save your life. If the lies being told sullies your name but does not put you in harm's way, keep going.

Get away from that person that is heaping lies upon you, and do not look back. Someday the truth will be revealed and if it is not. Comfort yourself with the knowledge that the heavens knows that you are innocent. If the lies are enough to bring you harm, you must fight, you must "leave it all on the field," as the saying goes to clear your name.

Expect the unexpected

You who are leaving must take courage. Expect the unexpected in the worst way possible, so that you can take pre, not post caution. Pre as in before, post as in after. Pre-pare for the worst, so that the worst does not destroy you. Expect your abuser to try to make themselves the victim. Expect that he or she will try to vilify you. If you pre-pare for it the blow from it will not break you and bring you to your knees; instead, you would have amassed the tools that are needed to fight, and to preserve your good name.

You must protect your moral high ground

Do not give up your righteous position, your moral high ground to your abuser; as others have done, due to the extreme desperation they are experiencing. Do not allow yourself to have a mental breakdown, to have a lapse in judgment brought on by your horrific circumstances.

Stay vigilant, and protect your position. You are the victim; you are the person that is being victimized. Do not allow what others have done to you, to cause you to turn around and victimize yourself also. What do I mean? Many have burned their own lives to the ground themselves; all due to their desperation on exiting their abusive relationship, or exiting their relationship. Many times, there is panic, desperation, and a lack of answers during exit. Suddenly there are thoughts, how will you feed yourself or your child or children? What will you do for clothing, household goods, and money for shelter? Where will you get money to replace your car, or to buy gas for your car?

Suddenly in your desperation you go shopping for an abundance of food and clothing although there is not enough money in the bank to cover your purchases. You write checks for cash to cover gas in the car, to pay for your journey, to pay for a roof over your head. Some of you have money in that bank account but once you left, your abuser closed out the account, or your partner closed out the account and took it all.

Listen to me please, **"LET IT GO."** The moment you write those checks in desperation, you Sir or Madam, have given up your high ground, you have destroyed your good name to the pleasure of your abuser, to the pleasure of the partner that you left, or the partner that has abandoned you. I have seen this happen over and over, and over again, to too many people.

Many times, unbeknownst to the victim, there is a mental breakdown when it comes to their judgment, when it comes to their decision making and the desperate situation they are in. Because of the trauma associated with the exit. You are running for your precious life, or you have been abandoned. This is enough to send your mind into a painful spiral of misjudgments and wrong actions taken; and all due to the breakdown in your mental health. Please press pause, focus on just getting out.

Oftentimes even when you are innocent, the abuser or the ex-partner will paint you in the worst light. There is one incident I know of where the rent was always paid from his account, he had stormed out and went to his mother for a few days, while he was at his mother his wife paid the rent the exact same way she had done in previous months. The husband never returned to the marriage and painted her as a thief. Think long and hard about that. She was turned into a thief for paying the rent from his account, when they had not even broken up as yet. Make no mistake, they will do everything in their power to ruin you.

Another incident happened, where the wife was stalked for months by a neighbor and her husband did absolutely nothing. She tried to get her husband to move, the apartment office refused to let them out of the lease, and the husband said he would not go against them. The neighbor broke in and raped her while the husband was away on duty. She was never the same. She had trouble responding in the marriage and it ended without her knowing.

He closed out every bank account and opened new accounts with only his name on it, and left instructions that he would pay for a one-way ticket back to where she came from. It gets better. He left on a six months work voyage the next day. She was finished, her life would never be the same.

The rapist destroyed this woman, and what little bit of sanity this lady had left, her husband took it from her. She wrote checks for food, clothing, and shelter. Remember he had closed the accounts, those checks were no good. This lady gave up her innocence to these monsters during her mental health breakdown, and she suffered the consequences of her actions. This incident has been repeated over and over, and over again, by countless victims, this I promise you. This is the very definition of a travesty when it comes to these victims' lives.

This is when you started/or will start contemplating suicide. You started accepting the thoughts of killing the person or persons that victimized you, and then killing yourself. For heaven and earth sakes **PLEASE NO**. Please do not give your abusers the satisfaction of your missteps, brought on by desperation. There is help for you on the outside, away from the structure of abuse that you have been living in.

You and your child or children will not starve, you

will not go naked. Push the desperate thoughts at bay and focus on your escape/exit. Allow your rudder to steer you in the right direction. Do not panic, do not allow hopelessness to consume you, and to direct your path; this I promise you, will take away the moral high ground, the victorious hill you are standing on.

Many Innocent men and women have given up their innocence, they were the victims, and due to their mental breakdown, they turned into perpetrators also. Guard your precious life I beg of you, do not be shaken by your circumstances. Hold on and find your way out, without doing damage to yourself. Spare yourself the violence of your very own hands I beg of you. You will find answers, relief will come. Someone will give you a job, and if that income is not enough, there are agencies, pantries and charities that will fill in the gap. Please I beg of you, please guard your precious life, please hold on and **LIVE.**

Please contact the **Suicide & Crisis Lifeline** at **988**, the 1-800-273-8255 has merged with **988, Active-duty members and veterans, please press (1)** when the call is answered, or text to **838255**. Non-military, if you are unable to speak, or you are hearing impaired, you can send a text to the **Crisis Text Line** 24/7, at **741741**. You can also go to **988lifeline.org.**

Please call the Violence Prevention number, if you are being harmed, at 1–800–799–SAFE (7233) or TTY 800-787 3224 **or** (206) 518-9361 (Video Phone Only for Deaf Callers). Please allow them to help you.

"Stockholm Syndrome, the characteristics within your abusive relationship,"

I want you to understand something important. The term "Stockholm Syndrome," was created from a kidnapped victim, that astonishingly, actually turned into the kidnapper's defender and admirer. After being kidnapped, over time the victim is drawn to the kidnapper, grow to like the kidnapper, sympathizes with their kidnapper, and even defend/make excuses for the kidnapper. About fifteen years ago I believe it was, I was in the middle of preparing my message for Sunday morning service. I was in a section that dealt with those who are being abused, and the need for them to leave the abusive relationship they were in. As I went over the victim's behavior in staying, and what I had heard as a pastor from victims, I was suddenly jarred into a realization and I said out loud, "LORD that is Stockholm Syndrome behavior."

That coming Sunday I preached the message, and in that message, I explained to the congregation that I believed Stockholm Syndrome, did not only exist between a kidnapper and their victims, I believed it existed within relationships between abusers and their victims also.

Many victims that are being abused make excuses for their abusers. Many victims refuse to leave their abusers. They are drawn even closer to their abusers, and they even defend their abusers. Their entire trust is in their abuser. They blame themselves when their abuser abuses them. "He or she hit me, threatened me, or cursed at me because of something I did. I caused my abuser to abuse me, it was my fault, I need to do better."

This is the very essence, the very identity of "Stockholm Syndrome."

If you superimpose the kidnapper and their victim's life with the abusive household in another country, they will fit perfectly together; they will not be at odds with each other, but will instead, fit perfectly together. Both victims' lives will display a perfect alignment continuation, when placed together. the same Stockholm Syndrome behavior intertwined perfectly.

If you the victims are wondering why you are still there and refuses to leave, perhaps it is time to face the difficult truth. This truth is the place to start from if you want to save your precious life, and your child or children's lives. Madam, please get out of there! Sir, I beg you please get out of there! **"AND YES, MEN ABSOLUTELY, THEY MOST DEFINITELY EXPERIENCE ABUSE ALSO."** Please look at your bruises, please I beg of you, please look at your scars, or please see the despair in your eyes, and tell me, why do you stay? The names you are called, the beatings you take, precious souls please tell me why?

"YOU ARE PRECIOUS, YOU ARE PRECIOUS, YOU SIR OR MADAM ARE PRECIOUS. YOU ARE PRECIOUS, YOU ARE PRECIOUS, FOR GOD SAKE, PLEASE ACCEPT THE FACT THAT YOU SIR OR MADAM, ARE BEYOND PRECIOUS."

CHAPTER 28

You are contemplating suicide, because you lost an opportunity within your career, within your employment

Before going down the road of suicide, instead of contemplating on suicide, please consider this. In days of old, in cultures throughout the world, failure within employment meant death. There are many souls that pleaded, that begged for one more chance, that begged for their lives, and while begging for their lives, their precious life was taken away. Those in leadership measured that precious life, based on one missed, or based on one failed opportunity.

You Sir or madam, are now offering the same lack of mercy to yourself, that those leaders offered to those men and women that lost their lives in days of old. Do you not deserve a first, second, fourth, or seventh chance? Is your precious soul not deserving of a chance to recover from your missed opportunities, or your disappointments and or failures? Do you not deserve the opportunity to try again and again and again, until you succeed?

Do you even have the slightest idea, of how very overwhelmingly dreadful, your suicide would be to your employer? Please become the employee that will not drive their employer to ruins through the employee's death, that is caused by self-harm.

Your employment journey and your life's journey

are a reflection of each other. There will be ups and downs. There will be failures and victories; there will be motivational seasons, and there will also be times when motivation will not be there, and you will have to motivate yourself. All of these experiences are a part of life, and they are also a part of your ebb and flow journey, that is within your career.

Instead of giving up, please give your precious soul the chance to prepare for your next opportunity in life. Instead of giving up, please prepare for the next opportunity as if it were your last. What do I mean? Please consider this, and hold it to heart. For you to be successful in life and within your career, you must work and study hard. Without a doubt, you must be dedicated if you are loyal to your goal. You must be fixated; you have your eyes trained on your goal. You are driven; you are going after it with fervor.

Make this commitment to yourself, "I will treat my next opportunity as if it were my last."

you must pursue hard after it; and treat all future opportunities as if there will never be another. In doing so, you are maximizing every opportunity that presents itself, whether through others, or through you. Lean into it and pursue hard and fight to achieve your goal, to its fullest. This will help you to avoid the pitfalls of wasted opportunities. In turn, it will prevent the discouragement that comes with never acquiring an opportunity, or a second chance. Again, please make each opportunity count to its fullest.

Here is the reality of your journey. If you put very little effort into your journey, you will get very little reward out of your journey. On the other hand, if you put in much study, hard work and dedication, you will reap the rewards; by becoming an individual that is well learnt, experienced, and knowledgeable when it comes to the particular journey you are on, and the destination you have in mind.

The importance of Social and Occupational Skills

For you to be a great employee, you must possess both Social and Occupational Skills. One without the other will prove to be disastrous, when it comes to your career. Having great occupational skills as in, being skilled in your particular area of occupation, and yet having little or no social skills to function within your workplace, to function alongside your colleagues will not work. They go hand in hand, and there is no escaping this, no matter how hard you try.

If you recognize that you are this very person I am speaking of. Please do not get discouraged; instead, do something about it. You must evolve and grow, and change for the better. You must set yourself to acquire the social skills needed, and all the while telling yourself, "As of this day, I am entering a new season in my life; I am starting a new chapter in my journey called life; and this change will most certainly be the catalyst for my success." Mark my words; this change can help to encourage you, and it will help to lead you far away from suicide also. There have been many occasions when a person's social skills surpassed their occupational skills, and yet brought them great success. Their kindness, and their willingness to go above and beyond, and their great rapport with their co-workers, them being a team player acquired them enormous success. Both in their professional and in their personal lives also.

You possessing good social skills will go a long way in building a great organization. Any organization built on discord, built on me, myself and I, and with no consideration for each other, instead of teamwork there is only individuality in action. This will only lead to ruin. It takes a team with the specific goals of that organization in mind to win. Different people with different ideas, coming together, working together, exchanging ideas, taking a little bit or a lot from each other, and honing their individual social skills for the good/goal of the organization they are a part of.

These social skills go a long way in the establishment of any organization, into a positive and a lasting company. You being a part of this movement, will help to motivate you, and bring you from that dark place, that is wearing you down and is pushing you towards suicide.

Yes, I am absolutely speaking from experience. As I said before, I was in a horrific accident that left me broken in both mind and body. I came out of it being a loner with the inability to let others near me. I hated conversing. I guarded my space while at work like a lioness; and the look on my face said, "Why are you speaking to me, leave me alone?" I had to change, I had to evolve, (and now I write a book). Look in the dictionary under miracle, and you will see me smiling back at you. Because of my lack of social skills, I failed in my occupation. I had tons of occupational skills, but I lacked the social skills that I needed. It was not until I evolved, I changed, I began to see others, I heard them, I listened to them, I understood them, and I communicated with them.

Only then did my life change for the better, and my career took off. Now here I am with the incredible ability to lead others. Through my faith, and much improvement in my social skills, I have stood before many audiences; and I articulated the undeniably importance, of them having good, honorable social skills; that are filled with honor and consideration for others. I have taught that the willingness to listen to others, to work with others, and the willingness to sacrifice for others; will go a long way in helping the outstanding individuals that are taking these actions, to live an accomplished, favor filled, successful life.

Humanity needs the better in us

Humanity on a whole demands the better us; yes, I am absolutely speaking to myself also. What we do for our fellow human beings is beyond important. Whether on the job, at home or out and about, who you are, and the role that you play impacts humanity; and there is no denying it. In your contemplations of suicide please consider this. If you impact one person or one organization, that person, that entity is a part of humanity; and it is just that simple. We all have a role to play within humanity; and it does not matter. if you are rich or poor, you are educated or not, or you are famous or unknown. No Sir or madam, you have a life to live; and people to impact on your journey called life, no matter your lot in life.

Please do not count yourself out, you too have something to bring to the table

Never allow yourself to believe that it is only the wealthy, the well-educated or the well-known that matters. NO! Our nations were built by little known, poor men and women. Nations were built by people that were educated and some were not. What these people possessed was the willingness to do their part; in the best way that they could; for the betterment of their nation.

Now it is your turn to work on your social skills. You should work on listening to others, and on you being more patient, and being a part of a team. This will help you as I said before, to bring you from the dark places. You must put in the work, if you want to motivate yourself, and to also present the improved you, to the organization you are a part of, or the organization you want to join.

To get help to recover, to be able to claw your way back, to fight your way back from the cliff's edge of suicidal thoughts and tendencies, or from a mental breakdown, or mental stress. Please I beg oy you, please contact the **Suicide & Crisis Lifeline** at **988**, the 1-800-273-8255 has merged with **988** as of July 16, 2022. **Active-duty members and veterans, please press (1)** when the call is answered, or text to **838255**. Non-military, if you are unable to speak, or you are hearing impaired, you can send a text to the **Crisis Text Line** 24/7, at **741741**. You can also go to **988lifeline.org**. Please tell them what you are feeling. You can express yourself without any fear that they will judge you. I promise they will not; they are there to help you. They are vested into you overcoming suicide, and or the restoration of your mental health, please give them a chance to help you.

You are the employer, and the weight from your employees is back breaking.

You are the employer and your business is failing, you want to give up and are contemplating suicide

As an employee, you must always fight to meet your Employers', your organization, financial goals at all times. Your company's financial goals must be met at all times; and there should never be any fear, resentment or discomfort within this area. You are a member of the staff, and you are never on your own. The entire team works together, whether they realize it or not, when it comes to any organization meeting its goals. You are all an extension of each other.

Whether you believe it or not, it takes an enormous amount of financial sacrifice, an immense financial burden, and seven times out of ten, it will cost the owner/employer of your organization greatly. Most organizations are not large corporations with endless profits. Please allow me to use this excerpt from my other book, as an example, so as to give you a clear and concise picture of what I am talking about.

The employer is a dentist. It is not by accident that I am using a dentist as an employer; for years, there was a very high rate of suicide, withing the dental field.

Let us talk about any employer, both large and small organizations, and their financial burden, by using the dental career, by using the dental field as the example. Please use this information to imagine the financial burden for your employer, within your particular career field also. Now, here we go.

For the dentist to provide dental treatment there are some things that are needed. There is the building to provide the service in, which will mean paying their business rent or their business mortgage. There is furniture specific to the dental practice; insurance coverages are needed for the providers of treatment.

There is the light bill, the water bill, the gas bill, waste disposal, linen service (for scrubs).

There is also the expense for Nitrous Oxide supply, and its delivery. Your employer has to constantly buy an assortment of dental instruments of all sizes and costs for patient treatment. From the endless supplies of gloves, to the bibs that are used by every patient. There are abrasion equipment of all types. Syringes, retractors, and burnishers are needed. They need to buy amalgam carriers, matrix retainers and matrix bands, and also LED curing lights and articulating papers. Your employer has to buy scalers, and carvers, also pliers, curettes, and forceps and pocket markers. They have to buy instruments for root canal treatment, files, reamers, and endodontic forceps.

They must also buy sterilizer cases to hold some endodontic root canal instruments, for when they are being sterilized. Rubber dams are needed, and also instruments for crown and bridge treatment. There is also instruments for fillings. They need instruments for cleaning, and there is also cost for their autoclave and ultrasonic, both to clean instruments. They need prophy angles, and suction instruments, trays and tray racks; they need probes, excavators, explorers, and handpieces also.

Your employer(s) will need elevators; no, not the one you use to go up and down in a building; this is the instrument the dentist uses to elevate the tooth during extraction. They need extracting forceps; they need curettes instruments and rongeur instruments to cut through tissue or bone during extraction. I could go on and on and on. With every instrument or material, I have listed, there are many I still have not listed. Do you have any idea the hundreds of thousands into millions of dollars it will cost to establish a dental practice and to keep it running?

How about the dentist, the employer? Let's talk about him or her, or both. They live in a home and more than likely there is a rent or mortgage payment; there is car payment, light, water, gas, trash disposal. Do they deserve to be able to buy food and clothing? How about student loans?

Do you actually believe they hung out in Boston, in Florida, California, New York or Montreal, or some other university that is located abroad, and went to university free of charge? They most likely owe a student loan, and not a small one at that. What if they are married with a family? Does this mean they will need less or more income? They went through hell and high water to become a dentist.

They spent years toiling and digging deep to hone their craft. They had sleepless nights, a strenuous schedule and uncertainty. It was pressure on the mind and heart, and discouragement. There were highs and lows, while fighting for their dreams. They deserve to live a financially secure life in accomplishing their dream. Now let's talk about you as an employee. Oh, you are so incredibly amazing; you are working in spite of a reduction in your paycheck. Did I get that right? "Nope," The moment any dentist/employer tells you that they are having financial difficulty, you are in all likelihood going to call in sick the next day. You know the proverbial joke. Your phone rings and you start to, "HU, HU, HU, HU, HU HUUUU." You are coughing like a crazy person; when in reality, should Mr. Cold and Mr. Flu see you, they would drive right by you, because they have not seen you in many years. You and Mr. Vitamin C became best friends; and you stopped talking to Mr. Cold and Flu. Now because your dentist/employer has told you that finances are bad; you guessed it, you are out job hunting and using Mr. Cold and Mr. Flu as your alibi.

Nine times out of ten, there are additional dentists that are employed in the practice, along with dental assistants, hygienists, front office staff, and possibly a sterilization technician; there might even be a lab technician on site. Listen to me and listen well, it is mandatory, I repeat, it is mandatory that the dental practice meets its monthly goals. It is not optional; it is not maybe or maybe not, it is not "this is my reason why we did not reach our monthly goals." I am sorry, but you have no excuses.

Without the monthly goals being met, you are setting the stage for your employer to go under; you are setting the company up to have to lay off workers including you, or close its doors; or to have to sell the company because it is going under. Always think of the revenue, think of the needs of your organization, and the financial goals that have to be met. Everyone has a job to do, and you must do yours also.

Please accept it now, and say it with conviction, "the company I am employed with must always meet its goals, and I play a great part in this." This will be your ticket to success. Your boss will respect and appreciate you. You will have job security, and they might even offer you a monthly bonus. If they do not, do not get mad, remember the overhead. Appreciate the fact that you have a good income and are able to meet your expenses in life. If you are not, do not blame your income if you are being paid fairly. Instead, create a budget; spend less, focus more on the things that you need to survive. Cut the frills and you would be surprised at how well you do financial wise. Financial pressures have killed many dentists.

Never forget, your employer's monthly goal is to be met at all times; this will not only help to give you job security, it is also for your employer's wellbeing. Please do not worry, meeting your employer's goal is not all on you, you will have help. Every member of the organization plays a role in its survival, and in its owner's sanity, believe it or not.

If you desire job security, please lead the charge. Please accept the personal responsibility, as you should, when it comes to your employer meeting their financial goals, and work towards it at all times. Remember, they go hand in hand in meeting your production goals, and in the financial stability of the practice for it to stay alive. Failure of any business after such investments, could absolutely cause any employer/owner to suffer a mental breakdown. Sir or Madam, make no mistake; failure on the job for the employer or employee, has led to suicide. This is a fact; this is without any doubt. Perseverance is a must for the employer or the employee; when things are not at their best, and when failure of your career or your business is staring you in the face.

Taking your life due to seasons of disappointments, due to this season of failure is not the answer. Give yourself the chance needed to rebuild, to start over, and to reach beyond your successes ever anticipated. Yes, accomplish what you never imagined. Please reach out and get some help to recover, to be able to claw your way back; to fight your way back from the cliff's edge of suicidal thoughts and tendencies; or from a mental breakdown, or mental stress.

Please I beg of you, please contact the **Suicide & Crisis Lifeline** at **988**, the 1-800-273-8255 has merged with **988** as of July 16, 2022. **Active-duty members and veterans, please press (1)** when the call is answered, or text to **838255.** Non-military, if you are unable to speak, or you are hearing impaired, you can send a text to the **Crisis Text Line** 24/7, at **741741.** You can also go to **988lifeline.org.**

Please tell them what you are feeling. You can express yourself without the fear that they will judge you. I promise they will not; they are there to help you. They are vested into you overcoming suicide, and or the restoration of your mental health.

You must persevere no matter the odds against you.

To be successful in your career you must persevere. Whoever you are, please, please, pretty please with sugar on top, please listen to me. Do not give up! Please do not throw in the towel in your pursuit of a successful life, or business, or a career, because no matter how much you try, no one is willing to give you the opportunity you are in need of. Perhaps you are living at home with mom and dad or one or the other, and need to move out and start living your own life. Perhaps you are about to enter into adulthood and this will be your first occupational skill; or you are already an adult and have yourself to take care of, perhaps your children, or a husband or wife to help.

Whoever you are, more likely than not, you have or will have rent/mortgage, or car payment(s), and all the responsibilities that come with being an adult. Whatever the circumstances you are facing, a job is paramount when it comes to your survival in life. This is the avenue by which you will pay your bills and live a financially secure life.

No matter how hard it gets, no matter the struggles, add to it a rude boss, rude employees, obnoxious co-workers, and on, and on, and on. Listen to me, you must keep pushing forward; you must keep a forward momentum; you cannot allow your spirit, your heart, your mind to become discouraged. You must not lose hope, no matter how difficult your circumstances may be, you must push forward. Many have taken the journey before you including myself, and have lived to tell the story, and have succeeded in life. Fight! Tough it out! Give it your best shot, and then give it some more. You my dear people, whomever you are, you are absolutely worth it.

No matter the circumstances that you are facing, you must survive them all and you must live. You must outlast your adversities; You must outlast your adversaries; and you must excel. You precious soul that you are, must never give up. In wrestling, using your hand to, "Tap, tap" means, you are asking your opponent to let you go, because you are giving up.

I am now saying to you, I am imploring you, I am admonishing you, no matter your circumstances in life as I said before, you Sir or Madam, young man or young lady, "no matter the situation, no matter your circumstances, please precious soul that you are, do not tap out of life." Do not give up, fight to the finish and then fight some more. No matter how difficult the journey, you must survive it. Crawl to your destiny, drag yourself to your destiny. Weep, cry, and moan in sorrow; and let it all out. And all the while still holding on for dear life to your dreams, to your precious aspirations; and telling yourself, "No matter the heartache, no matter the disappointments, no matter the pain, my dreams, my aspirations will not be denied, they will be accomplished."

The passion of the mind starts within the heart;

The passion of the mind starts within your heart; determine your success within your heart, and your mind will follow. Positive changes are now within your grasp, how do I know this? It is simple, it is because you are having this conversation with me. You are nodding your head, crying, saying to me, "how do you know exactly what I am feeling, how do you know exactly what I am going through?"

I know because I too believe it or not, have crawled through darkness of sorrows, cried oceans of tears while billows rolled over my Tony and I. I have wailed in the midnight hour, for my precious child and I, while suicide beckoned to me with lies, that it was the comfort that I needed. Here is an insight; to prove to you that I get it, here is one percent of my journey, anything more would cause you to come apart at the knowledge of my horrific journey.

My career Journey

As I mentioned before, I was in a truly horrific accident. This took place over twenty-seven years ago, and the very moment it happened my life as I knew it had ended. I remember weeks into my injury I said to myself metaphorically speaking. "Had I known what was up ahead, had I known what would have befallen me, I would have run ten thousand miles, I would have swum the ocean and climbed the Kilimanjaro Mountain." To my great sadness and regret there was no warning, just complete and utter devastation. No ankle in my left foot, no cartilage, just bone screwed to bone, some areas of my left fibula and tibia from mid-foot down looks like Swiss cheese; there are holes throughout my bones and screws to fill in huge chunks of bone that fell out. The surgeries were brutal, and my recoveries were even worse.

I was told to give up on any idea of going back to work. I was told the foot was hanging on for dear life, and that down the road amputation was every bit a possibility. My son was twelve at the time and I knew failure was not an option. I was told my left foot would not be able to touch the ground for a year; and that even then there was much uncertainty when it came to my recovery.

I set myself to find out all that I could about my injury, because as far as I was concerned, ignorance was not bliss. As far as I was and am concerned to this day, what you do not know can end your life. In my studies on bone anatomy, I found out that after a fracture, not immediately after but after a while, if you put pressure on it as in start placing the foot bottom to the ground as if to stand and allowing some weight to it, this actually helps in the healing of the bone. Remember I was told I had to wait at least one year before my foot could touch the ground. Three months into my injury I was placing my foot on the ground to apply pressure. (DISCLAIMER) This was my personal choice. I would not recommend this to any other person.

I knew my circumstances as a mother, and that I had no one to depend on. I had to persevere…I had to get back up, and I had to win. Six months into my injury, a few weeks after the metal fixator was removed from my left leg and ankle, I started applying for jobs so as to get back into the dental office, so as to start working. I would always wear my scrubs because it was loose fitting and it covered the extreme swelling of my left leg, ankle, and foot, and it also hid my secret.

Most employers would tell me point blank that my limp was so extreme that there was no way they could hire me. I became even more determined. I would fight to the point of nausea to stand straight, to walk steady, and to try and minimize my limp as much as was possible, during interviews. All-the-while feeling the most unbearable pain and nausea you could ever imagine.

After approximately two months of doing this, I finally started getting employment. Now here is where perseverance kicked in. They would hire me on Monday, and on Friday they would fire me. They would explain to me that although I knew the job really well, as in my occupational skills when it came to the dental office was just fine; but physically I could not do the job due to my injury. They would fire me on Friday and days later, by Tuesday or Wednesday of the following week, I would have another job. There was no giving up. I had to feed my child, I had to provide a roof over his head and encourage his precious heart.

Some days I could not go to work; I had to crawl on my knees to get to the bathroom. My foot and my ankle would just stop working. I had gotten rid of my crutches for Tony's sake. I did not want my injury to haunt him, and to be always on his mind. Those crutches would be a constant reminder. My help lived outside of the United States at that time. My immediate family within the United States was seniors that were retired. The non-stop pain from the time I awoke, until the time I laid down was causing extreme mental stress, was breaking me down; and it did not help that I refused to take any medication that was stronger than Tylenol or Ibuprofen.

The reason for this was simple, as I said before, narcotics caused addiction; and there was no way I was going to become an addict. I stopped taking any form of strong pain medication the day I left the hospital. They all had narcotics in them. I went from a morphine pump due to my extreme injury, and the incredible pain that came with it, to Tylenol. I know, crazy yes, impossible no, compulsory? Absolutely, without a doubt it was. There was just no other way to avoid addiction. I had to persevere, and I had to make it. Wow, such an incredibly painful journey. And yet wonderful joy, at the fact that I recovered, I did not give up. Instead, I persevered, and I made it.

My social skills were terrible, because I was always uneasy, due to the nonstop pain in my leg, ankle, and foot. I hated talking, and I was short tempered. My anger was always just below the surface, due to the trauma I had gone through, along with what I was still going through. These were all ingredients for a short-lived career.

As months grew into years, my desire and my will to be better at life, started to kick back in, and grew tremendously. In spite of my injury and the nonstop pain and limitations, I decided in my heart and my mind, that I would not use my circumstance as an excuse to live a pitiful, damaged life.

I persevered, I pushed forward, and I changed not only in the way that I was/am with others, I also changed my outlook on life. My career grew until I outgrew being inside any four walls permanently. I became a Dental Consultant, a Trainer, a Business Owner, a Community Leader, and an Ordained Minister and last but not least an Author. What if I had given up? What if I had quit? What if I had not forced myself to get back into the dental office? What if I had given up when I was fired from the 1st, the 2nd, the 3rd, 7th or the 10th job?

Look at it! Fired from the 10th job? And still I kept at it. Opportunities after opportunities to have the financial ability to pay for the things that I needed for my child and I, opportunities to put food on the table, to pay the bills, I lost, and I lost, and I lost, because of the horrific injury I had experienced. Yet I kept going, finding job after job after job. There was no other way, my baby, my precious child needed me to get the job done for the sake of his future, and I could not fail. You must keep at it also; you must not quit.

keep pressing, keep with your forward momentum, and do not stop. Your future depends on it; a better way of life is depending on it, and your determination will reap in the abundance, great, satisfying, and miraculous rewards for you.

You can absolutely do this; pen your journey; your actions are the pen that is doing the writing. Write strength, perseverance, tenacity, patience, strong faith, love for yourself and humanity. Write, "I will not quit; I will accomplish my dreams. I will live with honor and gratitude; I will show mercy."

Write your story precious you; write a great one that is filled with perseverance, love, and passion of the heart and mind. Be fearless in writing your story; conviction of the heart will lead the way. it is your story, and thus, only you precious, can write it.

Never forget, it is your actions that are writing your story, and not your pen. With these actions, trust me when I say to you, you will become a bestseller that everyone will want to read, talk about, and emulate. Write your story my love, and never forget; they are your actions, and thus it is your story and no one else.

Proof that perseverance reaps great rewards

Due to my injury, I was constantly being fired from my job. I would start another job a few days later; I became immune to starting over, or being in a new or different environment. The fear of the unknown was no longer a part of my life; my confidence when I stood in a new arena was phenomenal. I am so very grateful; I would start in a new dental practice, and it was as if I had been there for years. I gained and built a vast wealth of dental practice knowledge; so that after a while I was able to run the dental practice with my eyes closed. How did this happen? How did I accomplish this? My answer is this, I worked in many, many, many dental practices due to my horrific injury, and I learned from them all. This came about through a horrific accident, an incredibly horrifying injury with very few options, and my not giving up. But instead, pushing through and clawing, reaching, and fighting my way through some of the most horrific circumstances, that could befall any human being.

My success came about through my believing, my hope, and my strong faith. I had a never, never, never say die attitude, after surviving the desire and the intention to commit suicide. I persevered under the greatest of circumstances. My journey could have gone another way, had I given up; had I not fought for the saving of my life, and for my child's life; I most certainly would have gone under. Perseverance is the catalyst for a great life, this I promise you; and the fight to the end is a must, if you want to live a successful life and have a successful career. Do not give up, please do not quit no matter the odds against you, or the amount of no's you are told whether you are the employer or the employee.

Instead, I encourage you to plant your feet with determination; believe in the gifts and the talents that are within you; and tell yourself destiny is on your side. Start your business, grow your business; and if things falter, please tray and try and try again. Outlast failure, and when failure tires and goes to sleep, that is your time to build, and or make your comeback.

For you the employee, work hard, study hard, and pursue hard after your career, and your desires in life. You will achieve great results, and accomplish much in life, through your hard work and perseverance. For all of you please remember, your life is only as good as the effort you put into it. Your very own actions are what will count the most. Give it your all, give it your best and allow your change to happen. I bless you; I bless you with courage of conviction, and strength to finish your journey. I bless you with faith to believe in what you do not see, in spite of the many difficulties and hindrances, and the willingness to pursue hard after your dreams; so as to live out the gifts, the talents, and the authentic blueprint for your life, for your career, and for your business. Be brave, be enduring in the face of adversities, believe in yourself, your gifts and your talents are your own.

CHAPTER 29

The hostage situation, where the weapons being used to hold the victims are, "Threats of Suicide."

You are holding someone hostage, because they have told you they no longer want to be in a relationship with you.

Your Threat:
"If you leave, I will kill myself."

The Ransom/payoff:
"If you stay, I will not kill myself."

Your will is to force them to: Remain in the relationship between you both.

Your will is to force them to: Not end the season of life that they have been sharing with you.

Your will is to force them to: Live within a space where they no longer want to be.

Your will is to keep them from: moving on with their life, where it will no longer have you in it.

For The Hostage Taker. Please let he or she go. Please do not travel down this road of hostage taking, to feed your obsession. This is the absolute wrong direction for you to go in, please let them go, please walk away with your head held high and your integrity still intact. Yes, it hurts, yes you do not know what you will do without them, but I promise you, you will be just fine without them. Think about it precious; there are countless people that have gone through breakups and they are just fine. The breakup allowed them the opportunity to find the person that is truly meant for them. Please precious, let them go and LIVE.

Think about it Sir or Madam, what is the point of forcing someone to stay with you, if they no longer love you or want to be with you? Please let them go and LIVE. Give yourself a chance to find long lasting love. Give yourself the chance to find a partner, that wants to be with you. Please give yourself the opportunity to find lasting companionship, with the person that is truly meant for you.

Precious please hear me, forcing someone to stay with you is not right. It is and obsession, and hostage taking pure and simple. It is a prideful action that is filled with your selfish deeds. Please let he or she go, and move on with your life. Letting go allows you the opportunity to look forward to the new chapter of your life, that is brought on by this breakup.

Do not worry about what the people around you will think, because you were together for many years. It is better to let go than to waste additional years of your life. This person might want to love you, but find it impossible to do so. Do you know why? Because you are not meant to be. Please, please I beg of you, precious, please let them go. Go on in your new direction, and live your newness of life. Claim what is meant for you, and speak it into existence. Enjoy your new season of being single, and give yourself the chance to heal from a broken heart. Be good to yourself; and do not turn yourself into a hostage taker. No, you are not a villain; instead, you are victorious. Live a fabulous life without them, and be encouraged precious, this stranger loves you.

You have help, this I promise you. Please Call or text the **Suicide & Crisis Lifeline** at **988**, the 1-800-273-8255 has merged with **988** as of July 16, 2022. **Active-duty members and veterans, please press (1)** when the call is answered, or text to **838255.** Non-military, if you are unable to speak, or you are hearing impaired, you can send a text to the **Crisis Text Line** 24/7, at **741741.** You can also go to **988lifeline.org.** Whether by voice or text, please tell them what you are feeling, they are there to encourage you. PLEASE I BEG OF YOU, PLEASE LIVE.

Here is insight into the other side. For you the hostage taker. This is the reality of the person you are holding hostage. This is how ugly, how dangerous things can become.

The Hostage: Someone being held against their will.

The hostage: Someone being held against their will through the threat of suicide.

You the hostage, are allowing yourself to be held hostage, because you believe it will save the person, that is holding you hostage life. This while wanting

232

to end the relationship. Unbeknownst to you, that same person is slowly ending your life.

Your will: Is to end the relationship between you and the person that is threatening to harm themselves, or commit suicide, if you breakup with them.

Your will: Is to end the season of life that you have been sharing with that person.

Your will: Is to stop living within a space where you no longer want to be.

Your will: Is to move on with your life, which does not include the person that is threatening to harm themself through suicide or otherwise, if you leave.

The Prisoner
The moment you told your partner that you wanted to end the relationship, you wanted out. Make no mistake, the relationship as you knew it ended.

You deciding to stay, because they threatened to harm themselves, is you allowing yourself to be held hostage. **"You both know it is over."** You are there out of fear, that they will kill themself, and make no mistake; they are quietly and meticulously buying their time; and they will destroy you, because you no longer want to be with them.

There is something that you, who are trying to walk away must understand. The moment you spoke into existence, the fact that it was now over, and that you wanted to end the relationship, your heart, your mind started reacting as a person that is no longer in a relationship. You stayed, but there is no longer that loving relationship between you both. The relationship has now changed over to hostage and prisoner.

Your heart and mind will start noticing others, liking others and showing interest in others. The moment you act out your feelings, because you feel no emotions towards your ex. Yes, your ex; you are only there because you are afraid they will kill themselves. Your heart and mind has left the relationship. You know it, and I know it also.

Here is my advice to you. Speak with family and friends, speak with a mental health specialist. Tell them all that it is over, and that you are only there because you are being told your ex will kill themself if you walk away. That's right, say your ex, to emphasize the fact that you are only there out of fear they will kill themself. Listen to me please. Do not play into their hands. They know you want out, they are biding their time, and is looking for the first opportunity to burn your life to the ground, and turn everyone against you in the hopes, that you will be destroyed. Why? Because you broke up with them. You know the proverbial, **"If I cannot have you no one else will?"** There is a likelihood you will fall for someone else, because your heart has already exited that relationship. Your ex will rally the world against you. They will burn you at the stake as a traitor, a cheater, as a monster and a lowdown villain. This is while the hostage taker is painted as the victim. Your ex will use this to steal your joy, your assets, your friends and even your family; all because you told them you wanted to end the relationship. Do not allow yourself to be held hostage. If you no longer love this person, and want to walk away, please do so. Them threatening to kill themself or you, is a sure sign that you need to get away from them. As I said before, speak with your family and friends, speak with a mental health specialist. Tell them all that you are being threatened, you are being forced to stay with your ex, because he or she might kill themself if you leave, and that you need their help to handle the situation.

Ask their family and a mental health specialist to step in, and you let go. Do not hang around them please. Because mark my words, **"there is a bullseye on your back,"** and the arrow is already out of the quiver, and is into the bow. If they cannot have you, they will shoot that arrow straight through your heart. Please protect yourself, call the hotline and tell them that your ex is suicidal and you need help.

Please note, there are some hostage takers that is calculating with every single step they take. They will not use the word suicide, that way they can deny their actions. Here are some examples, "I never said I would kill myself, I only said if you leave my life is over. I did not mean I would kill myself." Or "I never said I would commit suicide, I just said if you leave, I am no more, but I was not talking about suicide." Call them out, make them explain what they mean by "no more," and "my life is over." Ask them if they mean they will kill themselves, they will commit suicide? When someone attempts to hold you hostage, you need to know exactly what you are dealing with, when it comes to that person. That way you know how to function from that point onwards. Do not allow anyone to use suicide to hold onto you. If they are willing to commit suicide, they might decide to take you with them.

Give them the hotline information, encourage them to seek help, reason with them. Help them to face reality. Ask them to see the reality for what it is. Them letting go of you, is them giving themselves a chance to find the true love of their life. Explain to them that they deserve better, than to hold onto someone that no longer loves them, or want to be with them. Explain to them that it is not about going to someone else. Instead, you both are no longer what you use to be for each other, and your seasons of being together is no more. Encourage them to give themself the chance they deserve, to find what they truly need. Thank them for the love, the happiness, and the joy that they gave to you. Assure them that you are grateful to them for your time together, and please Sir or Madam, **"You Need To Let Go."**

Please do not allow yourself to be held hostage, where to onlookers you are a free human being, but in reality, you are an actual prisoner. **Please call the Violence Prevention number, at 1- 800-799-SAFE (7233) or TTY 1 800-787-3224 or 206-518-9361, Video Phone Only for Deaf Callers**. Allow them to help you to gain your freedom without being harmed.

CHAPTER 30

For the precious soul that is unable to read, they are illiterate.

If they have not told you that they are unable to read, please do not embarrass them, by you revealing their secret. Instead, sit in their presence and mention out loud how good this book is. Mention to them that you do not want to be annoying, but you want them to listen for a moment.

Start reading from the beginning; and write down the suicide hotline number on a piece of paper, and give it to them. Tell them to keep it, and to pass it on-to anyone they know, that is going through extreme stress, and anyone they know that might be suicidal. Please be sure to tell them, that they can tell everyone they pass this number on-to, that no one will know that they called the **988 Suicide & Crisis Lifeline,** and be sure to tell them that the people on the **988 Suicide & Crisis Lifeline,** is there to help them.

Continue reading to them, and keep reading if they do not stop you. If they stop you, mark where you left off, and start from there at your next reading session with them. Be strategic in where to stop, until your next reading session. Stop at a place where the words will leave a significant impression on them. This will ignite a hunger within them, to hear more, and will cause them to look forward to the next reading session. They might even initiate dialogue.

This is the moment to discuss with them, how you want to join a reading and answer meeting, together with them. Tell them that you will do the reading, and they will give the feedback. Tell them that all they need to do is talk about what they heard, and how they felt after. **"Do not read this chapter to them."** As you are reading, please break down any words you believe they might not understand. Please stop and make certain you repeat sentences that you believe are significant, and need to be repeated.

Go slow, take your time, give them a chance to take in what you are saying. Keep at the forefront of your mind, the fact that you are fighting to save that person's life. Take your time, speak clearly, be gentle when need be. Be strong and forceful when you need to be; and yes, it is okay to be funny also. Laughter is medicine for the soul; a man or woman that is filled with sorrow, does not have much of it. Feeding them with kindness, with consideration, with laughter, is food for the soul.

Prepare for their tears, prepare for them to open up to you, please do not worry. You are not expected to solve their situation, you have this book, and you have the **Suicide & Crisis Lifeline** at **988**, the 1-800-273-8255 has merged with **988** as of July 16, 2022. If they open up to you, please encourage them to call the hotline. If you are able to convince them, call the hotline while you are there with them. If they are unable to speak or are hearing impaired, please speak or text on their behalf. You can send a text to the **Crisis Text Line** 24/7 at 741741. You can also go to **988lifeline.org.** Nod your head in agreement, while helping them. Tell them that they are doing great. Tell them they are not alone; tell them you are with them. If you need to speak on their behalf, I beg of you, please do so. You Sir, or Madam, young man, or young woman, are saving someone's life.

Do not end your reading session even after they call the **988** number. Please keep on reading to them. At some point mention to them, that this book was written for everyone, and that no one is left out. Tell them this book was written for the government of nations, for the fisherman, the billionaire, for the student, the grandmother and grandfather, the person that cannot read or write and the doctor, dentist, attorney, baker, cook, scientist and everyone else is included. Tell them no person is left out of this book because every soul is precious; everyone matters and everyone must be saved.

Please gather as much information as you can, on how to help someone that is unable to read

During this journey with them, please do this for me. Please call your local community college, and find out what options exist for an adult, that is unable to read and or write. Get the information and keep it until the moment presents itself, where they tell you. Or the reading sessions have now brought you closer, and you now are presented with the opportunity to discuss it with them. What you could not discuss in the beginning, you can discuss farther along in the journey, because you laid the groundwork with this book, and with your contribution in them finding, in them getting the much-needed help, that they so very desperately, desperately needed.

Please leave them with hope, when you finally close out your reading sessions. Tell them to remember the encouraging words from the book. Tell them to consider starting a session of their own with others. Tell them that all they need is a reader, and others to talk about what they are hearing.

Sir or Madam, "I thank you, and I bless you." Thank you for your selfless actions towards someone that needed your help, someone that was limited in their ability to get the help they were in need of. I am beyond grateful to you, and again, Sir or Madam I thank you, I thank you, I thank you.

CHAPTER 31

To you the owner, the manager, or the human resource representative, or any other person that is doing the hiring for your organization. Please give someone with no experience, their much-needed chance to start their career.

I ask with the most respectful heart, that is filled with tremendous gratitude towards you. Please give those without any experience a chance. Please do not turn them away because of their lack of, or their limited experience. Please give that individual, that person a chance to be gainfully employed, and to grow within their chosen career field. Please keep in mind that you and I, were once without any form of experience, and yet someone took a chance on us; and now years later you Sir or Madam, are a force to be reckoned with within your career.

Please bless these individuals by opening your doors to them. I am asking you Sir or Madam, to please give them the life changing opportunity, that will pave the way for their success in life. Never forget, someone opened their doors to you; someone said yes to you, when you had no experience.

For the seasoned employee, I ask on behalf of those who are now drawing close to their senior years. Please do not abandon your employee because they are now much older, and you believe new blood, young blood will serve you better. Actually, you need both. You need the young blood that will take chances that the seasoned person might not. They will help you to usher in the next chapter of your organization; and they are the future strength of your company.

You also need the seasoned employee. This is who will train your young-blood and show them the way. The seasoned employee during times of crisis will be the rock within your organization. They are the ones with the years of experiences within their career, at your organization, or at another. They are the ones with the wealth of knowledge within that career field. Make no mistake, your seasoned employee without a doubt, plays a significantly important part within your organization's success.

Your seasoned employees, nine times out of ten, are vested into making your organization the success that it is and will continue to be. Older and wiser although not all the time, is definitely far more than not. Yes, experience is your best teacher, and also, the best motivator. Yes, this I truly believe. I am absolutely speaking from my own experiences. The years of my experience has definitely made me stronger, wiser, and has given me an undeniably strong resolve, and it has filled me with an abundance of wisdom.

The resolute human being that I have become, was birthed through experiences, and years lived upon the earth. In the same breath make no mistake, our young men and young women have much to offer also. There are some situations that are suited for the young mind, for the brash mind. Yes, the brash mind will step out and seize the day; even though they might get knocked upside the head while stepping out. You need that attitude when going for success.

Trust me when I say, that attitude comes in a large amount when it comes to young folks. The seasoned employee will help to reinforce the young folks. The seasoned employee will help the young-blood to get back into the fight, when the young-blood comes back from the fight with one shoe on, shirt barely hanging on them, and a bruised ego that is there for all to see. In other words, when they jumped out to manage the task, they failed. Every company needs both the young and the seasoned employee; this is to build your organization, and to make it a successful company.

Always remember this information I ask of you. Any human being with employment, will find that they are more likely than not, guaranteed a better way of life, than someone without employment. This is that person's safety net; to provide a better way of life for themselves and their family. It gives them the ability to lead a productive, financially secure life; that is empowered by their hard work, their dedication, and their very own accomplishments.

A human being without employment, without the ability for financial gain, can fall off a cliff, due to their lack, and financial desperation. Please see you employing someone in a different light, I ask of you.

Please see the life changing significance, that you employing that individual before you will bring, and please act accordingly. I beg of you, and I thank you.

Last but not least, please consider placing this book within reach of your employees. Place a stack of this book on a table for them to read. Someone within your company could be suicidal. Or their family member could be, and your employee is desperate for answers, is desperate for help. Even if they do not want to tell you out of fear that they might lose their job. This book being within their reach, could make a world of difference for not just them, but for their family members also.

CHAPTER 32

You are entrenched within the ghetto, or you live in a shantytown, or you are without any form of resource and you hate and pity your life, to the point of wanting to die. You do not believe you can make it out

Yes, I agree, your chance of making it out from the place where you are, is slim to none. The odds are completely against you. Tell that to those of us who have suffered in the most horrific ways and are still alive. That one percent that have survived is now an army of millions. **"Join us,"** stake your claim in the journey of survival and betterment for your life, for your existence, for your future accomplishments, and make it out and live. Look around you, look at the lack, the wretchedness and feel the heartache within you. That Sir or Madam, that young man or young lady, is your motivation; that is the inspiration that you must grab hold of, and allow it to push you away from where you are now, away from that place of sorrow and extreme wretchedness and lack.

Can you make it out? **"YES YOU CAN."** At this point what is there to lose? The answer is nothing. Go for it, stake your claim for the survival and the restoration of your life, Sir or Madam, young man or young woman, and live. Your beginning is not your middle, and your middle is not your ending, give yourself a chance to live, to experience a better way of life. Push through, punch through, crawl through, cry, wail and moan through, and find your way out from the pit of sorrow that is your life.

Here are the tools that you will need, to make it out, and to build a new life, with new opportunities, and new accomplishments.

Food: as in nutritional sustenance for your existence.

Money: As in the ability to live a far better life due to your financial gain.

Humanity's Input: Humanity will offer you much needed direction. Humanity will offer you advice, will help to grow your wisdom, your knowledge and your understanding. Humanity will help to provide provision, provide supplies for your journey, and will help to point the way to your success.

You must be stoic: Here are some other words for **"stoic"** that I want you to lean into and live out, while finding your way out of the extreme poverty, the financial misery that you are living in.

Enduring: You must outlast the place where you are now, and the people that are after your demise within that place.

Understanding: Do not rush to judgement. Be kind, be considerate towards others. Even while suffering greatly, while being under much pressure, and while needing an abundance of help to get from where you are; still give of yourself to others. Your giving of yourself I promise you, will come back to you, in the most wonderful way. A smile doesn't cost a penny, a hug, carrying someone's heavy bag, speaking kind words to someone, and encouraging them is without financial cost, and yet, is beyond valuable. Is worth more than diamonds, rubies and pearls all together. These attributes, when extended to others, could save someone's life, and will make you feel encouraged, that you did these things for someone.

Be Patient: This is a must, your journey so far has taken your strength, and left you weak, and with a broken spirit. Be patient, take your time and nurse yourself to good health while preparing to make your exit from your place of extreme poverty and great sorrow. Take your time and start removing the hardened scales that you are covered in, that are due to the wretched experiences of your life.

Where you are going is new and different, and is a place where you will turn your life around. If you do not remove the hardened scales of where you have been, you will bring the same way of life into your new existence. You will accomplish great wealth, and achievements; and you will live the way you did in the ghetto; you will live as you did in your shanty town. Face who you are now, face how you have had to live and accept that you will need to become a new man or woman for where you are going.

You have spent your entire life looking over your shoulder, expecting to be killed, expecting to be forced into a gang, expecting to be shot and killed if you resist. You perhaps have done things you did not want to do, to ensure your safety and survival. These are things and ways that you must stop, you must change, you must let go of, if you are truly desperate for a better way of life. You will need to give yourself time to change, to reinvent yourself, to become a better human being. Your harsh existence has shaped your heart and mind into a, **"I will kill them before they kill me person."** I see a person coming towards you smiling, you see that same person at the same time coming towards you, with the intention to cause you harm. You must take your time; **be patient,** and allow yourself the time needed to renew your mind and heart, to the knowledge that you are heading towards a brand-new territory. This territory needs the new you. Yes precious, it needs **your patience** for the exit from one life; and for the entrance into your new life. This new life that will be filled with joy, with financial gain, and with an enriched life and living; must be saturated with **"your patience."**

Where do you go, how do you gain finance, how do you survive, in going after your new way of life?

For you, the person that needs to get out. What are you willing to do to make it out?

Are you willing to live in a shelter? Are you willing to grovel, to beg for help when it comes to finding a job? Are you willing to work eighty hours in a week to get to the life you want to live? Are you willing to take the job that no one wants so as to give yourself a chance at life? Are you willing to do what needs to be done to get your GED? Are you willing to go to college, go to a trade school, get vocational training so as to give yourself a chance at a better career? Are you willing to use your funds to accomplish your dreams? If they will not let you in, **are you Sir or Madam, willing to build your door, that you can open yourself? If they will not give you a chance, "are you willing to create your own chance?"**

With an almost dead foot being dragged along, with horrific pain being inflicted upon my body and my mind, and the call of suicide haunting me, I still did it, and you can also. I crawled, I begged, I negotiated, I created my opportunity. I studied for a new career, after researching, realizing I stood a better chance of getting my son across the finish line with that career. I put in forty hours in three days, so that I could get Thursday and Friday off to build my dental consulting business. This is while dragging an almost dead, extremely swollen foot, that hurt beyond measure, and while suicide had me by the throat.

My goal was to give it my all, while I was upon the earth; so as to get my Tony to safety, and I did just that. My end date would be the day he graduated from college. Tony would be equipped to take care of himself, and I could end my life. If a human being as I, that was broken in heart and mind, could survive those traumatic heartbreaking seasons, that was filled with unrelenting sorrow, horrific abuse, and pain after pain and still made it. Trust me, believe me, and rely on my words and be encouraged when I say, "you can make it out also, and you can live. You can outlive the mental stress, you can outlive the mental health breakdowns, and you can outlast these suicidal thoughts and tendencies, and accomplish your dreams, your aspirations and all the while, finding your way to your comfort, your happiness and your peace."

What are your gifts and talents?

Can you sew, draw, bake, or cook? Are you good with numbers? Are you Tech savvy, good with repairing automobiles, or are keen to learn? What are you good at? Please tell me, what is that ability that has been lying dormant within you, because of the oppressive circumstances you were living in, you were surviving in? Can you paint, make furniture, do you have a high IQ score and yet have done nothing with the incredible intelligence that you have?

Stretch out both your hands or your hand, palm or palms up, so that I can inspect. What can your hand do? What can these hands do? Can it, can they clean, do plumbing, type, teach? What can the work of this hand do? Can these hands be trained to heal wounds, to administer treatment to the sick? I ask you, and I ask the heavens, what can this hand, these hands do? What is the potential of this hand, these hands when it comes to you as an individual?

Now is the time to do your part in saving your life. If you have no skills, are you willing to fight hard to get one. If you cannot read or write and someone is reading this book to you, are you willing to tell someone about your limitations when it comes to reading and writing; so that you can get the help that you are in need of, to get from this place of utter misery? This is so that you can turn your life around, and create new, or you can maximize the potential that is already within you. As in the gift and talents that are already within you and waiting to be used. You can also maximize possibilities, as in the vast ocean of anything is possible if you pursue hard after it, and give it your all.

Decide on the location you want to relocate to. If you can save enough to rent in your new location please do so. Check for one room rentals. You stand a better chance budget wise by starting out in a one room. That one room will allow you the ability to save for a while, until you can move into the space you truly desire.

Please note, it is better to live with a senior than a younger person if you are in your twenties or thirties. You will not party as much or spend as much. You will save more and you can learn a lot from them. In your case less is truly more. You need peace, you do not need chaos. Yes, one person can inflict chaos on a thousand people, but you stand a better chance of resting, with fewer people that will come with their own emotional characteristics, and you having to deal with them all. The seasoned roommate will also help to shape you when it comes to being grounded.

Their journey can help to lighten your load, when it comes to your journey. Listen to them, ask them questions and seek out their advice. At the same time limit yourself, do not become a bother. Respect their space and pay attention to their personality. No, my statement is not a blanket statement when it comes to living with an older person. There are people in their twenties, believe it or not, that are far, far more mature and grounded than people in their fifties and sixties, and their decision making is superior to those that are decades older than them.

If your life is threatened and you must leave now, please do so. If it means you have to stay in a shelter, then so be it. Save your life first, save your life second, save your life third, save your life fourth, save your life fifth, save your life sixth, save your life seventh, save your life eighth, save your life ninth, **"find your comfort tenth." This is my way of emphasizing, that you must be willing to forgo your comfort, in order to save your precious life.**

Apply for positions before you leave, or while you are on your way out. Tell them you are relocating and can start on ____ date. Consider joining the military. You will have a steady job, a support system, you can travel the world, you will get free education for the career of your choosing. You will even get support after you leave the military. For you who will seek out non-military employment. Save enough to stay in a hotel on your first day at work if you have not found a permanent living space. Staying at the hotel instead of a shelter will give you less chance of anything going wrong. After the first day on the job, you can check out of the hotel, and check into the shelter. Take comfort, you are employed; you will find a living space, do not lose heart. You will spend more time at work and less time at the shelter; you can do it, be encouraged; it is for the saving of your life.

Stake your claim in life

Brick by brick, moment by moment, and you will get there. The deprivation you have lived through, that almost broke your mental health, that almost caused you to take your life, or almost had you killed by someone else, will finally be behind you. **"This is where you must stake your claim in life, and nourish what you are claiming."** When those of old staked their claims for their land, and they eventually planted their crop, so as to accomplish their financial journey. They nourished their land with water, enough sunlight so that their crop would grow, and no drought please. They prayed that their land would not be overrun by pestilence that could wipe out their crop.

You do the same, stake your claim for your changes you desire in life. Stake your claim for your future prosperity in life. Work hard, pray for rain as in blessings to saturate your life. Plant and reap as in work hard and reap the rewards from your hard work. Save and invest your time and talents into your future. Never forget pestilences and the need to prevent them; by staying away from people, places and things that will consume what you have worked hard for, and accomplished; by wiping out your hard work and investment that you have made into your life.

change for the better, bring back the essence of the person that existed before the trauma.

Change for the better, some of you have had to live without a conscience to survive, whilst others of you have stayed on the straight and narrow. You without conscience must fight to change your heart and mind, and to bring back the humane you. The angry, the battered and traumatized you, will not help you on this journey of redemption.

Some of you, like myself, have had to send away the very essence of who you were, so as to persevere, so as to not lose the kind and gentle you. Please allow me to explain what I mean. There is something about me that I have always known. I have an ability to extend mercy beyond my own capabilities. I have always treasured this characteristic about me and never wanted to lose it.

A few days after my accident, while I am still in the hospital, the rehabilitation specialist came into my room, and told me I needed to try to use my crutches, and that I would be taken to rehabilitation within the hospital; so that they could teach me how to function with one healthy foot and crutches. They sat me up and brought my feet over the side of the bed, so that my feet hung down towards the floor. I almost lost my mind. A pain and cramp and buzzing and more pain, more brain freeze shot through my leg and brain in the most horrific way. It took about fifteen minutes to stop, and then they helped me into the wheelchair. They pushed me in the wheelchair, and once there, they helped me to stand between two bars, that I could hold onto, I remember nothing after that. When I awoke, I was back in bed, with no memory of how I got there. I had fainted due to extreme loss of blood

My doctor came in a few minutes later, and told me that I had to accept a blood transfusion. I had fought against getting the transfusion, even though they said I needed it. Since the accident, I had been bleeding out profusely, and needed blood. I was terrified of getting blood. Back then hemophiliacs, people going in for transplants, people going in for surgery that needed blood, some were coming out of the hospital and testing HIV positive. The moment I entered the hospital, I told them not to give me blood during my surgery, no matter what. Days later, my doctor tells me that without the transfusion I will die.

They attached what they needed to attach to me for the transfusion and a sorrow came over me like you could not imagine. Hear me please, imagine taking ice out of your freezer, blending it, and then pouring it into an I. V. bag, and pumping it straight into my bloodstream. You feel the frozen ice inside you, you cannot touch it, you cannot use a thousand blankets to warm it away. It is too deep, too far within, to get to it to warm it, you feel like you are at death's door and you are beyond helpless. Knowing that blood could be infected with the HIV virus your mind feels like it is dead, time does not exist, and you are in a vegetative state of madness, confusion, and utter and complete despair.

Just then the phone in my room rang, I answered it. It could be my Tony, I needed to tell him I was okay and that everything would be alright. How in such a moment, in such a state you could answer the phone and say, you are okay? This is what parents do every day for their children. It was my insurance company calling. **"Remember the condition that I was in."**

Before my accident I had finished my internship. During the internship I was not paid, and right after my internship, I was planning to relocate; to find better opportunities for Tony and I. I had just gotten done with my internship, and was about to relocate when the accident happened. To prepare for my internship and relocation, I had done my budget. I turned off any services I could do without. I turned off my cable, paid off all bills that I could payoff, and I also stocked up on groceries. **"I canceled our apartment rental insurance,"** and paid the balance of my car insurance premium off.

My landlord knew how clean, how impeccable I kept my apartment; and so, they allowed me to pay just the difference after including my deposit also. My insurance company had me drop off a letter, that requested that they terminate my renter's policy. **"I dropped it off the day after they told me to do so."** We were all set. I would get through my internship and days later we would be gone from there for good. The day of my move, while heading back to my apartment, after checking on the moving truck, someone hit me head on, and sent the engine, and the axle in my car, straight to the firewall. My left foot resting next to the firewall, took the entire impact.

Now back to the phone call that came in, during my blood transfusion. **The representative from my car insurance company, told me I had no insurance coverage; they never received my letter to cancel my renter's insurance,** and so instead of posting the full payment to my car insurance, which would have paid off the premium balance in full. They had split the payment, and posted some to my rental insurance, which left me still owing on my car insurance. He continued by saying that when they did not receive any additional payment from me, they canceled my car insurance. He said they had sent me notification; I had not received any notification from them.

I hung up the phone, and something happened to me. I started shivering a thousand times more. I have no words for that moment, let's just move on. The next morning, I sat up and helped my legs over the bed, I waited for about twenty minutes, for the pain to subside, and for my brain to work. I reached for my crutches and made my way to the mirror. I looked into the mirror dead into my eyes and I said to my precious soul.

"Leave, get out of here, and don't come back until I tell you to. Hide, hide deep within me, and no matter what you hear, do not listen, do not come

back please." **"Find a deep dark place and curl up and go to sleep. No matter how hard I cry, do not come out. No matter the screaming, do not come back; I will come for you someday, but not now, not here, for now you must leave."**

If you are wondering if it worked here is one moment that took place, days later. My orthopedic doctor picked up my foot, all toes are broken in multiple places, my instep shattered in pieces, no more ankle, leg ripped from foot, no more cartilage. He picks up the foot two weeks and days into injury and uses his hands to try to reshape my instep back into being an instep again. I am laying on the bed, I turned my head to the side, and the tears just poured out, no sound, no reaction, just uncontrollable oceans of tears. May I share something with you?

I felt a deep heartbreaking sorrow for myself. I felt a deep abyss of utter sorrow for myself. My doctor said to me at that moment, "you are completely different, you caved on me, you had a determination about you, you had a fight in you, but now you are completely different." Unbeknownst to him, I had to send myself away; so that that horrific season in life, of the utter devastation would not crush who I was, when it came to the kind, the gentle, the humane person that I was.

That was me protecting my heart and mind. That was me knowing that what my insurance company did to me, could turn me into a monster. That was me knowing that the man that hit me, had no insurance, and had been drinking. The person that helped me away from my car, smelled his breath. The man had no insurance, he was riding a huge Harley Davison bike going almost 65 in a 15 mile per hour zone, in the deepest corner you could imagine. To stay on the bike, he had to take the corner wide; which meant entering my oncoming lane. I met him in the corner and he let the bike go and rolled away. That huge bike sent my engine, my axel and all else straight to my left foot.

He came away with bruises and went home to rest, while my life as I knew it ended. I could have burned to death and left my child at the mercy of this world. I had just filled my tank; I was leaving town for good that day to start our new life, it ended there. My gas tank ruptured and poured out on the road, one spark, one car driving through, and there is no telling if I would be here today. I, who worked two jobs right up until my internship to pay my insurance and other bills, was told I had none by my insurance company, and was abandoned to hell.

My work day started at 4:00 am and ended 11:00 pm. I did it all for my Tony and I, and it was all in vain. Everything I had gone through, in my teens, my early twenties, and in my late twenties; the accident, the treatment from my insurance company; the horrific betrayals from my family, and my acquaintances. It was enough to turn my heart wicked. It could have caused me to spiral in the most violent, and the most venomous of ways possible, when it came to my treatment of others. Revenge could have taken over.

You must beat back the angry person, that wants to steal the very essence of who you truly are.

This is where **"the rubber meets the road."** This is where you must dig in, and fight, to not become the person that boils beneath the surface; that wants to retaliate, for the monstrous mistreatment that had been poured out upon me by these people. Please hear me and hear me well. **"They are not you, and you are not them."** What they did to you is who they are, not who you are. You must respond according to who you are. Do not get drawn out into madness and mayhem. Stay your course of decency, and if you already left your course of decency, please return.

That is why I had to send away the kind me. I had to send away the merciful me. I had to send away the dreamer; that loving human being that cared so much for humanity; so that that human being would not be destroyed, and to prevent me from destroying others. That human being would someday help me to finish my journey; and so I had to protect her, and keep her alive long enough to get my child to safety. From that point on, I would go it without all of me. I would take the pain, and the sorrow, and the betrayal, the return to poverty, and the embarrassment; of having to beg and dumb myself down. That after investing into my education, after investing into my life; so as to give my child a great life, this is where I found myself.

We lost the first and last month's rent, along with my deposit that I had paid towards the apartment, for our relocation. Instead, I had to move my Tony and I, into a filthy, horrifically roach infested, dilapidated dwelling place, so that we could survive.

It had no air conditioner, we had to live through the blistering summer, and we had no heat for winter. My foot looked like an old crusted bark of a one-thousand-year-old tree. My furniture was in storage, there was no way I would place our things inside that roach infested rotting mobile home. I received two hundred and seventy-five monthly I believe it was, to pay rent, light, water, and household supplies.

My son and I had never ever experienced such filth. I am borderline germaphobic, some say I am, I say I am not. I just crash when I enter a dirty place. For you who might live in a damp home, or roaches are caused by neighbors, that is no comparison to what I am describing. Walk to your kitchen cupboard, you are unable to see the surface inside because plates are sitting there, cups are sitting on the surface or even pots and pans. The surface in the mobile home was not seen because they were covered in roaches. In the cupboards, furniture drawers, the television, shelves, dresser drawers, the oven, all had roaches stacked on top of roaches on top of roaches.

In spite of the circumstance, you must improvise to overcome

I called supermarkets within the area, and told them my situation, they dropped off insecticides to spray around the outside of the mobile home, and gave me raid sprays and foggers also. Tony carried the outside insecticide container for me, and I sprayed all around the mobile home while balancing on my crutches.

When Tony was at school, I would spray throughout the mobile home and sit outside. I would set off one fogger every few days. I planned to set off two in each room, for a total of ten, and we stayed overnight at a former neighbor. Shockingly! The day before I did, it came on the news that a house blew up in another state, because they set off too many foggers. I promise you; I am telling the truth. One day before I set off all ten foggers, it came on the news, about the explosion because of too many foggers being set off at the same time, and it was less than what I had.

I used two hundred dollars for a cleaning company to clean the mobile home and the furniture included. It was horrific. They cleaned out the dead roaches as I asked them to do, and sprayed the areas I could not get to. They told me to get out, and that with my injuries I could develop an infection and die. What could I do? My son and I needed a roof over our heads. My poor son would turn on the TV that came with the mobile home and scream. Roaches would pour out from the TV, it was truly horrific. I gloved up and wore a mask. I wiped down everything over and over again with pine-sol and bleach water.

Retaliation, your acts of vengeance, will march you towards the death of you and others

Thank GOD I sent most of who I was away. The filth in that mobile home would have been the final straw that sent me over the cliff and driven me insane. The condition we were forced to live in, would have turned me into someone, who would have been able to do anything in retaliation, because of all that was done to me. If I had not protected my heart and mind, and sent me away, there is no telling where my pain would take me, and what I would do to retaliate.

For some, after the pain society has inflicted upon you, something inside you will still take you towards your redemption. For others, it will want to take you towards destruction. You, Sir or Madam, young man or young lady, "you must always fight that urge with all of your might, retaliation is death." The death of your life, the death of your bloodline, the death of your destiny that is up ahead, that will bring you relief, joy and rest. You must fight, resist the urge to punish the innocent and the guilty for your pain.

Someday I knew I would come back for me. for the kind and gentle me, for the considerate me, for the loving me. But not now, not here, not yet. I became a shell of a human being. I was very cold, distant, I trusted no one. I knew I had to bear it all, and get us out of there. Believe it or not, by October that year I was back at work. I had to get it done, winter was coming and there was no heat in the mobile home, GOD willing it was on me. I just had to get it done.

Yes, there are changes that take place in all of us, for our journey in life; and this includes you, who are trying to get out from where you are, to get to a better way of life. We change, we soften or harden; we evolve for the better or worse. Something inside rises or disappears, and our outcome is based on this.

Invest into yourself to become a better human being. Bring back the kind and gentle you, the considerate you, the loving you. Go after the things that will help in your evolution; when it comes to your education, your insight, intellect and the willingness to listen. Work on the building of your strength. Rebuild your patience, your understanding, and your ability to weather any challenges that are thrown at you. These things will nourish your journey, and take you a long, long way in the positive building of your life.

Do not restrain your abilities, because of your humble beginning

Allow yourself to go the distance. Do not restrain yourself because of what people will think or say. Yes, you came from nothing, **"OWN IT."** That is what is great about you. You did it, you made it out. Let them talk about how poor you were, and that you are a nobody. Wear it as a badge of honor. Your hard work, your determination, your refusal to give up on yourself, along with heaven's help; brought you here, or will get you there. Live it, own it and never stop being grateful for it.

When it is all said and done, please don't forget Sir or Madam, **"you have help,"** to encourage yourself, to pull yourself back from the brink, to help you with your mental health. If the journey out has weakened your mental health, if it has broken you to the point that you are considering suicide, please I beg of you, I admonish you, and I implore you, please contact the

Suicide & Crisis Lifeline at **988**, the 1-800-273-8255 has merged with **988** as of July 16, 2022. **Active-duty members and veterans, please press (1)** when the call is answered, or text to **838255**. Non-military, if you are unable to speak, or you are hearing impaired, you can send a text to the **Crisis Text Line** 24/7, at **741741**. You can also go to **988lifeline.org**. Please tell them what you are feeling, they are there to help you. Please LIVE!

You cannot return; while returning someone's jealousy could kill you.

Mark your surroundings well, make certain to survey the land. You need to know where your boundaries are located. If you are leaving, believe me when I say, there are places that should be off limits eventually; once you make it out. Eventually you will have a limited amount of time to return. The clock will run out; and your ability to return to your old places will run out right along with it. Yes, some of you will hate to read these words but face it. Returning to these places could cost you your life.

For those you leave behind, when and if you can, please help to bring them out also. If they choose to stay, say the physical goodbye in person, and keep in touch by any manner of communication, that allows you to communicate from a distance. You fought with everything in you to get out, some of you had to run for your lives. Believe me when I say to you, nothing in these places have changed, and they will take your life if you go back.

There is a serial killer that roams the earth, his or her name is "jealousy."

Jealousy is something that will be added to your detriment. It could absolutely impair your safety, and add to your ruin. The jealousy that now exists in some people's heart, because you made it out, will be palpable, you could almost cut it with a knife. Someone could walk right up to you and kill you, because you made it out. Make no mistake, this will be your reality. There are ninety-five percent of the people that wish you well within that community. They will read this and some might get very angry, and feel that I am telling those who made/make it out to forget where they came from, and forget the people they left behind. My answer to them is this,

"Leaving does not mean forgetting."

"Distance does not prevent me from making a huge difference within the lives of those I leave behind."

"Distance does not prevent me from making a huge difference within the community I chose not to return to in person."

"It only takes one jealous person to take your life."

While you wonderful people within that city are so very proud of that individual, and are encouraging them for their accomplishments, and are encircling them with love, loyalty and lots of support, that one ignoble, jealous human being, has just joined the circle. Suddenly a shot rings out, he or she just died, because you refused to love them from afar.

"It only takes one out of the gang that the person walked away from, to end that person's life." Them being even five miles, ten miles, or thirty miles away could make a difference between them living or dying.

While many of you reading this book will say you would never harm your community's favorite son or daughter, the person standing right next to you would in a heartbeat. "They have the gun on their waist, and the person that made it out name is on the bullets."

For GOD sake, please let those who have made it out go. Wish them well, and tell them to send help from afar, but to not return in person. This advice, I promise you, could save their precious lives.

For the sake of that person's sanity, and for their safety-their-wellbeing, for the greater good of the distance they will travel, and the lives they will change, and for their accomplishments that are up ahead, please help to preserve this person's life. Please help them to stay alive. Please pray for them, wish them well, and please let them go.

Be their resolute inspiration; tell them to run far, encourage them to climb high, to swim wide, and to never turn back to this place, where they felt lost, where it brought out the worst in them, and had them imprisoned without hope, and almost killed them. Tell them to not forget to send help if and when they can but,

"do not come back here, we will come to you, but you can never come back here to us, because returning to this place could get you killed."

Some of you are haunted by the memories, and want to die, so as to erase those horrific memories.

There were days when I would sit at my desk in my home office, and I would stare out into the abyss of my sorrowful journey. I would see my life, my future, my destiny being burned to the ground, and being replaced with abuse, and humiliation, along with the wickedness of foul and crushing words, rolling off the tongues of those who loathed me, the victim.

I would mourn, I would burst out in tears at my rerouted life, along with the unbearable pain, the unbearable sorrow, and suddenly I would whisper, "thank YOU LORD, I love YOU LORD" and burst into an ocean of additional tears. I knew and accepted early on, that GOD did not give me the sorrow that I had; **NO,** humanity did. Please do not blame GOD for our wretchedness, that we have poured out upon each other, and on the earth.

The sorrow that family, so called friends, and the stranger has poured out upon you is for the ages. Lifetimes will not erase it, oceans will not wash it away, and there are no mountains that can keep your sorrow hidden from view, and no depression within all the valleys combined could outsize the depression, the sorrow, the horror that haunts you. There are many of you that have gone through sorrows of the heart and mind, that are enough to drive countless men and women mad.

Nevertheless, I say to you, nevertheless, I say to each and every one of you precious souls, "you must live." Believe me when I say to you, amongst the sorrow you will find joy, amongst the pain and confusion you will find peace, amongst the heartache you will find love, and you will find healing. The tears will still come, but not as often as they used to. Eventually it will become less and less each year. You, Sir or Madam, you, young man or young lady, will look back with gratitude in heart and mind, and you will be thankful that you survived your mental health struggles. You will be grateful that you survived suicidal thoughts and tendencies, and **"YOU LIVED."**

Please do not use your very own hands, to rob you of your redemptive life that is up ahead

I give you my word, you will get there, but for you to do so; you must fight to save your life. You must fight to save yourself from the violence of your very own hands, and you must live. Some of you, the ignoble, left you for dead. They pounded you. They pounded your life into ashes and left you for dead. Sickness, disappointments, failures, and lack has you by the throat; and the fight in you is no longer there. Nevertheless, I say to you, **"you must live."**

Live through oceans of despair, live through failures,

live through heartbreak, and live through lack and through loss. This moment in time is not forever. These moments will not live on forever, your change will come. Yes, the memories will linger, but the moments will die off one by one. The experiences of constant unrelenting sorrow, unrelenting pain will subside, and your brand-new redeeming, redemptive experiences will come alive around you, and within you also. But for this to take place, you must give yourself a chance, and please precious, you must live.

Your yesterdays will no longer weaken you, and you will find strength within your tomorrows. The years of sorrow behind you will not eclipse, will not block out your years of joy, that are up ahead of you. Please hear me when I say to you, I have seen the weak, the broken, the never acknowledged, I have seen people with mental health sickness, and those that are covered in suicidal thoughts and tendencies, I have seen them survive, thrived and found their way out of these dark places, and you will also.

Be strong, be resilient and please do not doubt your ability to overcome. The hidden you that you have not given a chance is brave; is strong, and is filled with determination and fortitude, and wants to live. Please stay alive and live out your dreams, and your aspirations upon this earth. Please give yourself the precious chance to survive, and to live out your life upon this earth. Sir or Madam, young man or young lady, **"please live, I beg of you. Please give yourself this chance I beg of you. Please precious soul that you are, embrace your newfound life, and LIVE."**

CHAPTER 33

To Our Armed Forces and Their Families

A note to your precious spouses, or to the loved ones of the active-duty member, and or veteran. Further along within our journey, I will be sure to pick up from here, for you the family members.

You must never forget, your spouse or loved one's wound, could be seen or unseen. A deep wound does not need to bleed. Blood being a part of their wound, is not a specific requirement for a wounded soul, and you must never forget this. There are many, many, many active-duty members or veterans, that are sitting at a desk job or they are home, that have no outer wounds on their body, and yet their wounds are very deep and some are festering, because they are left untreated.

Make no mistake, every single member of the Armed Forces is included in this journey. Those who handle information, those who work with satellites and other data, and other information i.e., including technology experts. Their burden and their wounds can be as debilitating, as the wound that is visible to others. A pressured heart and mind can wreak enormous havoc on the body.

Pressure on our hearts and minds can bring us all to our knees. The decisions they have to make with the information they acquire is life changing, or nation changing, and could save or destroy nations. The intelligence they work with could protect not only our nation but countless others also. The pressure to get it right, I am all but certain, is all consuming and taxing. Any missed information could cause damage that could reverberate across the globe. This is a tremendous pressure on their hearts and minds and on their psyche.

No visible wound, and yet gaping wound, within the heart and mind, based on decisions they have had to make throughout the years. Yes, they too are very much included inside this book. Their smile reveals nothing, and their unresponsive demeanor is a facade for what they are hiding; the pressure and pain of the decisions they have had to make. Seen or unseen, make no mistake, their wound does exist also. They too are in the fight for their precious life, and you can never forget this.

Never forget, they too are also very much included, into everything I am about to discuss. The unspoken words when in pain, causes the most damage. The active duty-members or veterans, not telling you that they are hurting, does not mean all is well. Pain and heartache when nurtured by silence, will flourish and grow into an abundance of sickness. The harvest the unspoken words produce, are a multitude of misery, within the active-duty member or veteran's heart, and mind; with never-ending weed tentacles of confusion; that can reach into every corner of your lives. It will quietly, and oh so meticulously, tear apart your household. Confusion will reign, when anyone is forced to come up with their own answers, for someone else's actions. The spouses of the active-duty members or veterans, must never create answers for yourselves, or assume all is well; because your spouses, they are not telling you they are hurting. You must remember, they are our active duty-members or our veterans, they are brave and resolute, and will fight to keep it together. You, the spouse or loved ones, must quietly, with much consideration, get them to voice what they are going through. **You Sir and Madam, are an active duty-member or veteran. You are, or you were the protector of nations. You have been, or you are now your nation's bulwark, your nation's defense.**

I was not going to have a section for active-duty members or veterans inside this book. My reasoning was this, you are like no other. You are a warrior, you are the line that is drawn within the sand; and you are the blood, the sweat, the tears; and the hope of your nation. We ask for your blood and we give nothing in return.

I say nothing, because no amount of money or material goods could compare to the service you have given, or you are giving to your nation. Precious you, I thank you. I am in no position to think that I can help you. Some of you I do know have gone a thousand miles through hell; and the damage to your heart and your mind, and to your overall health, tells your story. **"Sir or Madam of valor, on behalf of many, I thank you for your service." I am beyond grateful for your sacrifice; your nation is forever grateful to you.** You cannot give up, I beg of you, I plead with you man or woman of valor, please live, please hold on, do not destroy your precious soul; help is on the way. **"Please Live, Please I Beg of you."**

I know that your nightmares, your day-mares, your evening-mares, and then rotate back to your nightmares all over again, exist. This is all consuming and debilitating. I know that some of you see the enemy in your living room, you hear them in your bedroom, and any sudden sound or movement places you back into the battlefield. The battle rages on and on within your mind, and your heart; and some of you use alcohol or other vices, to dull the memory and the sounds; and to keep the pain and the sorrow at bay.

The physical pain is horrendous; and you are taking medication on top of medication, to keep yourself from going insane. How can I not acknowledge you? Although it is not much, please accept these sincere words of encouragement from my heart. Please use this book as a part of your recovery, to help you with your survival. Yes, I know that it is not much. Never-the-less, the little that I have I give to you. Please stay close to someone at all times, please train him or her to get help for you, if they see you losing control.

Please call the **Suicide & Crisis Lifeline,** they are there twenty-four hours of the day, and are waiting to help you. **The number is 988. "Please press (1) when the call is answered." If you are unable to speak or you are hearing impaired,** you can **text to the Crisis Text Line 24/7, at 838255.** You can also go to the **988lifeline.org** website.

PLEASE LIVE! Please give them, give us a chance to get you the help that you are in need of; please do not end your precious life. You must fight for the saving of your precious life. If you are able to, you must do your part also. Please create a peaceful, a kind and a gentle sanctuary, for your heart and mind. Fill your space with music that will soothe your heart, watch movies that will make you lose control in laughter. Avoid war and violent movies or TV shows, it will only send you back to the battlefield. If you find a book that helps you, please keep that book next to you; and read it a million times, if that is what it takes for you to survive. This quiet gentle space will assist you in your recovery. Your goal is peace of mind, heart and spirit.

Eat the foods that you love to eat, it will make you feel good, but please try not to overeat; you must protect your health. Create a life within your mind if you are able to, and go there when you are tired. Travel to the UK, Middle East, Europe, to Montana, to Hawaii, the Swiss Alps, and Africa. You might not be able to travel in person to these places but you can dream, dream magnificent dreams that will soothe the savage beast that is inside you. That savage beast kept you alive on the battlefield, but has now become your Achilles heel. Aggression is ruining some of your lives. But no matter how much you try to explain where you have been, and the reason you are the way that you are, no one understands you.

Please fight this last battle I beg of you. Please do not give up on life I beg of you. I know that what you are going through is crippling. Where you have been now keeps you frozen in time, you must fight this one last battle to keep your precious soul upon the earth. Please, please I beg of you, please know that you Sir or Madam are our nation's valued treasure. You are irreplaceable, and the annals of history know you by many names. You are known as a warrior, a fighter, a protector. You are a preventer of lost lives, a gatekeeper; a hero, and a human being with courage and conviction. You are a brave soul; a leader, a willing follower to the battlefield from which there might not be any return. You are known as the courageous one, even in weakness and fear you hold strong. You are known as the Army, the Navy, the Air Force, Space Force, the Marine, the Coast Guard, and The Armed Forces for your nation. You are called Valor, POW, MIA; "I pray that you make it home." The annals of history will forever know you, and will never, can never forget you. You are loved beyond measure and you are cherished. You are the precious jewel of your nation. Precious you, **"PLEASE LIVE."** Please live I beg of you, please live I implore you, Sir or Madam of valor, **"YOU MUST LIVE."**

You must create the opposite of where you have been. Here are some names and descriptions of where you have been. It was pure hell, it was as if you had sailed through Drake's Passage, and had climbed Chogori Mountain all at once. It was ground zero annihilation. It was death that awaited your precious soul, and life that said, you would live. For some of you, your blood poured out, your flesh, your organs, and your bones gave way; and your body is no longer what it used to be.

"I experienced pain that was no longer pain, instead it was far more than pain, and there are no words to describe it. It was the five oceans of the world, all in one, as it billowed over and over again, over my soul. There were bullets, grenades, there were bombs that ended bloodlines, and created carnages that made the strongest men and women weak, and I had it for breakfast, lunch and dinner. I returned from the pit of hell, and now I am expected to act the same, and be the same person that I was before this experience."

I will finish talking with you, and then I will speak with your family and friends, your neighbors and even the stranger. After such an experience, I am not worthy to give you any form of advice, but still, I must. I cannot turn away from you who have fought, sacrificed, and have watched your brothers and sisters that have died next to you, to protect this precious nation I call home, and other nations also. Regardless of how small my contribution is to you, when it comes to keeping you encouraged, and keeping your precious soul upon the earth, precious you, I would rather give it to you and have you refuse it, instead of never giving it to you at all.

You must create paradise within your home. Until you are better, if you need to be in a space of your own, then so be it. Create a space **within your home** for your recovery. That space will be the place where you can let out your pain in whatever way you need to; as long as it is not destructive. Whether through your tears, in shouting, in sleeping, or through daydreaming, use any safe formula to survive and to recover, as long as it is not illegal, or addictive drugs that will turn you into an addict.

Please use whatever is needed for your recovery. Please step back from responsibilities that will push you over the edge. While you are at work, do not get into situations that are aggressive and that will take you back to the battlefield. Go to the park or somewhere with lots of greenery if you can, during your lunch break, or a break from home. Take off your shoes and socks and lie out on a blanket, listen to the birds, look at nature, listen to some soothing music while you rest. Avoid drinking much alcohol if any at all, alcohol can increase your aggression; and cause you to drink to escape, which is the last thing that you need. Make no mistake, there are many, many life ending actions that have been taken while drunk.

Mourn Those You Have Lost

Remember their smile and their laughter, and their silliness; and share a joke with them as you think about them. Do not think about how they died; instead, think about how they lived. Their death was five minutes, one hour, one week; but the life they lived was thirty years, forty years, fifty years upon the earth. Please remember them in those years, not in the time of their death, this is what they would want. Enjoy your wife, your husband, your children, and your parents, your friends, your co-workers, and your neighbors. Do not be afraid to ask them for help to move on from where you are. You cannot go back to where you were before the battlefield, you cannot undo the past, you cannot undo history, what is past has already passed. What you can do is create a life that will overshadow where you have been, and will strengthen you, and help you to go on, and to live out the rest of your years in peace. Weep for you, and for those you have lost, please let it out. Do not be embarrassed because you need psychiatric treatment, there are those with far less trauma and are seeing a psychiatrist. You have earned the right to be at the front of the line.

Use the tools that are available to you, so that you can recover. Your recovery is very important. Unless you are permanently injured, to the point that you are unable to function without help, you must fight to recuperate from where you are.

Your family, your friends and your co-workers are in the fight with you, but you must help them also. They too are also traumatized. They sent off their husband, their wife, their friend, they sent off their neighbor, their sister, their brother, they wished their uncle, their aunt, their son or daughter well, and watched them as they drove away; and a stranger returned to them. This stranger looks or does not look like their loved one, but their actions are that of a stranger.

Their pain is also valid; you need each other for your recoveries. NO, do not take what I just said to feel guilty and as a reason to walk away. The stranger that returned to them has their never-ending love, loyalty and everything else that is needed for both sides to heal, and to become complete again. Love them, respect them, and work with them to rebuild your life. Your life will probably not be the same; things might be different. Expecting what you left behind is not the same as rebuilding for your new life. What you left behind has changed, because you are not the same. Now they have had to evolve to help you also. Rebuilding is what is needed. You must use the tools that are available to you; and find or create those that you need but do not have, for the rebuilding of your precious life. You have help, you are not alone.

My precious, precious, precious man or woman of valor; you are loved and you are appreciated. You must improvise to overcome, and you must survive this battle. Brick by brick, tears by tears, anger by anger, thinking it through by thinking it through, music by music, visit to the park by visit to the park, psychiatric by psychiatric visits, book by book, and each day unbeknownst to you, you will get better and better, until Sir or Madam of valor; the rebuilding of your precious wonderful life becomes complete.

Please live precious you, I beg you and I plead with you, I even admonish you. You are the treasure, you are the pride of your nation, and you must keep your soul alive. Man or Woman of Valor, please I beg of you, please live. Please contact the **Suicide & Crisis Lifeline at 988**. Please remember the 1-800-273-8255 has merged with the **988** number, as of July 16, 2022. **"Please press (1)** when the call is answered, or text to **838255."** If you are unable to speak, or you are hearing impaired, you can also text the **Crisis Text Line** 24/7, at **838255.** You can also go to the **988lifeline.org** website. **Please Live! Please give the Suicide & Crisis Lifeline a chance to help you.**

As I promised; I have not forgotten about you, the spouses, and the loved ones of our active-duty members and veterans. "I THANK YOU ALL."

Please read about sailing through the Drake Passage; where three different ocean currents meet, and how deadly those waters are. Now, please combine it with climbing Chogori Mountain, and then add bullets, and grenades, and bombs that ended bloodlines, and produced horrific carnage; that would make even the strongest of men and women very weak. Some of your loved ones lived through what I just described. they had it for breakfast, lunch and dinner, and made it back home to you, when others did not.

They do not deserve your frustration, what they need and deserve is your precious love, your patience, and your understanding. "I thank you and your family for the sacrifice you have made for your nation, we are beyond grateful." I am well aware that the spouse, the son or the daughter, who went to the battlefield, they were not the only ones that made this incredible sacrifice.

You too have also sacrificed. Yes, you, the spouse, the parents, the children; have gone through the fear of loss and you experienced loneliness. You had to do more than normal, because your loved one was away. Yes, I understand completely. Now they are back and they just stay to themselves. You are in pain, you are frustrated, you have run out of solutions; or you need additional advice on how to be there for your spouse or family member. The first word I want to bring to your attention is **"loyalty."**

You must place loyalty within your heart and mind, and within your spirit. Many of us no longer live out loyalty. Loyalty is now shunned, and walking away now occupies that place. Many have gravitated towards the, **"me myself and I syndrome,"** and it is now worn by many, as a badge of honor. Here are some meanings for loyalty that should help you.

Being **steadfast, devoted, dependable,** and **reliable.** Having an **allegiance** to someone, being **faithful.** Live out these words with your partner or family member that has returned from the battlefield, or their deployment. Be **steadfast** in your love, and in the care that you give to them. **Devote** yourself to their wellbeing, because they need you to do so for them. Show them that they can **depend** on you, and that you are **reliable** through these trying times. This is the meaning of **allegiance,** within the framework of marriage or a relationship with your loved ones.

Within the relationship with our loved ones, there is the duty to be there for each other in sickness and in health. What do we do if our loved ones, our mother or father, our children or our spouses are sick? The answer is; we love them and we nurse them through their unfortunate journey. We do all that we can to help them to get well, and therein is our **faithfulness.**

You too must take some time for yourself when needed. If your loved one should not be alone, please have someone there with your loved one, while you are away. Go to the park and lie out on a blanket, and dream about times past with appreciation. This will encourage your loyalty towards your loved one. Find the honor that is within you, and ask yourself, does this person deserve to be abandoned, after fighting to protect you, their family and their nation, or do they deserve your **loyalty?**

Eat something that you enjoy, and release the stress that is within you. You must get counseling also. These sessions will give you a chance to release your anger, your fear, and your disappointments. It will also help you to find the resolve you will need for the rebuilding of your lives. You also need your space to shed your tears of pain and heartache. Find a place where you can shout out in anger, and let out your frustration, without causing pain to your loved one. Our tongues, whether we admit it or not, can at times place the bravest of men and women into the grave.

Be patient, be kind, and on the really bad days, go to the closet and pull out a pair of their military shoes, place them on your feet and stand. Now, close your eyes and imagine bullets coming at you, grenades being thrown at you, and bombs going off all around you.

You are forgiven, please hug your loved one and tell them how much you love them. Yes, I understand your frustration; your pain is real, and there will be times when you might lash out in anger. All is forgiven, dry your eyes and get back into the fight. You can do this; I believe in you.

Absolutely yes, you both need your spaces. But

the rebuilding of your lives, <u>will only happen if you work together as one unit,</u> with the same goal in mind. That goal is the rebuilding of your lives together as one.

I repeat, yes, yes, you do need your space, but please remember; you must work hard together to rebuild your precious lives, and your relationship. You who have returned, you also owe your spouse and your loved ones your **loyalty.** You must sit together and talk it out as much as you can. Be honest, and loved ones, please do not be offended if the man or woman of valor tells you, **"You do not understand."**

How can any individual, any person that has not been to the battlefield, say that we truly understand? We have an idea, but that is all that it is, just an idea. The experiences of the battlefield belong to the man or woman of valor, and no other.

Remember; There are different battlefields with the same end results. The battlefield inside that war-room can break minds and hearts the same way boots on the ground can. Imagine preparing the data and sending out twenty servicemen and ten come back alive. They hear their men and women coming under fire and can hear them being hunted and gunned down. Yes, the battlefield inside the war-room exists. They too can be broken by the experience.

Even missions where every member returns alive and well, can still bring extreme pressure. Before every mission, I am all but certain that our men and women of valor, accept within their hearts and minds, the possibility that this could be the last mission; they could die. They are determined to come back alive, they and their brothers and sisters next to them, but it is not guaranteed. That is pressure like no other. This is a constant way of life for our members of the Armed Forces, including veterans before they retired from service. Please give them their well-deserved respect and honor. Acknowledge the honor of the victory, the pain, the sorrow, and the loss that came with them going to the battlefield, no matter the form of battlefield experienced.

You the man or woman of valor must respect and give those you left behind and have returned to, their just deserve also. Imagine their pain, their sorrow, and their loss. They waved you off to the battlefield, and you returned to them broken in body or in mind or in both. Your wound, seen or not seen with the natural eye, absolutely exists. It has caused you to be filled up with great sorrow, and with a mind that is no longer as strong as it used to be.

You, the man or woman of valor, if you are able to, must also help your spouse and or loved ones to rebuild with you. Both of your pain is real, both your heartaches are real, and you must both do your part in the rebuilding of your lives, and your families' lives also.

Please learn and embrace your new directions, your new way of life together. Please Improvise, and fight to overcome, the tremendous maze of new directions, the new way of life that are before you both.

You lost your spouse; you lost your loved one during service to their nation

Sir or Madam, I am so very, very, very sorry for your loss. I thank you for theirs, and your service to our nation, or to your nation. Please know that your loved one's blood was not shed in vain. A precious life lost in battle for their nation, is an honor like no other. Please know that they will never be forgotten, and believe my words when I say to you; **"They will be cherished throughout history."**

You must hold on, please I beg of you. I know that the pain within your heart and mind is severe; and some days you just simply breathing, it is incredibly hard, and it requires tremendous effort. Please do not give up. You must withstand the unrelenting storm that refuses to cease, I promise you, you will survive it, and you will be victorious.

Celebrate your man or woman of valor. Talk to them, laugh to them, and go for walks and invite them. Do not worry about what others will think, if this is what you need to survive, please have it. All I ask of you is this, please understand that you cannot, you must not stay in that place forever. Your man or woman of valor would not want you to do so.

At some point, you must embrace those who are right in front of you, and accept the fact that your spouse; your loved one is no longer amongst the living. Weep in sorrow, cry out in pain; you must let it out or it will destroy you. **"The broken heart syndrome is real,"** we do not want to lose you also. Please I beg of you precious, please stay amongst the living. Please live the way your loved one would want you to live. Again, I am truly, so very sorry for your loss, Sir or Madam, **"you must live."** Please seek counseling. Stay with family and friends, and allow them to take care of you; until you can take care of yourself.

Please call the **Suicide & Crisis Lifeline, at 988.** If you, the spouse, are an Active-duty member or a veteran; and yes, that is possible, press **(1) when the call is answered.** If you are unable to speak, or are hearing impaired, you can **text the Crisis Text Line 24/7, at 838255,** non-military members **741741.** You can go to **988lifeline.org** website also, **Please Live!**

Please give them, please give us a chance to get you the help that you are so very desperately in need of. Please men or women of valor, or family members, do not end your precious lives, because the pain is just too unbearable to cope. Give yourself a fighting chance to survive. For you to stay alive, you must keep the fight going inside you to not give up. Hold on for dear life and keep that oxygen in your lungs.

Your child, or your children that are suffering from extreme loss, due to them losing their active-duty protective services, or veteran parent

Please close ranks around them. Surround them with family and friends, and keep them close. Allow them to cry; but you must pay attention to their health. They can actually cry themselves into convulsions, which is very harmful. Once a seizure takes place, it can return repeatedly. Seizures are quite harmful, as I am certain you already know. You must keep your child, or your children, within a safe emotional state; where they can mourn and have their meltdowns, but not become harmed by their emotional condition.

You must be selfless. Yes, this is tough, but you must put aside some of your sorrows, for the sake of your child, or for your children. Watch their actions while they mourn. Children will react to trauma sometimes by causing harm to their body, without meaning to. For instance, through uncontrollable nonstop crying. Another example is your child banging their head against a wall. Ironically, the saying, "it is as if I am just banging my head against a brick wall." Which means, I am doing something, but I am not getting any result from it. There is no result from my action.

That is exactly what is now happening inside your child's emotional aura. They are unable to find their way through this incredibly hard, earth-shattering experience. Their problem-solving skills have not yet developed, or are not fully developed; and so that banging of the head is their way of beating against the blockage within their minds.

Be warned, that action could be quite harmful. They could cause damage to the frontal lobe area of their brain, if they bang their head hard enough. At their age as children, they are still in the developmental process. It is within the frontal lobe that decisions are made, and this is where our problem-solving skills are developed, amongst other things. The possibility does exist, that they could harm themselves, even without them trying to do so, while banging their heads. You must shape the information, so that it can fit into your child, or into your children's mind. This needs to be understandable information, so that your child or children can find their answers. This will give them clarity; and will allow them to be able to process what has happened, in the healthiest way possible.

Did you notice I did not say in a less painful way? There is no less painful way for a child to lose their parent, or their loved one. You must fill them with assurance that you will be there for them, and that they will be okay. Have them sleep with you or their grand-parents. Hold them close, your love for each other, will help you to survive. Explain to your child or children, that their parent or their loved one, is a hero of their nation, and that their life was lost, while protecting their nation. Explain how large the nation is, use your hands, and draw pictures.

The nation is, **""THIS BIG,""** and your mommy or your daddy will be remembered by everyone within the nation; and is loved by them all. Use their super hero, use the military to make your point. Please give them the much-needed clarity, and some peace that they desperately need. There is no complete peace in the loss of their parent, or their loved one. But you can give them some form of peace through clarity, and through emotional support, and through your selfless, never-ending precious love towards them. Call on your man or woman of valor squadron, or your protective services members. Whether Police, the Armed Forces, FBI, the Secret Service, CIA, or the Protective Service in your nation, they were a part of. Ask members of the protective services family, to please come and spend time with your child or your children, and with you also. Knowing the military, or the protective services, and the bond that exists; you will probably not have to ask them, they will simply show up, out of their precious desire to be there for you all. Give your child, or your children counseling sessions. This is where they can talk, ask questions, and where a professional can walk them through their painful, their very sorrowful loss. Please encourage their hearts; and look out for their meltdowns, and wrap him, or her, or them within your arms.

If they need to be pulled out of school temporarily, go ahead and do so. Imagine your pain as a grown human being; their pain is far more severe. Forcing a child to sit in a classroom, during the early days of them losing their parents, or their loved one, can be extremely hard on some children. Some children will want to go to school, but others will want nothing to do with school.

Please respect the differences that are within their coping mechanism. You must cry with them, laugh with them, and mourn with them. You, the parent, must fight to be strong; you must live for you, and you must live for your child, or for your children. Their strength will come through you, and your strength will also come through them, and you will all survive this season of sorrow, this season of loss that you are all now going through.

You are a part of the Armed Forces, you are healthy, you have not been wounded.

Sir or madam of valor, I thank you for your service. You Sir or Madam, you must take good care of your health, and this is both mental and physical also. You must acknowledge the magnitude of your service, in the protection of your nation and others, and the risk that comes with it. Please pay close attention to your health, you are in a high-risk job when it comes to pressure on your body, and also on your mind. Take nothing for granted, if you feel something is off, please get medical help or counselling. You must seek answers immediately.

You cannot give the best of you to your nation, or to other nations, which is what is required, if you are not in the best of health. You will instead fall apart at the slightest pressure. Pay attention to your way of life and the sphere of people that is within it. You Sir or Madam, are someone that can face battles; where your split-second decision can-not just save your life; it could also save an entire unit that is with you. Or it could save someone, or a group of people, that are depending on you to bring them out alive.

You do not need people whose lives are the extreme opposite of your way of life in a negative way close to you. Here is an example. A selfish, mean-spirited person, who only cares about themself. They have zero loyalty, and will tell you that a hyena is about to bite your buttocks your (butt) only after they have jumped the fence, and are safe from danger. That kind of negative influence you do not need. You man or woman of valor are the opposite of that human being. **NO,** in this case the opposite does not need to attract. It is your unselfish actions that will save your nation, and other nations. It is your unselfish ways that will bring the wounded that are next to you to safety. The exceptional traits that are within you, are needed and special, and must be protected.

Even your selfish ways are night and day to theirs. Your selfish ways are, "I do not give a damn about you and yours; I am here to protect mine, and mine, I am always going to protect, no matter what. This includes other nations placed under my protection."

Their selfishness is running for cover and shouting **"in coming"** once they are safe, after the bomb has already dropped. Selfish to the core, and little do you know, they are also allergic to your noble intent. The closer they are to you, is the worse they look; and this is the quiet anger, and contempt for you, that lives within them. They act as if you are missing out on life, as if they have cornered the market on fun. But little do you know; that it is all an act to make you miserable.

Active duty-members and veterans, please take note I beg of you, I implore you.

It does not matter if it is a group of them, wolves move in a pack, and they all have the same agenda. Every time they guilt you for your noble military service, give them the passive aggressive treatment.

Treat them like a can of raid inviting roaches to a birthday party; this invitation will always cause them to scatter. "Hey guys, I am having a bootcamp party tomorrow. After we work out, we are going to serve food at the VA Hospital, and then on to the Rescue mission, and then, we are going to wash the floors at the Salvation Army, after that we will stop at the kindergarten school to wash the toilets and paint their building. Trust me when I say, they will scatter.

Believe it or not, these negative influences will cause you to hate your job; cause you to second guess your commitment to the Armed Forces; and build within you a complete resentment for your journey within the military. Suddenly you will find yourself having a complete disdain for your job, and not knowing why. The answer? Outside influences. They are able to party all night they say, while you are having to lead a disciplined life unlike them. Your resentment will boil over, and turn you into a terrible employee. You will start having mental breakdowns, because you are now feeling imprisoned. Suddenly suicide has developed somehow, into your way out.

Unbeknownst to you, this started with the wretched outside influences that you allowed in, without ever realizing how incredibly far reaching, these harmful nefarious influences could reach. Suddenly you are suicidal. Suddenly suicide has taken away your life, without anyone ever having an inkling, that you were suicidal. You had a great life; there were no triggers of any kind, and your command is at a loss, while being bombarded for answers that they do not have.

The explanation, or the elusive crosslinking answers, that no one thought about is this. It was some of the people in your life, it was some of the friends that you kept. Their negative contribution to your life is what led you to the decision to take your precious life. This all due to their abhorrent character, and their way of life, and its destructive influence on you. Yes, I know, this might be a new insight on suicide; and how it enters into someone's life; through the jealous enemy, that was camouflaged as a friend.

Listen to me, man or woman of valor, **"this means all of you."** Your health is beyond valuable, "even if you are already wounded." You must protect your health; protect you from even that ninja that might try to attack you in the dark. You know that you are off, suddenly you, who loved your job, are starting to resent it. You are a very disciplined person, always an orderly person; but suddenly you are changing and not for the better. **"Admit it,"** ever since you met that man or that woman, you have been completely off.

Dude or Dudette of valor, put one finger on your left hand in the air, use a finger on your right hand to make a cross with it, raise it high in the air and shout **"vampire,"** and run for your precious life. The same goes for those groups of friends you now hang with, remove them all from your precious life. Let them go, get as far away from them as is possible. Invite your unit, your regiment over to your home, or to your barracks/quarters for support. Ask them all to make the cross and shout, **"vampirerrrrrr,"** with you, and remove those people from your life; for the sake of your health, your well-being and the very sake of your precious life.

If you are the Army, Marines, Air Force, the National Guard, Coast Guard or Space Force; tell the members of your regiment/your team/unit, that if he or she or them, come looking for you, they should tell that nefarious person or wolfpack, that you switched to Navy; and left on a seven-year deployment tour. The Army, the Marines, and the Air Force, just tarred and feathered me, for switching them to the Navy. Okay Air Force, switch to Space Force, and tell them you left for mars, and will not be able to return for forty years, because Elon Musk got mad, and took back his return spaceship.

Okay let's bring it in, let's get back to being serious. Man and woman of valor please listen to this stranger that cares for you and loves you. Not all so-called friends are friends. Not everyone that tells you they love you actually does love you. Please for heaven and earth's sake; you are your nation's treasure. Correction, you are multiple nations treasures, and you must all protect yourselves, and guard your inner circle, for your very own safety, for your mental health; and for your much needed peace and your happiness.

For your reinforcement, I want you to contact the **Suicide & Crisis Lifeline.** If you ever feel yourself inching towards the idea of suicide. Take nothing for granted, and do not second guess your feelings. Call them at **988. <u>Press (1) when the call is answered.</u> If**

you are unable to speak, or you are hearing impaired, you can text the **Crisis Text Line 24/7,** at **838255.** You can also go to the **988lifeline.org website.** Yes, I keep repeating it. Please take care of your precious health. Tell them what you are feeling; no matter how small or large the feelings.

If there is any abuse, any violence involved, please call, 800-799-SAFE (7233) or TTY 800-787 3224 or (206) 518-9361, (Video Phone Only for Deaf Callers.) You man or woman of valor, you precious soul that you are, you must live. Pretty please I beg of you, and I admonish you, **"PLEASE LIVE."**

If your negative changes, including the suicidal feelings you are experiencing, are due to your strict military training. They are because of the stringent military regulations; and also because of the great sacrifice your job entails.

No, Sir or Madam of valor, they are not being mean to you in your training, not at all. "They are being the very kindest, any person or organization will ever be, could ever be to you in their lifetime. You do not believe me? Please allow me to explain my statement to you. Man or woman of valor, please hear me when I say to you, <u>**"the military's treatment of you; is to save your precious life; and to help you to make it home to your family."**</u> <u>**"Man or woman of valor, the military's treatment of you is to ensure, is to help you to protect your precious nation, or a nation and its people when they need you most."**</u>

For this to materialize; the toughness, the grit, the determination that is asleep inside you, needs to be awakened and developed. The fortitude, the courage inside, that you had no idea that you have, it must be awakened. That remarkable, unquenchable desire to protect your nation; will come alive in their harsh, (or so you think) treatment of you, and therein is the person that you will become.

You with the uncontrollable courage, and the passion and the red-hot fire inside you, that is without any cause or control, or direction. Everyone thinks that you are a pain in the donkey. You will be right at home in the military; but you must give it time. Your uncontrolled emotions that are inside of you; has to be reshaped and redirected; it needs to be molded for military service to your nation.

The Armed Forces justifiable treatment of you, is to prepare you; to meet your destiny, your moment in life. The moment when you cross over from being a man or woman, to being, **"Theeee Man or Woman of Valor,"** the warrior, a fighter, the protector, the bulwark for your nation, and other nations also.

Do not allow their treatment of you to cause you to be discouraged. NO, instead, allow it to fire you up. Tell yourself, "Their goal is to turn me into who they are." Which is an incredible man or woman of valor, that can storm any enemy and their territory, in order to protect nations. This man or woman of valor is the true reality of your situation. Do not allow yourself to be discouraged by your training. Instead, crazy as it may sound; embrace it, dig deep, and make it through; for the sake of ours and other nations; that will be graced by your valor in the future. Do not get discouraged by the drastic changes within your life, because you are now a member of the Armed Forces. The drastic changes are needed for your military journey. Embrace it, love it, and hold your head high. Square your shoulders, you Sir or Madam of Valor, **"YOU ROCK."**

Do not shrink from your military life, do not fear it, do not think, "my friends back home are having a blast while I am tied to the military." **NO,** your friends are not the bulwark of nations, Sir or Madam, **"YOU ARE!"** Please allow that to sink in. The life you fear, or want to back out of; is a life that only incredible men and women can live. Yes, that Sir or Madam is your life. Take courage, stick your chest out like Foghorn Leghorn; who would always walk around like he was King.

If your discouragement persists, and you now find yourself accommodating any thoughts of suicide, please get help. Please call the **Suicide & Crisis Lifeline;** at **988**. Please keep in mind; the 1-800-273-8255 has merged with **988** as of July 16, 2022.

"Please press (1) when the call is answered." If you are unable to speak or you are hearing impaired, you can send your text to the **Crisis Text Line** 24/7 at **838255.** You can also go to **988lifeline.org.**

Yes, I keep on **repeating the information, for the Crisis Lifeline,** over and over again. It is so that you will remember it without fail. I want to make certain that the information of help is always with you. The more you see it, in all likelihood, the more you will remember it. The more you hear it, is the higher the probability becomes that you will take it in.

Sir and Madam, you are the best that your nation has to offer. You are loved, and are appreciated beyond measure. Sir and Madam, perhaps one day, dear precious GOD, if only one day, I could hear the words from you man or woman of valor,
<u>"I LIVED."</u>

<u>"Your words helped me to live."</u> I touched your book inside my pocket, or I reached for your book and read the words; and I was encouraged and,
<u>"I LIVED."</u>

Please be encouraged I beg of you; and please watch your six. Please know that my prayers are with you in the cold dark night when you are hurting; and you are wondering if anyone cares for you. The answer is yes, man and woman of valor. It is the resounding unquestionable, yes! Your nation cares for you in the absolute abundance; and we love you; we love you; man and woman of valor,

We

LOOOOOOOOOOOOOOOOOO
OOOOOOOOOOOOOOOOOVE

YOUUUUUUUUUUUUUUUU
UUUUUUUUUUUUUUUUUUU

CHAPTER 34

You must see and recognize suicide for what it is; it is an evil wretched monster, and it wants to kill you.

I want to first apologize to every sovereign nation, and your King and or Queen. It is not my intention to be disrespectful, by using the term I am about to use, it is only an analogy, to make my point. The term, "scarecrow King or Queen," was used to describe a King or a Queen that was on the throne, but he or she had no power.

A sinister force, or sinister forces held the power, and the King or the Queen was their hostage. Due to this sinister arrangement, the King or Queen was only a symbolism of power and nothing more. Precious you, please hear me; until you overcome suicidal thoughts and tendencies, you are a scarecrow on the throne of life, and a sinister force is holding you hostage. You have no control over your life, and you are only a symbolism when it comes to your life.

Suicide has the control, depression has the control, addiction has the control, un-forgiveness has the control, anger has the control and on and on. You know what that sickness or vice is, that has control over you. The same sickness or vice that has now led you to a place, where you want to take your life, and end it all. Now is the time to battle, now is the time to lay it all on the line for your recovery. Do you want this wretched monster called suicide to hound you year in, and year out, until it devours you, or do you want to fight for the saving of your precious soul? The longer your enemy is with you, is the more likely it is, that your enemy will destroy you. Please allow me to explain this statement. Your enemy has stayed with you long enough to know what makes you weak, and what makes you crumble into a thousand pieces, and what causes you to give up.

Suicide has your number, and it knows when to show up. The moment anything goes wrong; suicide shows up as your best friend, and your closest confidant. It beckons to you with the most alluring argument; of how you will finally be at peace, and the pain will cease; and all you need to do is end it all.

"END IT ALL," are keywords. **"END IT ALL,"** means not just you; but also, the thousands of souls that are to be affected by your life. Yes, they too will be harmed or all together destroyed. Some will come to an end before there is even a beginning, they will not make it to the earth. Those words are just about right; in fact, they are spot on.

If you are an adult, you should know how important and far-reaching our decisions are. If you are a child, a precious wonderful child; a beautiful, a handsome child, a beloved child, I am telling you now; One decision can wipe out a nation. one decision can end a war or start one. Your decision to end your life will resonate throughout this world forever. I will say it another way, suicide done today can cause damage a thousand years into the future. Please I beg of you, both child and adult, please fight, you must fight for the saving of your precious lives. Please fight for the saving of not only your bloodline, but others also.

This fighting chance to survive belongs to you

Precious you, please give yourself a fighting chance to live long enough to finish your precious journey. Please live long enough to go to prom or not, to go fishing, or to go hunting. Give yourself a chance to go off to college or not, to drive your first car, or to enter your first rodeo.

Please precious you, give yourself a chance to bake the best apple pie, crème brulée or macarons, churros or flan at the county fair or cooking contest, or for your family. Give yourself a chance to raise the fattest animal and let him waddle with you to the fair and win against Peggy Sue, Garcon, or Consuela who is a pain. Hold that ribbon above your head and give Garcon, Consuela, or Peggy Sue, your, "yes I beat you, I won," smile.

There are many roads that are heading in many directions ahead. There are many twists and turns to come, and they are all worth you living for. For every loss, the victories will be far sweeter. For every mistake you make, your corrections, you getting it right in the end, will be incredibly gratifying.

Please give yourself a chance to get your first job, or to get your dream job, after having to work in some awful places. Give yourself a chance to drink wine, to eat ice cream, to celebrate Thanksgiving, Bastille Day, Hanukkah, Kwanzaa, Christmas, Passover, New Year's, Easter and on and on. Live life to the end. Go off to college and switch five different majors; but do not blame me, when your parents stop the flow of money to you.

Live long enough to fall in, and out of love. All of these experiences I promise you; will make you stronger, and more aware of what is best for you. Live precious you; live, and live, and live some more; find the strength in you, and **"LIVE."**

The seasons will come and they will go, and you must survive them all

You will have countless seasons that are before you, unbeknownst to you. There is the life of you being infuriating. There is the artistic era, or the season of you using your parent's credit card and begging for mercy. There is the era, "I failed my exam and I blamed my dog, my cat, my worm." There is the season of you landing the incredible job; that will catapult you into your future of greatness.

There is the startup that you will build from the ground up; and you will hire countless people; and change many lives for the better. You will marry and become a fabulous mom or dad, your children will have you as the rock of their lives; and you will shape their hearts and their minds in the most settled, confident, and loving way. In your older years, because of your experiences, you will use it to protect them, and others; so that they can avoid certain pitfalls; like the horrific sorrows in life that you went through.

You, the CEO, CFO, or the COO, will live through these traumatic times; and will turn the corner, and you will find peace. You will not always have this tumultuous period beleaguering your life or your company's life. The bankruptcy is not forever, you will rise again, of this you can be certain. Perhaps not as big as you were before, but that I believe is to your advantage.

Sometimes downsizing can be the best thing that could happen to someone. It gives them a chance to step back; it gives them a chance to rest. It removes the extreme pressure from their hearts and minds; and it allows for moments of introspection, the finding of nuances, that when you are busy, they go right by you without being seen. **Please I beg of you, please rise to the occasion, please outlast this season in your life and "Live."** Do not fear, do not come apart during these trying times; instead, rise to the occasion; and show them that you are the person for the job. Face the storm, and allow it to make you stronger. You must live; there is much to be done, and there is much that is waiting for you in the future. Please do not allow suicide to take it all away, please hold on and LIVE.

It does not matter your age, your gender, your class, or the color of your skin, we are all in this together, and we must fight together for your survival. You can do this, I promise. You can defeat this wretched monster called suicide. You, Sir or Madam, Young lady or young man, will live out your days, with your mistakes, your stupidity, your laughter, and your pain. You will live to see, and will experience your wonderful incredible accomplishments. They will be rolled up into one great feat, as the blueprint of your success over suicide. It will be your precious gift, and your encouragement for your family, friends and the stranger, on how you overcame suicide. Do not give up, **"PLEASE DO NOT"** cause the sun to set on your life forever. Please I beg of you. Please abandon thoughts of suicide, **PRECIOUS YOU, YOU MUST LIVE.**

CHAPTER 35

The death that was caused by a recreational adventure, or a social media challenge

The, "I am doing it to be noticed adventure." Or the social media challenge adventure. The, "look what I did" life ending journey. The, "I am going on this challenge or this adventure, because my buddies are going, or my fellow sports men and or women, or my family members are going on it. Although I could lose my life, I cannot say no, because of the peer pressure that is self-inflicted, or caused by my peers."

Please note the **"self-inflicted peer pressure."** You are doing this to yourself, out of perhaps wanting to impress your peers, or thinking that you not doing this thing, will leave a negative impression of you with your peers or family members.

This is another one of those topics or situations that I wanted nothing to do with. The backlash will be fierce and downright ugly. I have taken the most wretched beatings in life, and I am now at a place of safety. I do not want to be abused by humanity all over again. With that said, we do not always get what we want in life. Some of us, although already battered and bruised, we still drag our brokenness back into the pain of life and fight on, if it means saving someone else's life. All I can do is ask you to please go easy on me, after the conversation that I am about to have with you. "Yes, a conversation is correct." You, I am certain, will have something to say to me also, after reading this chapter. Now, let's get to it. Is my raincoat on, check? Is my leaf blower ready, check? Now I am ready for you to tar and feather me. Oh wait, "I SAID WAIT DARN IT." Goggles on, yup? Okay, now I am ready. Tar and feather away my friend, to save your life I am willing to take it, but more feather than tar please. As a matter of fact, let me help you, I am an expert at tarring and feathering. It is one teeny tiny tea spoon of tar, and two pounds of feather. I promise, that will teach me not to mess with you ever again.

I have often wondered to myself, how someone could partake in an extracurricular activity that could end their lives in an instant, just to be able to say, "I did this dangerous thing?" What is that kind of action truly like? How does any person digest, how does any person assimilate such a journey? How many people have embarked on the unnecessary suicide mission, knowingly and unknowingly, willingly and unwillingly? From my humble point of view, I will try to answer my own question. A suicide mission would be someone being given an assignment by others, or them giving the assignment to themselves. I want to talk about them embarking on the extra-curricular activity, knowing full well this activity could almost assuredly cause your death.

There are many that have inflicted upon themselves this suicide mission called "I did it." What do I mean? There are many that have caused their own untimely death, in the name of wanting to be able to say, "I Did this particular activity." It is truly sorrowful to me, and yes, I know, others will think differently. After all, every person is entitled to their own thoughts and actions. For some, this "I Did It Suicide mission," is not a big deal. For me it is a very, very big deal. Why? The precious value of your life, that is why. What will happen to your wife, your husband, your current and or future children? What happens to your parents, what will your death do to them? What about future bloodline, and your future accomplishments also, and so much more? You have No wife or husband, no children? My answer to you is perhaps not as yet. Is the value of this adventure worth more than all that I have listed? Count the cost my precious, and please tell me, is that adventure the sum of you? No one else counts, no one else matters. For this challenge, for this adventure, you are ready and willing to throw everything away, and cast your precious soul into the grave? Are you truly willing to pay that cost?

It is a huge difference to go on a suicide assignment to protect your nation. It is one thing to go on a suicide mission to make a difference; this is so that you can change the trajectory of your nation and your life, in a magnificent way. By blazing the path ahead for you, your family and your nation, in science, technology, aeronautics, or space exploration or medical breakthroughs and more. It is another to do it just to be able to say, "I did it." Imagine if you will, the adventure is dangerous to the point that one tiny mistake or no mistake at all, and your life, or your life and the life of the person (s) who are with you are over. For you to still go on this mission, for you to still embark on this journey, means the adventure is more valuable than your life, and the lives of those that are along with you. How do you reconcile this adventure, when it comes to your precious life and the future you are hoping for?

You have no future some of you are saying, and so you have no problem casting your precious soul into the grave? Dream, precious soul that you are. Dream way beyond your existence, kick the wall down that is in front of you. No man nor woman can stop you from dreaming; your dream is protected inside your very own mind. Dream and dream, and dream some more, until your precious dreams become reality, and please keep your soul from entering the grave.

This is not, "I am willing to jeopardize my life for the sake of my nation." This is not, "I am willing to sacrifice my life to save someone else's life." This is not, "I am taking a chance on my survival for the betterment of humanity." NO, this is, "I am willing to give up my precious life; for the ability to simply declare to others that I did this particular thing. And yes, I do understand, there is absolutely more than one side to this journey, and I completely get it. Is it worth being traumatized, your mind broken by the experience, while you are being taken to the brink of death, just for sport?

There are those that are motivational speakers, they do these death-defying actions to be able to motivate others. The question is this, am I able to motivate someone without swimming with sharks? Do I have the ability to inspire you without climbing K2 Mountain or Mount Everest? Please tell me, do you have to walk through the Mojave Desert when it is one hundred and thirty degrees hot in August, to be able to motivate someone? For you to inspire someone, do you need to jeopardize your life, when those you are trying to inspire, their life is not in jeopardy? Is swimming with sharks more important than your precious life? Is having your friends drive up to you while going sixty miles an hour, and then they stop just before their ATV or car hits you, is that more valuable than your precious life? Is standing on the edge of a cliff to get a selfie more valuable than your precious life? Is downing a bottle of fifty proof or one hundred proof rum while pledging, or while your friends watch, is it more important than your precious life that you have yet to live? Is a social media challenge, or to be known on social media more important than your precious life, and the magnificent journey that is ahead of you? Is it more important to be able to brag to your friends that you did this thing, is it more important than it is to guard your precious, precious, precious life?

In reality, these friends are not your friends if they are willing to jeopardize your life, for their nefarious fun, or their power-hungry cravings. Who was it that created the challenge you are doing, that could end your precious life? Was it a serial killer that figured out that he or she can kill countless people without ever touching them, or ever having to worry about being convicted? All he or she has to do is create a life ending challenge online, and then disappear. If this is a family member that wants to do this, it makes it harder for you to fathom that this could go very wrong. But you mark my words, it very well could. Saying no to family is hard, yes, I agree. But that no, could without question, save not just your life, but your family member's life also.

That action that you are about to take, for no other reason than to have a rush, always knowing you are jeopardizing your life. How about giving your life to humanity instead? If your life holds no value for you, then give it away to humanity. Do for humanity what humanity is unable to do for itself. Go and live at an orphanage, or how about dedicating your life to shut-ins. Create a camp for the underprivileged, dedicate your life to humanity, and I promise you, you do not have to swim with sharks to motivate them.

Give them your life and I promise, the rush you will get from your actions will be immeasurable. There are charitable organizations that are crumbling, and the pain the staff is feeling is palpable. There is not enough money, and not enough hands-on deck, not enough supplies, not enough of what is needed. Give them your life, they will consider you precious, and will see you for the precious soul that you are.

The wealthy hungers for more, when in reality; what he or she needs is far less. You are wealthy beyond measure, and you have everything you need and want. You Sir or Madam, Young man or young lady, you are mistaken. I promise you, you do not need more, because Sir or Madam, young man, young lady, "that, we both know you already have." What you need is less. The more you need is not higher, you have already ascended to higher heights. No, the more you are looking for is located in the lesser walks of life. And no, those you will meet in the lesser walks of life are not less in human value, not less in character, in strength or in wisdom. No, they are less in the ability to function, because of the limitations brought on by lack.

Travel to these unknown or forgotten people and places. Incredibly you do not have to jeopardize your life to do so. Wealth gives you long arms and legs. Wealth allows you to be inside orphanages even when you are not. Wealth allows you the ability to motivate others with sharks without swimming with them. Wealth allows you the ability to motivate yourself with mountains without you ever having to climb them. Wealth gives you height and depth, wealth opens countless doors of opportunities that most will not attain. This is in education, business, in philanthropic actions, in recreational adventures, and in danger also.

Yes, yes, and yes, a resounding yes, when it comes to danger also. Wealth gives you the ability to embark on adventures that there is a likelihood you will not survive. The reality is, the money you will pay to go on that deadly adventure, is the same money someone without wealth would use to buy a home, open a business, pay off their debts and move their bloodline out of poverty. Think long and hard about this statement. "The money that is used to pay for an adventure that will end the millionaire or the billionaire's life, is the same amount of money that would extend life for the poor." The same money depending on how it is used, can take lives or give life. It can end life, or give a new direction in finance, in education, in posterity, and in accomplishments, in innovation, in job growth, in hope and so much more. The financial blueprint of that three hundred thousand is different when it is in the hands of the middle class and the poor.

You do not see where I am going with this? Please allow me to draw you a picture in your mind. Instead of going on the adventure that would have ended her life, Mrs. Brown, blessed Mr. Hashford who asked her for help, to open his business instead. Mr. Hashford used the Three Hundred Thousand Dollars to open his business; and to the utter disbelief of us all, Mr. Hashford has now created material for construction of housing and businesses; that can withstand the most violent tornadoes, earthquakes, and hurricanes. Same money, different results; based on the decision that was made, and the journey it traveled through.

Why is the billionaire dead and the pauper alive? The answer is, the billionaire sought the more that ended their lives, while the pauper sought the more to extend his or her life's journey. My humble advice is this, always lead with the value of your life. I am willing to exchange my life for the safety and survival of my nation. I am willing to exchange my life for the well-being of humanity. I am willing to exchange my life for my family. I am not willing to give up my life for a selfie picture taken on the edge of a cliff. I am not willing to die for a social media challenge. I am not willing to give up my life to show that I can swim with sharks, or jump off a cliff. Yes, I know I am no fun. You all just ripped up and burned my cool kid pass. Guess what? The long-life group just approved my membership.

I hear you, yes, I hear you, I promise I hear you. Do you want me to prove to you that I hear you? You just said to yourself, "I could die from a heart attack without doing anything dangerous, or I could die while driving to work, or while grocery shopping." Yes, I completely agree. Please allow me to confirm to you that I totally agree with you. "I could already be dead while you are reading this book." But there is a difference. The difference is this, the death while heading to work, shopping, or the heart attack, is out of our control. The adventure, that social media challenge is very much, **"within our control," and yes, it can be absolutely avoided.**

Again, I beg of you, please count the cost
For everyone, wealthy or not, before you partake in the activity, that could end your precious life, just for fun, all the while knowing that you could be looking at your loved ones for the last time. Tell me this, when did this activity become more valuable than your child or children? How can you put more value in an adventure, more than your mother or father or both? How can you be willing to go on that suicide adventure knowing full well, you will probably not

314

get to live out your GOD given years upon this earth. "For fun, just for fun and nothing more," you are willing to destroy your wife or husband, and or children through your death, at the cost of just going on an adventure? Do you see the callousness in this?

For GOD sake, for humanity's sake, for your good, and for your families' good, precious you I beg of you, please use the incredible courage that you are about to waste, to save your very own life instead. Please I beg of you, please walk away from these misadventures; and please stay alive, so that you can meet your magnificent moments in life. Stay alive and meet that moment or moments that will catapult you into your GOD given destiny.

Yes, it takes courage to say no at times. It takes courage to tell your family, friends and neighbors, no at times. But you mark my words, that no could be the best no; you could ever express in your entire life. The grave is filled with **"yes men and women."** They knew that they wanted to say no, they knew that they needed to say no at that very moment in time. But instead, they gave in to their relatives, their friends, neighbors or colleagues, or even the stranger. Some surrendered to the momentary rush of a social media challenge, the social media pressure, and ended up dead.

Listen to me please I beg of you, you are precious beyond measure. There is but one of you. The world needs you; humanity needs you. Your gifts, and your talents even if undiscovered as yet, are needed. Your smile, your laughter, your precious aura; will make a difference to someone upon this earth. You, just you, the preteen, the teenager, or the adult or senior, you, by your very own self, is a precious human being upon this earth. Please live out your appointed years. Please stay alive and meet your moments of destiny, with courage and anticipation. Go it alone if you must. **The "No Road"** can be a lonely road at times, why? Many have said yes, and are no longer alive to travel down **the "No Road."**

Let's practice saying **"NO."** Put on your swimsuit and pretend that you are paddling water in your living room while saying **"NO."** Next, put on your business attire and walk around the living room as if you are on the clock working while saying "NO." Next, put on some shiny sixties outfit and do the sixties paddle while dancing and saying **"NO."** Next, stick your chest out like Foghorn Leghorn and march around saying "I say, I say, I say, **NO**." Next, put on your Pepe Le Pew, "there is no one that is more handsome than I, in my outfit," and practice saying **"NO."** No, No, No, while doing the electric slide. (Disclaimer), do not use this as an excuse to say no, when yes is desperately needed and you can say yes.

Be warned, after this exercise, the moment someone calls your name, a "NO" will roll off your tongue. Oh darn, that was your boss who was asking you if you wanted a promotion with a fifty-five percent increase in your current income, but you answered "NO." **Disclaimer,** that is the side effect from practicing to say "NO," that will happen, I am so very sorry.

CHAPTER 36

You want to commit suicide; you want to end your life, because of an internet, or a phone scammer

The human being that is ready and willing to use your very own hands to murder you. Please face the reality of the internet scammer, or the phone scammer. Your demise is their goal, do you doubt me? Here is your answer. Please tell me, what happens if you lose your life savings, is there a possibility you might harm yourself? If you no longer have ownership to your home, is there a chance you could commit suicide? What happens if you lose your 401(k), might you decide to end your life?

Make no mistake, do not kid yourself for a second, the scammer knows this; and still your demise is their goal. You are saying to yourself, "He or she is not a scammer, because they have given you money." Really? Do you know what they are doing? They are investing into your complete demise. Please allow me to explain. To get a return from the stock market, you must first invest into it. You first buy stocks, and those stocks hopefully will give you a return.

The scammer is investing in you, in the evilest way possible. He or she, they are willing to give you five hundred dollars, to get five thousand from you. He or she will give you a one hundred thousand dollars romantic make-believe pipe dream; so that they can get their hands on your four hundred thousand dollars 401(k) reality. Please answer these questions for me.

With the eight billion plus people that are on this earth, are you willing to give away your life savings, and all that you own to a monster? For all that you have worked for, for all that you have toiled for, or your family has toiled for, and left it for you, are you willing to give it all away to someone for romance?

Before you go down this road, please consider this. What is the value that you have placed on the work that you have done in life? What is the value that you have now placed on your accomplishments or your family's accomplishments in life? What is the value that you have placed on the quality of life that you live? Is the value zero, to the point you are willing to give it away for romance? Are you willing to give your finances to someone that does not care if they leave you dead or alive? Because their goal is you being destroyed. Please allow me to say it again, this person's goal is you being left with **"NOTHING."**

The murderer has entered in

You are laughing, and you are talking to a murderer; someone that is looking to use your very own hands to kill you. They want to kill your life savings, kill your bank account, kill your 401(k), kill your stocks and bonds, kill your assets, kill your business. And when it is all said and done; they will kill you by using your very own two hands, to take your life by suicide; and then move on to their next victim.

Read the words over, and over again. I want you to make your choice, while knowing the reality of the outcome. Say not to yourself, "I did not know." As I have said to others, I will say to you also. I beg of you, please count the cost. Out of eight billion plus people on this earth, is it likely you will find someone that truly cares for you? Another question for you, how likely is it that you will regain what the scammer steals from you? Zero chances, correct? Precious I will say to you once more, **"Please count the cost."**

Make no mistake, self-control is our saving grace.

Many times we will lead with our desires, our wants; instead of leading with our true understanding, and the reality of the facts that are before us. A monster is lying to you. Yes, they are telling you what you want to hear, and yes, it is absolutely convincing. But what about us? What about our understanding of life, people, and their ability to be monstrous? Why do many of us ignore what we know? Why do we ignore our gut instincts, and our ability to discern facts from fiction, and pretend that garbage is not garbage?

Are we not capable of going it alone if we must? Do we not have the ability to be by ourselves until the right person comes along, and if they do not, do we not know that we will still be okay by ourselves? Have we lost the ability to be by ourselves and be happy nevertheless? Does it take someone else to make us happy? Have we crossed the point of no return, where to give us what we want when it comes to an intimate relationship, we will give away our entire financial livelihood, by opening the door for the scammer to burn our lives to the ground? Yes, for some of you the signs were not there, but for most, the lights are blinking out of control, we are being warned by friends and families, and our greed, "yes, our greed for what we want is what will destroy our lives." "SHUT THE DOOR," GHOST THE HEAVENS, THE EARTH AND THE SEA OUT OF THEM." Show them that you are the master of disappearing, not them. Please walk away from this murderous scammer? Tip toe for half a mile; so they don't know you are making your escape, and then break out in an all-out sprint.

Save your precious life, save your mental health, and save your finances. "RUN FOR YOUR PRECIOUS LIFE; AND DO NOT LOOK BACK, THROW SOME SALT OVER YOUR SHOULDER WHILE YOU ARE AT IT." That salt part made me grin but I am serious, get far away from this situation before they burn your life to the ground, I beg of you precious soul that you are.

Meeting them does not mean that they are not scamming you; it means the danger is now in your physical presence.

Meeting them does not mean this person is sincere. To the contrary, they are even more dangerous. They can get to you in person. They can search while you are away, and rob your home; They can empty your home. They can forge your documents and sell your house from under you. Worst, they can gain access to your parents, and sibling's finances. How? You brought that person home to them. Again, yes, and yes, some of you both men and women had zero idea of the monster this person was. I completely get it.

How do you recover if the damage has already been done?

First thing is first, you precious soul that you are, "you must save your precious life." Without a doubt, many scammers shockingly, are hoping that you will commit suicide. Yes, they are hoping that you will end up killing yourself. "To these wretches, if you are dead, you cannot come after them."

"Toughen up," Your life has nothing to do with finance, your precious life has nothing to do with whether you were scammed or not. Your precious life, the soul that you are, is a life on its own. Money or no money, you are precious. House or no house, you are beyond precious. Stocks and bonds or no stocks and bonds, "YOU ROCK." Do you have any idea how many men and women would be grateful to you, as poor as you are, if you could just love them, be faithful to them, and be a kind gentle soul to them for the rest of your days? Do you know how grateful others would be, if you placed your companionship together with theirs?

The same goes for you if you are going it alone. You Sir or Madam, young man or young lady, you are precious, your life is not valued by money, you are a human being, a soul, a spirit within you; and you are beyond precious. How could your life be worth as much as the money that you have? Lots of money, you are worth living, no money, you deserve to die? On what planet is that correct? Yes, some societies live that way; but I am telling you, with or without money and assets, you are still beyond precious; and you Sir or Madam **"MUST LIVE."** Yes, Mr. or Ms. Pepe Le Pew, sweet talked you; and then he or she skunked you out of your finances. Yes, they skunked you; and it stinks up to high heaven, but don't give up. You precious must go on, "<u>**YOU MUST LIVE**</u>."

Please precious, please be encouraged. Please call or text the **Suicide & Crisis Lifeline** at 988, the 1-800-273-8255 has merged with 988 as of July 16, 2022. **Active-duty members and veterans, please press (1)** when the call is answered or text to **838255.** Non-military, if you are unable to speak or you are hearing impaired, you can send a text to the **Crisis Text Line** 24/7, at **741741.** You can also go to **988lifeline.org** website.

Precious please I beg of you, whether the signs were there or not, hear me, please hear me I beg of you, <u>**"you are not the bad person, they are."**</u> Please do not be embarrassed to get help. Whether by voice or text; speak with the **Crisis Lifeline,** tell them what you are going through please. Open a complaint with the police. Do not allow the embarrassment to keep you from getting help I beg of you. Please tell them what you are feeling; they are there to help you. Please I beg of you, <u>**DO NOT GIVE UP, PLEASE LIVE.**</u>

For you here in chapter thirty-six, and you back in chapter twenty-two, whether being scammed, or in a relationship and being taken advantage of. For your mental health, and for your wellbeing, please do not blame yourself. At this juncture the blame game will only break you down. You are not the monster, they are. "Please hold on and live precious." Your life is worth far more than any amount of wealth; your life is precious all by itself. Please I beg you, <u>Please Live.</u>

CHAPTER 37

Do not underestimate the importance of taking time off for yourself.

There is an incredible lifesaving, and life-changing machine called in its abbreviated form, (ECMO). E. C. M. O. stands for **"Extra-Corporeal Membrane Oxygenation,"** pronounced (EC-MO) for short. The ECMO machine is used to circulate and oxygenate blood throughout the body and at times work for the heart also. It is used when the heart and or lungs are not working, when the body needs a replacement lungs or heart, and when the body needs to rest and recover. Remember, I am not a doctor; this is my layman's term way of explaining this to you.

There are times in our lives, when we need someone or something to take over; so that we can rest and recover our strength and our health. Metaphorically speaking, attach yourself to EC-MO. Your EC-MO is called T. T. O. F. M. S. **"<u>Taking Time Off For Myself.</u>"** On many occasions, the stress that you are going through, can, and will wreak havoc on your cardiovascular, your respiratory, and or your mental, and neurological system/organs. T. T. O. F. M. S.,

"Taking Time Off For Myself." will give your heart, mind and lungs, the rest and recovery time that they need, and will save your precious life.

You going dark is one of the best cures there is for extreme stress, please shut everything down and rest, your life depends on it. Stress whether you believe it or not can end your life. Please do not ignore what you are going through. Do not ignore the fact that stress is pushing you over a cliff, and you are dying slowly but surely. For heaven sakes please act now! Please live and grow old I beg of you. Please live long enough to see and experience your children, or your grandchildren and great grandchildren, and tell them how you overcame great sorrows. You must tell your bloodline how metaphorically speaking, you swam an ocean of sorrows, climbed a mountain of pain as high as Mount Everest, you crossed hot desert lands of disappointments, or tell them how you went through valleys of sickness and overcame it all, and that they will also. They will hear of your incredible victory over mental illness. Lay the foundation for you, for your family, and for your future bloodline and **LIVE.**

Please live, survive and march towards the great life that awaits you. That great life does not have to be money; it could be incredible peace, precious rest, and laughter to fill every ocean; or it could be your life changing inspiration; that will continually draw others to you for encouragement.

Live out your life and allow your future incredible

life to manifest itself; where the greatness within you will somehow make it alright for others, when they are in your presence. Please live precious you, please live and give your family your blueprint on how to survive, and how to overcome under the greatest of circumstances; it is your duty to do so. Please I beg of you, I encourage you, and I implore you, please do not give up on your precious life. Take the timeout needed, to rest and rebuild. The timeout, you going dark; will go a long way in the rebuilding of your strength. No matter how discouraged you are, please precious I beg of you, please do not give up on your life. Please hold on precious soul that you are, and please never stop saying, **"I AM GOING TO LIVE."**

If you feel that you are in trouble, and you are now at a place where you are now entertaining suicidal thoughts, please I beg of you with unrelenting love, care, and compassion towards you, please speak with someone. You being overwhelmed can break you.

Please reach out to someone for the help that you are desperately in need of, you must do this with much urgency, and you must not delay. Please call the **Suicide & Crisis Lifeline** at **988**, the 1-800-273-8255 has merged with 988. **Active -duty members and veterans please press (1)** when the call is answered or text to **838255.** Non-military, if you are unable to speak or you are hearing impaired, you can send a text to the **Crisis Text Line** 24/7, at 741741. You can also go to **988lifeline.org.** Please LIVE! Please give them a chance to give you the help that you are so desperately in need of, I beg of you.

CHAPTER 38

Do not stereotype suicide; this I promise you, will be one of the biggest mistakes you will ever make

Suicide has a deep repertoire of skills to draw on-to take you to the grave. There are broken finances, depression, greed, or sicknesses. It could be someone with a broken heart, or loneliness, bitterness, anger, or aging. There is postpartum depression, bipolar, or the death of someone, or being abused. The reason for suicide could be pain, sorrow, or not being able to express oneself. It could be lack, or having an inferiority complex. It could be betrayal, sadness, or even wealth. The cause for suicide could be someone having an obsession. It could be their medication, or confusion. Perhaps negative thoughts and or negative influences. The reason for suicide could be addiction, or some form of embarrassing experience, or the traumatic loss of possession. It could be mistakes, or failures. The cause for suicide could be hate, and or extreme jealousy, ignorance and or arrogance. There is the overachieving reason, or the underachieving reason also. The cause for suicide could be the person committed a crime. This list is never ending; and many times, it is also without reasoning.

Please do not make the mistake of placing any person into any category.

Do not make the mistake of placing any person into any category; to eliminate you or them from the possibility of suicide. Please hear me; that could be one of the biggest mistakes that you ever make. Every single one of the above categories has caused someone to commit suicide. Do not take your eyes off someone because, "they do not fit a category." Please allow me to break it to you, **"suicide has no category."** Suicide works with them all; as long as the end result is death.

Now you know why yesterday, that person was filled with laughter, and today they took their lives. People have laughed, danced, cursed, worked, conversed, debated, invented, loved, hated, and cried their way into the grave; through suicide. Do not look at their actions alone, and do not listen to their words alone. You must give equal attention to both. Listen to their words, no matter how faint or even unbelievable their words may be, and give equal attention to their actions. You must act on what you see or do not see. Why is this person drowning, and yet they are not showing any apprehension, or any care, something is extremely off? Pay attention to verbiage, you must take them seriously when they say, **"They want to die." "They are going to kill themselves."** Them telling you they want to die is a gift from the heavens. This gives you a chance to take action before it is too late.

Do not say, "they haven't done this, and so they are fine, or they will be okay." You are wrong!

They do not have to do one set thing to be in danger of committing suicide. Your loved one, your relative, employee or coworker could be at a dinner party with you having the grandest of time, and all the while this person is quietly and meticulously, contemplating suicide; and intends to do it when they arrive home. Yes, I know, it is very shocking, and to my utter dismay, very true. If they tell you they want to die, it is their subconscious crying out for help, and is hoping that someone will stop them. Please I beg of you, please help these precious, precious, precious human beings, to live out the rest of their lives upon this earth. **"I THANK YOU."**

If you are the person I just described, please precious, please give us a chance to help you. Please give us a chance to save your precious life, I beg of you. Please contact the **Suicide & Crisis Lifeline** at **988, Active-duty members and veterans, please press (1)** when the call is answered or text to **838255.** Non-military, if you are unable to speak, or you are hearing impaired, you can send a text to the **Crisis Text Line** 24/7, at **741741.** You can also go to **988lifeline.org.** They will help you who are suffering from suicidal thoughts, and they **"will also"** help you who wants to save this person's life. Yes, repetitive, "I know."

Please use my journey as a confirmation of the fact that, you cannot stereotype suicide.

Please give very close attention to my journey. The characteristics demonstrated, were not of someone that wanted to die; and I was planning to someday commit suicide. I was determined, I was committed to my journey, I wanted to succeed. I fought hard, I worked hard, and I invested into my journey; and pursued hard for my success in life. This was so that

I could get my son into adulthood; where he would become a very successful, productive member of society. There is nothing inside these words I just mentioned, that gives you any hint, any idea, that I was suffering from suicidal thoughts and tendencies.

Nevertheless, I was. While fighting to live, so that I could get my son across the finish line, and into adulthood; where he could take care of himself. I had made up my heart and mind to die. While fighting to live, I had made up in my heart and mind to kill myself. This is the identity of many individuals that are upon this vast earth. They are across international borders; with populations of many, many inhabitants throughout nations. There is no denying this fact.

"Please do not place suicide into a box."

Please do not assume they are okay, based on their hard work, or their determination and focus. Do not eliminate the possibility of suicide, based on tons of smile or laughter, or because this person is always happy. While smiling, or with the most joyous of laughter, many are drowning in suicidal thoughts and tendencies; and are gasping with their last breath to survive. No, you cannot stereotype suicide, I repeat, do not stereotype suicide, because this will be to the detriment of you, and your loved ones, your friends, neighbors, colleagues and even the precious stranger; that is in extreme danger of losing their lives to suicide.

Please never ever forget
"You must not stereotype suicide."

Suicide can take place within any, and all known categories. There is no circumstance that is exempt from suicide. Suicide can affect any individual, any organization, people, location, and or nation. If you categorize suicide, it is going to be one of the biggest mistakes you will ever make. Please do not make this mistake, I implore you. It will cause you to overlook someone, because they are wealthy, because of the position they hold within their occupation, or their lot in life. You could overlook someone because they are cheerful, they are not bothered by anything, or because they are a great communicator.

You could overlook someone because the world knows them and loves them. This is all due to you placing them within a category. Do you know the world has lost countless people from every reason, from every career occupation, and lot in life, and from every characteristic of which I have listed? Yes, **"from every single one of them."**

"To you I say again"

"You cannot stereotype suicide."

"Suicide fits all categories."

CHAPTER 39

Sorrow is the spear that pierces deep within us all, and for some of us; it creates a mountain of fear, and silence also.

The Sorrow inside you is the spear that pierces deep within you; and much damage is done to you. **Your silence** is the obstacle, it is the barrier, the stumbling block; that prevents you from getting the help that you are so very desperately, desperately in need of; so that you can heal; and you can recover your mental health. Please precious, please I encourage your precious heart and mind. I beg of you, I implore you, and I admonish you.

Please call, please speak, please type, please text, please my precious love I beg of you, my precious heart begs of you; you must find a way to ask for the help that you are desperately in need of. I beg of you, I implore you, and I encourage you. Your silence is your prison. Your silence is the anchor that weighs you down; and will cause you to drown. Please give yourself a fighting chance to live. Please cry out I beg of you. Please speak with the **Crisis Lifeline,** please ask for help; and please precious, **"YOU MUST LIVE."**

Here is some additional information that I hope will help you to open up, and release yourself from the prison that you are in.

This is my way of saying to you, I truly, truly, truly understand your sorrow, and that you are not alone, in this journey that you are going through. I was in my late teens, and suicide was beckoning to me in the worst way. The brutal damage had already been done to my mind and my heart. I was living in fear of the world, and the hate they had for me. My precious heart was broken in a thousand pieces. I was a human being that had my life stolen from me. I had been betrayed by those closest to me, and I was dead more than I was alive.

Do you know what is the very worst torture there is to the soul? It is when a human being knows the nobility that is within them, they know who they are, and who they are to become at a very early age. They are to lead, to minister, to lay hands on the sick, and encourage the heart. I was to cross borders, and ignite the hearts of the people with much hope and precious encouragement, and I knew it from a very tender age.

I was not liked by most, no matter how I tried to be. I knew early on that those around me did not like the sight of me. I did not know why, but I knew they did not like to be around me. As I grew older, I found out why. I loved to laugh; I had the joy of the LORD within me. I had gone to a crusade when I was in the first grade, I was seven years old, and I fell hard for GOD that day. The love for GOD stayed with me as I grew older.

When you are seven years old and fall in love, that love is forever. I had a laugh like no other. I always had a grin on my face. Then it started fading. The laughter grew less and less, and then it was no more.

IT WAS REPLACED WITH FEAR.

IT WAS REPLACED WITH SORROW.

IT WAS REPLACED WITH ANGER.

IT WAS REPLACED WITH LOSS.

IT WAS REPLACED WITH THE INABILITY TO PROTECT MYSELF.

IT WAS REPLACED WITH THE CONTEMPT OTHERS FELT TOWARDS ME.

IT WAS REPLACED WITH THE BLOCKAGE INSIDE MY MIND, WHERE I AM UNABLE TO BE CLOSE TO OTHERS.

MY JOY, MY LAUGHTER, MY SMILE, MY PEACE, ALL STOLEN, AND WAS REPLACED WITH HORRIFIC SORROWS.

I trusted no one, and I feared everyone. I have been told that perhaps I am autistic. My inability to be close to others, and my being an extreme loner, they believed were symptoms. They had no idea that by the time I had my son, it was open season on me. People literally wanted me to die. I would take my son to church with me; not because I was proud to have a child young. No, it was because I loved GOD; and that was all I knew, and I wanted my precious son to love GOD the way that I did also. I was determined to raise him before GOD.

I feared the people at the church. I was trash to them. They did not hide their disdain for me. I remember I was working for a company that recorded weddings, and special occasions. The church had a national function, and a group had asked me to please record the function. I received the necessary permission from the church, and confirmed all documents and payments with my boss. My boss's brother, who was a director for a company, but loved working in the communications field, was my working partner. He and I would do the recording for the occasion. We were always paired in two or more, to do any job.

On the day of the function while I was recording, one of the leaders told me to get my stuff and get off his stage. Do you know what was strange? I felt no anger, what I felt was utter fear and inferiority. I quickly stopped recording and packed up my camera and tripod. My working partner asked me what was going on? I told him and he was livid. He told me to give him the camera and tripod. He went back up on the stage and finished the job. He explained to me after that the job was paid for; and unless it was unavoidable, we must always finish the job we were hired to do. He was a blessing in my life, I used to hide at his house. He would leave the key for me and I would hide there. I would be gone by the time he arrived home after work. He knew something was terribly wrong, he had even tried to get me to talk; but my brain had lost the ability to trust anyone, or to ask for help. I believe he allowed me to stay there, to protect me. I was living, but I wanted to die.

I finally had to stop going there because his girlfriend did not like it; and I appreciated his help too much to create any problems for him. She had no idea that unless we worked together, we never saw each other. I entered after he left for work, and left before he arrived home. His home was just my hiding place. When I could no longer go there, I would go to the country. I would take a bus to the country and stay overnight at any hotel I could find. No one knew where I was, I was dead to the world until they saw me again. I had my son to stay with his father during the week, and I would have him on the weekends. This allowed me to hide for five days, and build myself up to stick my head out for the weekend.

I remember there was an American televangelist that came to Jamaica during that time. It was a national crusade at the stadium. Many of us from our church went to the crusade. One of the members, a young man, sat next to me. I knew he lived near me; we had agreed to travel home together. We were not friends; I feared his family, I knew how they felt about me. The young man would get off before me, but not to worry, the van would stop right across the road from my subdivision. All I had to do was cross the road and enter. We had reached about a mile from my subdivision, and the van turned off instead of going straight. It turns out it was their last trip, and the driver and conductor were heading home. They turned off in the direction of where the young man lived, because they too lived in that direction.

The van stopped, so that I could get off. I had to walk about a mile home and it was close to midnight. My church brother came off the van with me, and said he would walk me home, and then he would head back home. I was so very grateful. The next day I went to church and he approached me. Immediately I knew that something was wrong. He looked flustered, he looked sad, and confused and he looked angry. I went up to him and asked him if he was okay? He said no he was not. I asked him what was wrong?

He explained to me that when he arrived home, his father confronted him. His father must have seen that his son sat next to me at the stadium, because he was already angry the moment the young man entered. He asked him why he was having anything to do with me? My church brother explained to his father that the transportation we took turned off before getting to my stop, and so he walked me home to protect me, and then he headed home. His dad cursed him out. **Please note,** I do not mean with curse words.

He screamed at him and shoved him. The young man explained to his father that if he had not walked me home, I could have been attacked and killed. His father said to him, **"let her die, let them kill her,"** and slapped him in the face. I was young, I was weak, and I was fearful. I quaked in fear of all those around me. They wanted me gone, but how could I leave the church? I loved GOD, and I wanted my baby to know and love GOD also. Please do not take this to talk bad about the church. The church is made up of you and I. We are imperfect people that are terrible at our best and at our worst; but nevertheless, are trying to change for the better, and please do not start blaming GOD for our own wretched behavior.

I had already tried to kill myself, and it would not be the last time. I had given up on life. I would move from pillar to post daily. I would avoid going home if I could. They would talk about me in the filthiest of manners. I was dead. I had no hope. I had been thrown in the trash heap of life and left for dead. I remember one day I thought I was going to lose my mind, I was a child, a little girl pretending to be okay, because I needed help from the very enemies that burned my life to the ground. I had to laugh with them, talk with them and kowtow to them. I asked one of the members of that family one day, what would she do if she was me? The answer given back to me I can still remember, and will probably never forget was, "**<u>I could never be you.</u>**"

By the time I migrated to the United States, the damage had already been done. There are countless people that have gone through horrific misery in life as I have gone through. They are doctors, active-duty military and veterans. There are fishermen, bakers and scientists. There are mathematicians, lawyers, home makers, teachers, professors, and dentists that have been where I have been, the list is endless.

There are many that are confused by military service members that are taking their own lives suddenly. Unbeknownst to many, they might have signed up with that horrific troubled past and broken spirit, without anyone knowing. Many of us by the time we reach the age of adulthood, we are already finished. We have already been betrayed, used and abused in the most horrific way, and left for dead. The ignoble actions of nefarious men and women found us, when we were most vulnerable, and they burned our lives to the ground. By the time we get to adulthood, we are the empty shell of who we were meant to be.

When I brought my son to the United States, I knew what needed to be done. I was going to ensure that people could not destroy my child the way they destroyed me. I was going to prepare and equip him to be the best that he could be, with the help of my MOST HIGH GOD, and then I would kill myself. I fought to give my son a good life, and to get him over the finish line.

The more years I lived, was the lesser and lesser I desired to kill myself. Instead of leaving the world, I left people behind, and then I started to live again. My family and others, might think something is wrong with me. They all know that I am an extreme loner. That lonely space has allowed me the ability to heal from my wounds, and to find peace of heart and mind. Many people think that my being a loner is weird, but that is okay. When you have been where I have been, a few disagreeable words do not faze me. My quiet space is exactly what I needed to heal.

Please listen to me all of you, I beg of you, with these tears filled eyes; please I beg of you, please live. You must live out your years that you were meant to live upon this earth. "Do not forfeit your destiny." I made it! Do you hear me? **"I made it, and you will also."**

Gird your grip on life. Tighten your grip on life and please I beg of you, I admonish you, and I implore you, please do not let go. It will not always be this way, you will make it, there is rest up ahead. Weep and moan for the journey of pain and sorrow that you have lived. Hold your head, or hold your chest, and wail for the pain and great sorrow that was heaped upon you, and drag and crawl your way precious, to your redemption. Please **Live,** I beg of you. **Live** and **Live** and **Live** some more. Great was the sorrow that broke your precious heart into pieces, and resilient, wonderful, superb, and so very splendid, brilliant and strong are you, the individual, that has survived the great and terrible horror that was inflicted on you.

Forgive all those who caused you harm, and you push forward. The memories that haunt you, they are not enough to kill you. Instead; it is your very own hands that are in danger of taking your life. **"Please Live precious, Live and Live, and Live again."** Your yesterday is not your tomorrow. Please rise like the phoenix from the ashes and live, I beg of you. You have much to live for, even if you do not see it, and your accomplishments are yet to be made. You are up in age you say? It is still not too late to accomplish great things in life. Do you know that one action from you in your senior years, can last for many centuries? Please all of you, please do not give up, **Please Live.**

Please survive your heartache, please survive and LIVE. I bless you all according to the will of GOD. I bless you with long life, joy and peace, I bless you with an abundance of precious laughter; that flows from your heart and mind. I bless you with fortitude, to go the distance, and to accomplish your destiny. I bless you with noble and kind people, that will point the way. The value of you is not based on what others think of you. No, it is based on who you truly are, or who you will become. The finale is not where you are today; you still have a way to go, more distance to travel; and your incredible evolution, the authentic you is yet to come. Give yourself the chance to live, I beg of you, and I thank you. Your beginning is not your middle, and your middle is not your ending, please precious I beg of you, **"Please Live."**

Precious soul that you are, please live. Never forget your precious blood relations, and your grafted in bloodlines. Please allow them the opportunity to make it to this earth, or to survive upon this earth. I beg of you precious soul that you are, please, I beg of you, **"You Must Live."**

Your today is not your year from now, it is not your five years from now, or your ten or twenty years from now, this I can promise you. Your beginning is not your middle, and your middle is not your ending, please give yourself a chance for your change to happen. There is much to live for. Please, you must give yourself time, and the chance to discover it all. **I love you; I love you, and I beg of you precious soul that you are, "Please Stay Alive." Please precious, stay alive, you must live. "PLEASE LIVE."**

Here is a note for your detractors

For those of you who believe that what you believe or say about your fellow human being, is the reality of who that person is. I will say this to you, there is honor in recognizing the strength and depth of your fellow human beings, and you acknowledging them. Instead of you pretending their gifts, their talents, and the value of who they truly are, does not exist.

You undermining that person could be to your very own detriment also. How do you know the value this person could bring to your life? Their worth could be your blessing, not your curse. Please give them your assistance to fulfill their journey in life. The mercy you show them is the rest that you are giving them. I thank you for your kind consideration towards them.

I cannot closeout, I need to keep trying to save your precious life.

CHAPTER 40

Please hear me, your life's journey is not just about you, it involves many others also.

Your life's journey will involve countless lives; It involves, or it will eventually involve, an enormous number of varied experiences, and possibilities. Its expanse is, and it will be through the joys and the sorrows of both you and others. It does not matter if we are extreme loners, or we are the extroverted

Individuals. The same goes for all of us. **"We are not alone."** Our actions, and our decision-making, will affect countless others. Whether through personal or business, or through a myriad of other forms of relationships, formed on a plane, a train, a bus, or at the gym. There are relationships formed in Saudi Arabia, in Qatar, Abu Dhabi, Dubai, at The Hague, Prince William Sound, or Nova Scotia. Relationships formed in Paris, Bahrain, in Jamaica, in Sharjah, Jeju Island in South Korea, or Ukraine. Relationships formed in Jordan, Australia or in Egypt or Berlin.

Every one of these relationships bears some form of significance, whether we understand it or not. Some form of cause and effect are born through these relationships. Something about that person, what they say to you, or how they treat you, their smile, their laughter, their eloquence of speech, or their not so great, yet caring speech; can cause some form of reaction, some form of behavior that will be relayed, will be passed on-to many others.

Yes, our journey is an expanse. It is a large never-ending cycle of our contact and communication with others, along with the impressions and our influences that are made on others. Our journey rallies others, or pushes them back. We can motivate others, or we can discourage them. We intimidate or we reassure them. We leave the impression that we are kind, or we are mean spirited; for some we give them the impression that we are a place of safety, or we are a place where turbulence is constant and never ending. We leave some of our smiles and our precious laughter in the hearts of others, or we leave some of our tears with them. There are times when we leave some of all three with them; our smiles, our laughter and our tears. We share our wisdom with others, or sadly it is our ignorance that is shared with them.

Our journey expanse, unbeknownst to many, are made up of interrelationships. Our lives and actions with others, with humanity are intertwined. We are woven together in unbelievable ways, wherein our lives affect each other, and the impact is far reaching; and sometimes surprisingly endless. We impact our family members, our friends, and our acquaintances and colleagues, and even strangers. We affect these people's lives in the simplest of manner, or in the most complicated, and or the most profound ways that are possible, and this is undoubtedly the truth.

Your words, your deeds can heal, or they can kill

With this in mind, how you treat others matters. What you say matters. For some of you, you were just joking you say? Calling someone out of their name while joking is still calling someone out of their name. Saying something vile and downright vicious while joking is still vile and vicious. Adding the hee hee, the haa haa, after your vicious, vile ugly words; does not soften the blow to the heart and mind of the receivers.

Please see the vast and significant impact you make in the lives of others, with your words and deeds. It doesn't matter who you are, and no matter your age, young or older. The same broken spirit in a child is in an adult also. The same broken spirit in an adult is in a child also. Please own your actions; please own your ability to damage your fellow human being's spirit, young and older alike. Because once you own your actions, you can now do something about it.

This includes changing your behavior; to prevent the hurt, the damage to others from happening again. Recognizing one's mistake, is the moment in time, when the possibility of change can start to take place. I say possibility, because some will recognize their damage to others; and instead of changing their behavior for the better, they will instead revel in it.

In this great expanse of life, you will travel many different roads during your life's journey. Some of these roads will be traveled simultaneously; while you are traveling one, you are traveling another at the same time. You will experience tumult and strangely peace at the same time. There will be joy and sorrow, loss and gain. You Sir or Madam, young man or young lady, will travel on a road, where suddenly or gradually, there will be an epiphany; there will be a sudden understanding, a sudden realization of who you are, and the impact you have on others' lives.

The road of forgiveness will be one of the most significant and tumultuous roads to travel; and in the end, it could be the place where you start to heal.

Another road will be the road of courage; where you will face your circumstances head on, and make courageous decisions for the betterment of your life.

There will be the road of preemptive actions. Where you will make decisions based on you looking out ahead; and making those decisions to prevent future mistakes, to prevent future damages to yourself and to others also. One instance of this, is you turning in your gun(s) to a police station, because of a fragile mind, and the need to make certain you do not end up using that gun on yourself, or on others or both.

There is the road of no excuses; where we accept the truth, that we do not get to use our pain, to use what was done to us; as an excuse to live a scorched earth lifestyle. Where because of what was done to us; we burn down, or destroy everything in sight, with no regards to life, to right and wrong, and the horrific end result, the ruin our nefarious actions will bring to ourselves and to others.

This is why forgiveness must absolutely enter within you.

Forgiveness is not just for the victims; it is for you the victimizers also. You the victimizer has changed for the better, and are sickened by your past actions. Forgive yourself please, and let it go. Apologize if you can. Make it right if you can, and if you cannot apologize or make it right, because of time, and or distance, please hear me when I say; you must still forgive yourself of your past mistakes, of your past actions.

Yes; forgiveness, believe it or not, is a brutal, brutal, unfair, gut-wrenching action to take. It is so very hard to do, but you mark my words when I say to you, it is one of the best things that you could do for your life. Some of you the victims I know are saying to yourselves in anger, "these people pounded me into ashes, and I am to forgive them?"

"I gave up on my life because of these people, and now you are saying to me, forgive them? Heaven to the no, no, no, no, no I am not forgiving them, nope, nope, and nope, not happening."

Do you know what the essential information about forgiveness is? Forgiveness removes the need to want to hear from those who caused you pain. After you have forgiven them, if you never hear a word of apology from your victimizers, you will still be okay. Forgiveness removes the restraints that keeps you bound to your victimizers, and it gives you the ability to leave it behind you.

Remembering does not mean you have not let go

Make no mistake, you still remembering does not mean you haven't let it go. Think about it this way. There are people, employers, places and things you have been finished with for years. You will never have anything to do with them again. In other words, you have let them go for good. Here is the epiphany, do you still remember them?

The answer is yes, you still remember them. In other words, letting go doesn't mean forgetting. Letting go and forgetting are separate things; forgiveness allows you the opportunity to let go. Yes, memories will surface, but because of you letting go; it will help to negate, or it will lessen the pain that comes with the memories of what you went through, due to others.

Please listen to me precious, your soul needs this. Your precious heart and mind need this, and your blood pressure is saying, "thank you." Forgiveness releases your body from stress, and from the horrific pressure; and pain, that those experiences inflicted upon you, and upon your life. Please think about it this way. The people that victimized you, will not give you the release that you are desperately seeking, or is in need of. Precious, it is you that must find a way, justifiable so or not, to release you from it all.

The burden that is tied to your victimizer saps your strength; eats away at you, and it breaks your spirit way, way down. Whether you believe me or not, forgiveness is the medicine, that will help to release, and to relieve you from all that hidden sickness, and increase the strength that you have, because some of your precious much needed strength, is being used up carrying that very, very, heavy burden.

Once forgiveness is given, it will help to remove that heavy burden. Forgiveness will help to transport you to a place of wellness, where your strength can be restored. Forgiveness causes you to let go; it causes you to unload the heavy burden caused by your victimizers, and forgiveness restores you to a place where you can be free of those who harmed you.

Please forgive them, please let it all go; so that you can release that constant pain, and that constant tightness in your chest. It will help you to release the constant sorrow that haunts you, and precious, please live. "I love you precious soul that you are, my care is in the abundance for you, Please Live."

During this difficult process, if you feel yourself being overcome by mental stress, or you feel like giving up. Please contact the **Suicide & Crisis Lifeline** at **988**, the 1-800-273-8255 has merged with **988** as of July 16, 2022. Repetitive yes, I know.

Active-duty members and veterans, please press (1) when the call is answered or text to **838255**. Non-military, if you are unable to speak, or you are hearing impaired, you can send a text to the **Crisis Text Line** 24/7, at 741741. You can also go to **988lifeline.org** website. Whether by voice or text, please tell them what you are feeling, they are there to help you, they will not judge you. Do not give up, please do not allow your pain to drive you into the grave. NO! Hold on, and fight to survive.

PLEASE I BEG OF YOU

PRECIOUS SOUL THAT YOU ARE

"PLEASE LIVE."

CHAPTER 41

A conversation and questionnaire, about your journey towards suicide.

While you are standing in the presence of suicide, I want to ask you some questions, and I also want to pass on some information to you.

While you are in the presence of suicide:

Please tell me, what type of transportation was it that brought you to suicide?

Your Answers

It was financial loss

It was physical and verbal abuse

It was the horrible beatings I received

I experienced the death of my loved one

I had to file for bankruptcy

It was the loss of my career

I lost my job

I experienced an extremely embarrassing situation

I experienced failure, or a missed opportunity

I am gravely ill

Your Answers, Continued

It was the crimes I committed

I went through a relationship breakup

I have never been loved

I am always depressed

I have no direction in life

It is because I am destitute

In the presence of suicide: Please tell me, who are you?

Your Answers:

I am a student, preteen, teen, or pre or post graduate

I am a scientist

I am a doctor

I am a baker

I am a teacher

I am a musician

I am a father

I am a mother

I am a member of the protective services; I am a police officer or an FBI or CIA agent

Who Are You, Continued?

I am an aunt

I am an uncle

I am a brother

I am a sister

I am an attorney

I am a maintenance worker

I am a technology expert

I am an active-duty member of the military

I am a veteran

I am an ambassador for my nation

I am an engineer

I am a farmer

I am a librarian

I am a millionaire or a billionaire

I am a fashionista

I am a brand ambassador

I am a singer

I am a gardener

I am a fisherman

Who Are You, Continued?

I am an actor, or an actress, or a host for a TV program

I am a motion picture writer or director, or staff

I am the CEO of a fortune five hundred company

I am a dentist

I am a maintenance worker

I am a veterinarian

I am a clergyman or clergywoman

I am a businessman

I am a businesswoman

I am someone that is lost in life, I have no direction

In the presence of suicide:

What are the experiences that has caused you to head in the direction of suicide?

I am a student that is picked on, bullied without mercy, ganged upon, and there is no help in sight.

I am a parent, I have no resources, I do not have the ability to care for my child, or my children.

I am ashamed of my life, and the conditions that I am living in. I am desperate, I have zero option.

I am an author that is suffering from writer's block. No matter what I do, my mind is blocked from gaining new material. I was already paid in advance for this work, or I am drowning in debt; and need this work to keep from going under. I have nothing, my mind is empty, and my pen is without movement.

I am a doctor, that lost a patient on the operating table, and it broke me completely.

I feel empty inside, I am without hope, or direction.

I am a millionaire, or a billionaire, and the pressures of life have me by the throat.

I am a husband or wife, that is about to lose my family, because I am going through a divorce.

I am a ballerina, a professional dancer that suffered a career ending injury, my career is no longer.

I am a Rhodes Scholar, or an individual representing my nation, in some form of educational training, and I am failing.

As an ambassador for my nation, I was tasked with partnering with my host nation on a very important project, and I am failing.

As a brand ambassador, I am not living up to my client's expectations. The pull that they thought I would have, they are now saying I do not have it. I am finished, I invested everything into this career.

As a dentist, my career is associated with pain. My patients come only when they must. The strain of the never-ending financial uncertainty has broken me.

As an actor or actress, or singer, or TV host, I am abused by the public in the worst way. I am hounded, talked about in the vilest of manner, and all I am expected to do is smile for the camera.

I am a clergyman or clergywoman, I am the lawyer, the doctor, the parent, I am the cook, the human being that sends home the dead and welcomes the living. I give my all, and get nothing in return. I am drained, I am tired, and I am completely burned out.

I am a fashionista with a social media following, that is envied by many. I am watched and criticized at every turn. Every garment I wear is scrutinized and will be spoken ill of by someone. I am suffocating, and I cannot take it anymore.

I am a singer, that has never produced a song borne from my talent, from my passion. I sing the way the world wants me to sing. I sing to sell records; I do not sing according to my gift and talents, and what I truly want to say. I do not exist in my true form.

I am a librarian; my place of employment is one of quiet peace, of eloquent speeches, amazing travels, unending knowledge and new discoveries every day. I am amongst the vast and significant repositories of history, accomplishments and magnificent journeys, and unbeknownst to everyone; I suffer from extreme depression and anxiety. I cannot take it anymore.

I am a businessman or woman; my business is going under, and I will have to close it down; everyone in my city knows me, I am ashamed. Failure haunts me, and the shame of it all has me on the cliff's edge.

I am an engineer, I desperately needed to win the bid, and I lost. My business needed to win that bid to stay alive. I am lost, how do I go to my competitors, to seek employment from them? I would rather die than ask them for employment, or for any form of help.

I am a scientist; my work has failed. The organization that was financing my work has pulled their financial backing, and my work will come to an end. My staff will be terminated; they will lose their jobs, and so will I. I want to end my life, from the trauma of it all.

I am an attorney, and I am not well known. I rarely get clients, because a very few well-known attorneys are constantly recycled. They are called on non-stop, and the rest of us are treated as if we do not exist. The few cases I get keeps me in a desperate grip of limitations, when it comes to building my practice.

My student loan debt, along with all of my everyday expenses to survive, is choking the life out of me. My debt is growing, and I am behind on all my payments, and have defaulted, I cannot take it anymore.

My response: Wow, many of you are from different nations. You differ in travel, in your career, and you do not know each other. Yet you are all gathered here today, at the same destination; to experience suicide. This is sobering, and incredibly mystifying.

My response: Interestingly, most of you potential victims have something in common. You have been hurting, you are having mental stress, and you have been silent; you have been quietly carrying some form of pain, some form of sorrow for a while now. This current circumstance pushed you over the edge. Onlookers do not see it; but there is far more sorrow within you; you have been suffering in silence.

My response to you:

I know that you are in a rush to stay with suicide, but did you know, did anyone tell you that you can return from this place?

My response to you:

"You do not have to leave with suicide," and you do not have to return on the same transportation you arrived in. You can leave on the transportation called **"hope," instead. Yes, there are many additional return transportations, that are available to you.**

My response to you:

Precious soul, I will list the **"Mode of Returns," the type of "Survival Transportations" below. Do not forget; "they are available to everyone," night or day, twenty-four hours of the day, seven days per week, three hundred and sixty-five days of the year.** They are waiting to take you as far away from suicide as is possible. There is no charge for your boarding pass, no cost for choosing the best seating, and no charge for baggage. As a matter of fact, they will help you to get rid of the baggage you are boarding with, and will give you brand new baggage, that is filled with hope, joy, peace and a brand-new redemptive lease on life. The conductors are ready to help you and are shouting, **"ALLLL ABOARDD!"**

"The List of Returning Transportations"

Returning Bus:
I am going to live

Returning Train:
I am going to live

Returning Car:
I am going to Live

Returning Ship:
I am going to live

Returning Airplane:
I am going to live

Returning Train:
Restoration is mine

Returning Airplane:
I am encouraged

Returning Airplane:
I am loved

Returning Car:
Healing is mine

Returning Car:
I am loved

Returning Train: I am loved

The List of Returning Transportations, Continued

Returning Train:
I will survive suicidal thoughts and tendencies

Returning Bus:
I will overcome Addiction

Returning Airplane:
I will take responsibility for my actions,
and I will not end my life

Returning Car:
I will forgive those who caused me pain,
and allow myself to be free of it all

Returning Airplane:
I will fight to overcome my panic attacks,
I will not allow it to break me

Returning Bus: I am loved

Returning Car: I am loved

Returning Airplane:
I am loved

Returning Bus:
I am needed

Returning Train:
My precious future awaits me

The List of Returning Transportations, Continued

Returning Train:
My bloodline thanks me for not committing suicide

Returning Car:
My husband thanks me for not killing myself

Returning Bus:
My wife thanks me for not killing myself

Returning Airplane:
My children thank me for not killing myself

Returning Airplane:
My family thanks me for not killing myself

Returning Train:
My career awaits me

Returning Bus:
Incredible opportunities await me

Returning Car:
I am loved

Returning Airplane: College awaits me

Returning Airplane:
My scientific accomplishments await me

Returning Airplane: High school awaits me

The List of Returning Transportations, Continued

Returning Airplane: College awaits me

Returning Bus:
The birth of my children awaits me

Returning Train:
My incredible accomplishments await me

Returning Train:
Joy and peace awaits me

Returning Car: Laughter awaits me

Returning Train:
Prosperity awaits me

Returning Car:
My future spouse awaits me

Returning Airplane:
I am loved

Returning Ship:
Breathtaking travel awaits me

Returning Airplane:
Breathtaking travel awaits me

Returning Train: Breathtaking travel awaits me

Returning Bus: Breathtaking travel awaits me

The List of Returning Transportations, Continued

Returning Car:
My years of growth and strength awaits me

Returning Airplane:
The rain, the sun, the moon, and the stars, the night-time and the daylight all awaits me

Returning Airplane:
The grass, the flowers, fruit trees, and rivers, the oceans, hills, valleys and the mountains, along with the spring, summer, autumn and winter awaits me

Returning Bus:
The rain, the sun, the moon, and the stars, the night-time and the daylight all awaits me

Returning Bus:
The grass, the flowers, fruit trees, and rivers, the oceans, hills, valleys and the mountains, along with spring, summer, autumn and winter awaits me

Returning Train:
The rain, the sun, the moon, and the stars, the night-time and the daylight all awaits me

Returning Train:
The grass, the flowers, fruit trees, and rivers, the oceans, hills, valleys and the mountains, along with the spring, summer, autumn and winter awaits me.

"ALLLLLLLLLL ABOARDDDDDDDDDD!!"
"YOUR REDEMPTION AWAITS YOU!"

This Is an Announcement, From The "I AM GOING TO LIVE" Transportation Authority

Please Note: <u>The Return Transportations</u> listed; Is available for every individual; and will take you to all return destinations that are listed. Feel free to try them all. Every transportation listed will take you far, far away from here; and will keep you away from suicide.

Please Note: For <u>ALL</u> those who wishes to board the suicide transportations

Every time you think about going in the direction of suicide, be warned. The cost for your seat is your life. The cost for one baggage is your life and your child's life that was to be born three years from now. Due to your suicide, precious you, that will not happen.

If your baggage is one-pound-overweight, not only do you have to give up your life to board, but now due to your overweight baggage, you must now give up your future generations also.

Please Note: There are no charge for seats, and no baggage charge, on the "Return Transportations"

be sure to board one of them instead, they will get you away from suicide; and they will also keep you encouraged. The transportations listed, are there for your encouragement and for your survival. Once you are aboard any of them, you will feel encouraged and loved, and you will survive. The food will be great also. From the roast "This is my precious life and I will not give up on it." To the grilled, "My future of joy and peace awaits me." You can also have the baked, "My future accomplishments will come to pass, I will not give up."

The Return Transportations has everything you need, to get away from suicide. Please get on board, and please live a great life. Please drive far away from suicide; Fly away from suicide, or sail far, far, far away from suicide, **"AND LIVE."**

The life that you save could not only be your own life; there are countless other lives that could be tied to your survival. Your survival is their existence, or prosperity; and your demise means they will not exist, or they will miss out on the life they were meant to have.

Please precious you, for you, and for their sake, you must hold on. Please live; please give them the much-needed, precious chance they are meant to have, that will flow through you. Your impact in life does not only cover your life. No, it covers countless other lives also. The depth and breadth of your life is beyond comprehension. The significance of your life when it comes to others is unfathomable. Your action can change millions of lives for the better or worse, whether you are rich or you are poor. The heavens made it so, not I. **I BEG YOU PRECIOUS SOUL THAT YOU ARE, "PLEASE DO NOT GIVE UP ON YOUR LIFE, PLEASE LIVE; PLEASE HOLD ON AND LIVE."**

CHAPTER 42

The murderers that walk amongst us

The only thing holding them back is the fact that they do not want to serve time in jail, or have their lives taken by corporal punishment. They will instead drive you to take your own lives. The evil in their hearts is soaring due to your misfortune, that is caused by your mistakes. There are those who grow fat; due to others misfortune. They will spend their days and their nights debasing you. They will do things to break you, to embarrass you, to make you want to take your life out of their relentless pursuit of your destruction.

Social media is their darling; it gives them the power to tear at you while summoning the killer Wolfpacks to finish you off. They want your destruction, and will do just about anything to achieve their goal. Their thirst for your demise is palpable, and make no mistake, they are without conscience and are void of any fairness, mercy or truth. Your destruction is their pleasure, and your mistake is the opening they needed to attack you.

What does a man or woman do when someone seeks to force them to take their very own life by their very own hands? The answer is, **"YOU MUST LIVE."** No matter the fierceness of the storm that swirls around you, precious soul that you are, **"YOU MUST LIVE."** Bow your head, crouch down low and let the storm pass overhead. Precious you, you must survive these wretched monsters, and **"YOU MUST LIVE."** Be brave, correct the mistakes that you are able to correct; and the ones that you cannot correct, let them go; and you must work hard to do better, and live. Hold your head up high within your heart and mind **"AND LIVE."**

You cannot underestimate the cruelty of those that are attacking you. There are souls that have spent ten, twenty, thirty years and even more in jail, because of someone's lies. The mistake many of us have made, is not being able to imagine or accept the reality, that a person could be that wicked to us. Precious, please listen to me, please hear me when I say, "they can, and they will," Because evil has no limit.

I was an innocent child that was thrown to ravenous wolves. They created false sins against me and used it to bury me. There is one family member, he is dead now. I will not say who he is, the dead is unable to defend themselves. That person knew exactly how innocent I was, and painted me as a wretched person.

The darkness of those who talked about me, and took pleasure in the type of cruelty that could send any soul to the grave. Do you know what that does to an innocent child's heart and mind? Do you have any idea of the massive mental breakdown that took place inside me? The righteous mob robbed me of my very existence. I was a teenager who created in my heart and mind, the ability to disappear from sight. Living but not living. In a home but not there. on the bus but not there. In school but not there. As a teenager based on what these people said about me, I was judged relentlessly and cursed at. No matter the sin, if I was around at that time, I did it. A thousand people in a building, and if it is robbed, burned to the ground, or anything else, it was me. Read these words over and over and over again and let them sink in.

Please allow me to break this down for you on how this could happen to any person, from the billionaire to the pauper. There are those who relish in others' calamity, their misfortune; as long as that misfortune makes them look better than the person that is going through their tribulation.

There are those who will be happy to join the crowd in lying about someone, if it means they will gain from it, whether it is monetary or otherwise. There are people that will hound others to death, because they are filled with hate and malice, and can get away with it. Why? because the person they are hounding has now been painted as a bad person, when in reality they are actually innocent of the accusation.

Sir or Madam, young man or young lady, pre-teen or teenager, please listen to me. Evil monsters come in all ages, all positions in life, and from every type of family, friend, neighbor, colleague or pedigree. As in blue blood aristocrats, middle class, lower class and all else. They are from every career field, as in white collar, or they are blue-collar working class. They are everywhere and the mistakes many of us have made is to say, "there is no way, he or she could be that evil, he or she could not be deliberately trying to push me towards suicide." **Guess what, they are?**

Build your strength, build your resolve to survive this season in your life. You must pay special attention to this. You are not a machine. No, you are a precious human being that feels pain, that feels heartache; and you are someone that can absolutely have a horrific mental breakdown. Due to these wretched monsters and their vile actions.

In a blink of an eye when no one is there to stop you, you precious soul that you are, could kill yourself, because of these self-righteous monsters that have made countless mistakes also. The only difference is no one knows about their mistakes, or their mistakes await them up ahead. Little do they know that their horrific treatment of you, will lock in what becomes of them. Please hold on and live precious, I love you, I pray for you, please precious soul that you are, **"Please Live."**

The crowd that is led by the, "Hijack the Crowd; For Influence" individuals.

There is something I call the, **"Hijack the Crowd For Influence Action."** The human being that is being accused could be innocent, or here is a scenario to think about. A family member, a friend, or a business partner is the accused. You then write a letter to the judge on their behalf. **The letter is not in denial of the person's action, because you do not know if the person is innocent or guilty.** Your letter is not declaring that the person is innocent; your letter is only saying to the judge, **"please allow this human being the chance for redemption."** I am a pastor remember, I too have written these letters on others behalf. The letter is saying, **"Your Honor, please allow this person the opportunity, to serve their time for what they did, and at the same time, please also give them a chance at redemption."**

Suddenly, to get your clout, you **"Hijack the Crowd for Influence."** You start cancelling the person that wrote the letter; and you accuse them of siding with the criminal, instead of the victim, which is a lie. This human being is not siding with them, they are saying, "please allow for restoration in sentencing, after they serve their time." Suddenly, your name and who you are, is on every website, because you are leading the crowd, why? For influence and nothing more.

You have sent someone's life to the grave, because they wrote a letter that is saying, "please allow the person, while they will serve time for what they did; please allow them to still have enough years on their life; to come back to society and contribute to their family, and society in a positive way."

<u>Please sit your buttocks down, an adult is speaking. "NO, not every crime, NO, every person should not get this opportunity." There are those that have to be locked away for life, or given long extended sentences.</u>

You going off on the wretched deep end, is your way of whipping up the crowd, to say I am not on the side of victims, **<u>"which is a lie."</u>** We need to recognize the **<u>"Hijack the Crowd for Influence,"</u>** when it happens, and shut it down. A person has the right to speak on their friend or family's behalf; as long as they do not ignore the crime or disparage the victim. The crowd has sent many a people to the grave; when in reality, if it were your friend or family member, you would speak on their behalf. This is the reality of society.

The **"Hijack the Crowd for Influence,"** allows social media the ability to be far more wicked in its attack on innocent people. The crowd wiping out people's accomplishments, their hard work, and their ability to just plain live. This is wicked, it is vicious, and it is a thousand times more enhanced by social media. They even check throughout the day, to see if **"they are trending"** based on their actions of them actively destroying people's lives.

As a child, as a teenager, I lived it. I experienced the crowd crashing down on me in the most vicious of manner. I witness others using false, filthy narrative created by the crowd; to make themselves look good, at the expense of an innocent child, an innocent teenager, that had zero ability to fight back.

There were many days when the self-righteous crowd of monsters celebrated my demise, but little did they know that strength and honor was deep within me, and would someday stand before them, and there would be nothing they could do about it. Build your resolve from within, whoever you are. Survive their filthy evil jokes, survive their sneers and their violent intentions towards you, by words and deed, and **live!**

Listen to me whoever you are, do not allow the crowd to influence your actions, because they are now attacking you. Do not take actions to placate to them. This I promise you, is them getting you to destroy your life by your very own hands. I did exactly that, and it almost killed me. The crowd would talk about me, sneer at me, and say filthy things about me; and it hurt me to my very soul.

During that time a young man approached me. He wanted to befriend me; but I wanted nothing to do with him. I was always a loner. I saw people through a sorrowful lens of despair; and I knew without fail the pain they had already inflicted up on me. After a while, I decided to be his friend for only one single solitary reason; **"it was for protection from the crowd."** If I had him as a friend, the crowd would leave me alone, the crowd would stop attacking me, the crowd would give me peace. He was from a well-known and loved family in the neighborhood, and everyone respected them.

And so, I became his friend. One day, while walking home, I had to go pass his home. He and two of his friends were at his gate. He stopped me, and wanted me to enter his home and I said no. While his friends stood there and watched, every time he told me to enter and I said no, he slapped me in my face with every bit of his strength, it felt like that to me.

Remember, **the crowd led me to him.** To survive the hate, the filthy lies, and the malice of the crowd, I made the decision to be his friend; so that I could **"get protection, because I lived in fear of the crowd both young and old alike.** He beat me in my face and head until his friends left in fear. I suspect they thought I was going to collapse and die right there, and they wanted no part in the situation.

Now, listen carefully to what I am about to say to you and think it over. Society took me the innocent victim; the crowd took me the innocent victim and marred me. They tarnished me, they ruined me. The crowd sullied me, they vilified me to the point that there was no one, not one person I could turn to for help. The crowd turned an innocent human being into trash. Which means I had zero credibility.

All I could do was stumble home and hide under some covers, and sleep. I could tell no one of the beating I took, because I would not enter his home. I walked in a fog for days. I lived in terror of that community. I lived in terror of him. He would visit the owner's family that we rented from, and they would all look at me as if I was dirt itself.

Yes, the crowd has the ability to turn victims into abusers, and the wretched abusers into innocent victims. The crowd for its very own self-satisfying nefarious hunger and clout, will blow the trumpet of destruction throughout your life, and rejoice at your destruction. For some of you, inside that crowd is the person you broke up with, and the grudge they hold against you is deadly. Inside that crowd is your former business partner that you left behind, because they would not pull their weight; now that you made it, they despise you and want you destroyed.

Inside that crowd is the friend you had to walk away from, because they were no good for your mental health. Inside that crowd is that woman or man that was great when you were strung out on drugs; but now for your sobriety, you had to let them go, and you now have nothing to do with them. And now your demise is their goal. The idea that you are now doing great is the fuel that feeds their hate for you.

Many of you are running scared of the crowd. You are making bad decisions based on their threats, and you are giving up your very existence; due to their unending bullying. Listen to me please, do not give in to the crowd. Do not give away your life because of the crowd. Fight for the saving of your life; and for your accomplishments.

Where were these people when you had nothing? Where was the crowd when you were beaten within an inch of your life? Did they help you; did they defend you; did they provide for you? Where were they during your sleepless nights that you went through to build your company? Can the crowd decide that no person within the United States of America or anywhere else, can speak on someone's behalf in a judicial environment? And if they do, they will be canceled?

Do not capitulate to the crowd. This could be to the death of all that you hold dear in life. Your life is worth more than one mistake. How many mistakes do we make from childhood, until the end of our lives? Your life is worth more than the stumble you have made. Ask yourself this question, what is the chance that someone in the crowd has made the same mistake you have made? In all likelihood, they have.

That someone or some people in the crowd, is now

demanding your destruction. Yes precious, I know that the crowd is ferocious. Yes, the crowd seeks to destroy you. Yes, the crowd is filled with malice towards you. Yes, the embarrassment causes you to want to kill yourself. I promise you; I completely get what you are going through.

Their relentless attack on you, is driving your soul to the grave. You just want to die, so that their attack on you can finally end. I see you, precious soul that you are. I hear your deep, sorrowful grave, soul piercing cry; that comes from your soul in the midnight hours. Please stop precious, stop checking the internet to see how bad their attacks on you are. Precious please, get away from the thundering of their death cry and live.

Please precious, **"you must live."** Whether the storm and live precious, I beg of you. Fight for the saving of you and yours. Do not allow anyone to burn your life to the ground. Please call or text the **Suicide & Crisis Lifeline** at 988. **Active-duty members and also veterans, please press (1)** when your call is answered, or text to **838255**. Non-military, if you are unable to speak, or you are hearing impaired, you can send a text to the **Crisis Text Line** 24/7, at **741741**. You can also go to **88lifeline.org.**

Whether by voice or text, please tell them what you are feeling, because they are there to help you. Yes, this information is repetitive; this is to ensure it lives within your heart and mind continually. The more you read it or hear it, is the more it will stay with you. Which is the exact result that I want to take place.

For everyone that reads this mental help book, please consider these questions before joining the crowd.

What if you were the person that the crowd wanted to cancel? What would you desire from the crowd instead? Would you want the opportunity to recover? Would you want the crowd to leave you alone, so that you could deal with the tumult in your life? Would you want the crowd to consider your journey in life before cancelling you?

Would you want to be able to speak on a friend or a family member's behalf, without any of the fear you feel of being cancelled? Would you want the crowd to accept the fact that the words they type, while they are unseen behind their computer screen, could place you into the grave?

Would you want the crowd to give you a chance to stay alive? Would you want the crowd to give you the chance to recover from your mistakes? Please accept the same chance that you have given to others when they were going through their tumult.

I am certain you allowed them to live. I am certain you gave them the chance that they needed to recover from their mistakes. You Sir or Madam, young lady or young man; deserves the same chance that you gave.

"PLEASE NOTE"

Make no mistake, within society, there are those that do not deserve any chance, and no support should be given to them. Any support given should be held in disdain. To the

offended I say to you, "this is not complicated, you creating scenarios just so that you can attack me is futile."

Remember, the crowd has already beaten me, cursed at me, they have hated me, and maligned me in the worst way and,

"I LIVED"

Do not speak for me please. I am certain at this point in this book, you already know that I am not a coward, I am not afraid to speak my mind, and you, the crowd, does not scare me. I am not ten, twelve, fourteen, fifteen, sixteen twenty, twenty-seven or thirty years old. I am older, stronger, and wiser. The crowd does not own my destiny, GOD does. If you burn my life to the ground; my GOD will rebuild every bit of it. My providence is not of you, it is of GOD. You take it away, and GOD will give it back to me.

Here is my statement, to help you the crowd from having to create answers about my statements inside this book.

Is the crowd always bad? NO

Do we need the crowd at times to take a stand? YES

Are there times when someone, some people, or a business needs to be cancelled? YES, YES, and a resounding YES.

Are there times when someone will rally the crowd, and they are not the, "Hijack the Crowd individual?" YES

Are there times when someone will rally the crowd, and they are not, "Hijacking the Crowd for Influence?" YES

Are their crowds that will form for a cause; and there are both honorable and also nefarious individuals within that crowd? YES.

Are there times when the crowd will gather together for a

purpose; and bad people will try to take over that cause, that crowd? YES.

Please "do not lie," My statements are to specific situations that fits, within what I am saying. Please do not cast a blanket over the entire earth's situation; due to my words. Everyone is not the same, every situation is not the same.

"NO," I am not talking about every crowd, or every leader that is leading or rallying every crowd.

"NO," every crowd does not turn its back on the victim.

"NO," every crowd does not treat the victim as the abuser, and the abuser as the victim.

"NO," every crowd does not sneer at, malign, or spread lies about the victim.

"Yes," I have been the victim in the most horrific way. The worst has not been, and will never be told. I will spare you the horrific heartache you will go through, after reading it. "My experiences," does not give me the right to use my experiences to judge all others. I do not get to throw all men into a fiery pit. There are good men and there are bad men. There are good women, and there are bad women, we are not all alike.

I do not get to burn another man's life to the ground, because of what someone else did to me; the same way a man does not get to burn any woman's life to the ground, because of what a woman, or women in his past did to him. With some people, their vengeance is without a name, it has no address, no face, and no actions to it. Everyone is fair game. The rich man will be accused, when in reality the poor man did it. The poor man will be accused; when in fact the rich man did it. The rich and poor innocent men have been turned into monsters, and are being cancelled, with no fair process in sight. Every person is fair game in their thirst for vengeance. Please do not for one moment turn me into that type of individual. My statements are specific to the individual and crowd that are deserving of such statements.

CHAPTER 43

Do not allow the numbers to influence you. It does not matter if it is one, or one thousand, do not join them in any suicide pact

Do you know the popular saying, "there is strength in numbers"? Please keep this in mind. "There is weakness in numbers also." There are many, many individuals that have made the very worst decisions in their lives; and it was all due to the number of people that were involved within the decision making.

Because one hundred people agreed to take the action, because one thousand people agreed to take the action, many others have gone along, although it was the worst action to take. The crowd saying yes, made this very, very horrendous decision okay or attractive.

There is comfort in numbers when all are like minded, when all are in one accord and are taking the same actions. Some would say these people are followers, and that is why they are following the crowd to their detriment.

Please allow me to take a momentary detour to say this. We need to be careful in painting a follower in a negative light at all times. Imagine this if you will. If no one was willing to follow the Walton's when Walmart was being built, the Meijer's, when Meijer Supermarket was being built, if there were no followers when Amazon, Apple, Google, Samsung, were being built, would these companies exist now, if it was the leader all by themselves and there were no followers to help them? Would Vanguard exist without followers following their leader to build this investment company?

Would many leaders have acquired their wealth, without their followers helping them to accomplish their financial dreams? These followers helped these organizations to build, to grow and to flourish. There are people that are born to follow, they flourish within these spaces. They are the Owner, the CEO, the President's anchor. The term follower should not be used in a negative connotation at all times.

You who are a follower, and see yourself within the previous statement, I thank you for your insight, your dedication and your hard work. Your willingness to be the person that is able to grab a hold of your leader's dreams, and fight right along with them to help them accomplish their dreams. Your blessing will come from your hard work and your loyalty to the journey, and if it does not; please do not be discouraged; your blessing will find you even if it is delayed, or rerouted.

Now, back to what I was saying. I apologize for the detour, please forgive me. I have spoken about the positive follower; I will now talk about the follower that is willing to follow others to their very own destruction. Why are you willing to do this? Because the crowd, or others are willing to do this particular thing, you are willing to do it also? Do you realize that the crowd on many, many occasions are just plain wrong? Do you know that the crowd have actually turned to me and said, "why did you not say anything? My answer, I did. Then their answer to me was, **"you should have screamed at us until we listened."** I promise you with every bit of my heart and mind, please hear me when I say to you, those other two, three, four, or four hundred people that are pulling you into a suicide pact are **"WRONG."** Them being a part of it does not make it right. **"NO, IT IS HORRENDOUSLY WRONG."**

Listen to me, precious soul that you truly are. Please I beg you, walk away from them and save your life and theirs also. You will do this by calling the Suicide **& Crisis Lifeline at 988,** or by telling someone, or some people about what you are feeling and what you are planning with them.

"No, snitches do not get stitches." You telling on them and yourself, will save your precious lives. Please I beg of you, I plead with you, wonderful soul that you are, I admonish you, and I beg you, **"PLEASE TELL SOMEONE; SO THAT YOU CAN SAVE YOURS AND THEIRS PRECIOUS LIVES, PLEASE I BEG OF YOU!**

If you are a student, tell the teacher, and your parents and their parents also. If the parent or parents are the ones that have actually driven you or them to the point of contemplating suicide, then tell the teacher instead; and call the **Crisis Lifeline at 988.** If you are an adult, please precious, call or text the **Suicide & Crisis Lifeline** at **988.** Active-duty members and

veterans, press (1) when your call is answered, or text to **838255.** Non-military, if you are unable to speak, or you are hearing impaired, you can send a text to the **Crisis Text Line** 24/7, at **741741.** You can also go to the **988lifeline.org** website.

"PLEASE I BEG OF YOU." Please do not follow others to the grave. I beg of you, please speak with someone; they will help you to break the influence of the majority. Do not go anywhere with them by yourself. If they are contemplating suicide, they could force you to go along with them, even if you are unwilling.

Please break the "suicide pact" that is between you all; and fight for the saving of your precious life. I give you my word, precious soul that you are; you have help, you are not alone. Many others including myself cares for you and the others within the pact, and will help you. This book is my way of helping you, the **Crisis-Lifeline-staff** cares for you deeply; and is waiting to help you. The people around you want to help you; if only you would give them a chance to do so. Precious, you and your pact have it wrong.

You can make it, things will get better; and you and the pact killing yourselves is most horrific. Please I beg of you, please listen to me. The, **"no one cares"** reason is now null and void. I have shown you with this book, that many of us cares for not just you, but for every person inside that suicide pact. Your true reality at this present time is this, the information that you needed to survive, has been given to you. Now, please use it to survive this horrific place, and live precious, please I beg you, **"PLEASE LIVE!"**

CHAPTER 44

Humanity, your precious kindness is medicine to someone's soul

You and I, should never forget about our treatment of others. When we say no to someone, we can be as kind, respectful, and as gentle as when we say yes, it is up to us to do it. The person standing in front of you; they could be going through the most horrible, the most sorrowful, wretched horrific season of their life, they are just hiding it well. Please I beg of you, whomever you are, please be kind, please be gentle, even if you are about to say **"no"** to someone.

Even if you are about to say the words, **"I cannot help you,"** please saturate your words with mercy, please I ask of you. I ask this of you, because I can remember the horrific suffering that I went through; and what a second of kindness meant to me. Please pour out patience towards that stranger, please give them a glimpse into the fact that someone does care for them.

Please I beg of you, please, you must never forget; your simple, your very precious actions of thoughtfulness, of benevolence that is shown to someone; is the much-needed kindness, it is the much-needed consideration, that could absolutely save countless precious lives. By saving that one person, that one precious soul that was on the brink of suicide, that one person could save millions. Case in point, when my books are sold throughout nations, how many lives will be saved? **I am one person,** that was saved from suicidal thoughts and tendencies. I am now trying to save countless lives throughout nations, throughout the world. Think about it, **just one, "save one; and you could be saving millions of precious souls, that are throughout the earth." That is an undeniable fact that will live throughout the ages.** For you the person that is struggling, please do not hesitate to contact the **Suicide & Crisis Lifeline at 988**, **Active-duty members and veterans please press (1)** when the call is answered, or **text to 838255**. Non-military, if you are unable to speak or you are hearing impaired, you can send a **text to the Crisis Text Line** 24/7, at **741741**. You can also go to **988lifeline.org**.

Precious, please, tell them what you are feeling. You can express yourself without any fear, that they will judge you. I promise you, they will not; they are there to help you. They are vested into you overcoming suicide, and or the restoration of your mental health.

Please precious, please give yourself the fighting chance that is needed, to restore your mental health; to remove your mental stress, and to pull you back from the brink of suicide. Please give us the precious chance that we are asking for, to help you. As long as there is breath in your body, oxygen in your lungs, you Sir or Madam, young man or young lady, little boy or little girl, you are alive, and we can help you.

Please I beg of you, please live! You must live, the precious soul that you are. Be encouraged I beg of you, and never give up. Please do not kill yourself, I beg of you. Precious soul that you are, please hold on for dear life, your much needed change in life will come. Please precious, "PLEASE LIVE."

Please take these words to heart, to recover from a mental health breakdown, to recover from suicidal thoughts and or tendencies. You precious must claw, you must fight your way back from the brink of destruction. Please I beg of you, whenever you are at that critical place, where it is conceivable that you might harm yourself. You are at a place where your mental health is failing, and you are losing control.

I say to you again, and again, and again, precious; please contact the **Suicide & Crisis Lifeline** at **988**, the 800-273-8255 has merged with **988**. **Active-duty members and veterans, please press (1)** when the call is answered, or text to 838255. Non-military, if you are unable to speak, or you are hearing impaired, you can send a text to the **Crisis Text Line** 24/7, at **741741**. You can also go to **988lifeline.org**.

Make no mistake precious souls yes, I am well aware that I keep repeating this information, over and over, and over again. This is to save your precious life. This is to restore your mental health. This is to reduce or all together remove the mental stress that haunts you; and eventually could cause you to take your life, through the violence of your very own hands.

Please precious you, please capitalize on the advice, on the love and encouragement that is being given to you inside this book, and live I beg of you. Please do your part in the saving of your precious life. Do not cast your precious soul into the grave. Please allow the fullness of your life to come to fruition, and live I beg of you. **"You must live I ask of you, and I admonish you, and I encourage you!"** Please live.

CHAPTER 45

My closing statement, along with my thank you, my heart-felt sincere apologies, and my request and acknowledgements also

My Request to Humanity

Suicide is no respecter of persons. It does not matter the class, the race, the nation, or the educational background. Suicide has removed bloodlines and caused countless sorrows. It is our responsibility as a part of humanity, to do whatever we can, in our own way, to make a difference in the lives of those who are under attack. Please make a difference, if you have the slightest inkling that someone is in trouble, please I beg of you, please help him or her to get the help they are in need of immediately. Please make a difference within someone's life, humanity needs your help.

Humanity, "I Love You."

I must do my part no matter how small, no matter my limitations. Please let it never be said when I die, "She served no purpose upon the earth."

Sir or Madam, Young man or young lady, little boy or little girl, please know that you are loved, this stranger loves you, this stranger cares for you far more than you could ever imagine. Yes, I do love you, and GOD willing; if I am here twenty years from now, my love for you will still remain. I love you, and I beg of you, to please hold on. Please be encouraged, **"PLEASE LIVE."** No matter the odds against you, no matter how difficult your journey, please never stop saying, **"I AM GOING TO LIVE."**

Please Note:

You will notice that the title of my book is written in three languages, English, Spanish and French. I initially had **"I Am Going to Live"** written in all three languages for this book. I was not comfortable with the quality of the translation that was done, for the Spanish and also the French version, which is why I removed those two languages.

In the future, I will use representatives from each nation that I partner with, based on its government referral, to translate into that nation's language. I will also hire interpreters from that nation, to interpret my Suicide prevention training program also. Along with this book, I have also created a program, to train others on the active real-time actions that are needed, to save lives. The suicide prevention program, allows for the interactive actions between governments and their citizens, between readers and I the author, or between employer and employees, or interactive, amongst a group of people. All with the goal in mind, of preparing governments and citizens to understand the inner workings of suicide, its ramifications, and to counteract and save countless lives in the process.

Acknowledgements

I Thank You

I will never forget your kindness, from my birth to my death, whomever you are, and wherever you are located. I remember you. It does not matter that I have not seen you in ten, twenty, thirty or forty years, I still remember you. **"Sirs and Madams, <u>I thank you for your precious kindness towards me, I am forever grateful, and again, I will never forget."</u>**

To you Doctors, Sirs and Madams, I thank you. The days were brutal, you had no idea that your kindness gave me a chance to catch my breath, and to live another day, again I thank you. By the time I arrived at work, there would be extreme swelling to my foot; and the horrific pain was beyond brutal, throughout the entire day. It was as if my foot was in a permanent beehive. By noon my foot had given out, and I was dragging it along, just picking it up and putting it down, and dragging it when no one was looking.

I was short tempered, and at times aloof. I was guarding the secret of my injury. The pressure of life, and my plan to commit suicide had me by the throat. Some of you worked with me, you actually worked around my personality; and allowed me the much-needed space to function. You gave me chances again and again, Doctors, Sirs and Madams, I am so very grateful to you; and again I thank you, I thank you and I thank you. I am forever, forever, forever, so very forever grateful to you.

"PLEASE LIVE PRECIOUS YOU." Please survive the journey.

My grandson Moriah, was born in 2019, and his dad; my precious son, my Tony is doing well. He is a productive member of society; he is a servant of GOD; he is the iron that sharpens the iron, and I am beyond proud of him. My Tony understands what it means to survive the harsh winter and the hot burning summer, and to come out on the other side. We survived the journey; **"Thank YOU GOD,"** and you will also. Please do not give up on your life; your change will come. Please hold on for dear life and live, **PRECIOUS PLEASE, YOU MUST LIVE ON.**

Please live on, please tell your incredible hard-fought story of survival, of fortitude, of recovery, and of gratitude. I promise you, the gratefulness inside you will consume you, it will drive you to do everything in your power to pass on your survival to someone else, drive you, to save the precious lives of others.

You are a precious soul upon this earth, and within humanity. You have a life to live, and a journey of restoration to cover. You are far from being finished. Please do not cast your precious soul into the grave. Please I beg of you, I plead with you, and I admonish you, I implore you; please sir or madam; young man or young woman; please boy or girl, do not end your life, please do not betray yourself, **"PLEASE LIVE."** I feel desperate, an urgency is within my heart to save your precious life. I am trying, GOD knows precious I promise you; I am truly trying, please help me.

Please precious you, please see my journey as a confirmation that you can survive the pain; and that you too can make it. Even in my apologies to others that I have hurt; I have found some form of strength and encouragement.

I Apologize: The days when I never showed up for work because I could not walk. I had to hide how truly horrific my injury was; out of knowing I would be fired if my secret was known. Some of you fired me, but others forgave me, I thank you. The dental community was tight knit. If my injury was known, my limitations would have been known within the community.

I preferred to be called unreliable, with the hope that once I was hired, my skills and my faithfulness to getting the job done, would make up for it. I chose that over not being hired because I had an injury that prevented me from doing the job. I cannot blame you who was angry with me, and lost faith in me. I apologize, I had a son to take care of, and no matter how very bad my injury was, I had to work.

Yes, it was not fair to you, but my child and I, we had to survive. Again, please forgive me for the days when I just never showed up. I was unable to walk, I would awake, and my foot would not plant to the ground, the way a foot should, and I just could not tell you, I apologize. A mother does what she has to do for her child/children. Yes, I admit it. It was at your expenses, but I had to work. My son, my precious baby, my Tony needed food, clothing, shelter, and everything else that my employment would provide for us. I had to survive, I had to work. When I think about it, I judged you all instead of giving you the chance to work with me. I just assumed that you would not understand my situation. There is one family in particular. I needed to go into another city to look for work, and I needed them to keep my Tony for me for one month. After one month I would relocate us to that city. I decided in my mind that if I dumb myself down, if I make myself into an uneducated, ignorant person, they would feel sorry for me and help me. Now that I think about it, how could I be uneducated, I already had a career.

The ignorant part, yes that could have been me. Even the most educated with a PHD can be ignorant in some form. There is not one human being upon this vast earth that knows everything. If you could ask Mackenzie Scott, Bill Gates, or Mary Barra, Mark Zuckerberg, Jeff Bezos or Tim Cook, I promise they will tell you, no matter the lofty places they hold, they do not know everything.

Now back to what I was saying. No one would hire me in the city that I lived in because of my injury. I decided to look in a city seven hours away. I faxed my resume in, and interviewed by phone. I received five different offers. I waited to give four answers. I needed a couple that I knew through church to keep my Tony for a month. I would save for the month and then relocate us to the new city. I feel so very bad now that I summed them up as arrogant people that would help me because I was not on their level, they would not see me as competition, instead they would see me as an illiterate, an ignorant person worthy of their pity, and was in need of their hand out. That was so very foul of me. I was so very, very wrong.

May I share something with you all from my heart? I believe that an uneducated person, could be the master of his destiny, while someone with a PHD hasn't a clue when it comes to life. Case in point? How many Irish, Caribbean, European, Asian, and Middle Eastern and African parents entered foreign lands without education, without literacy, and yet they are the ones that built nations. Their children became doctors, engineers, inventors, scientists, mathematicians, bankers, and so much more.

Their children are chefs, cooks, sanitation workers. Ask yourself what would we do without cooks and sanitation workers? I rest my case. I pray that we will remember one of this world's life altering sayings; that many of us live by, and hold dear. **"Despise not humble beginnings."** That is a statement that points the way for us all to become better human beings, with the much-needed humble insight into the way we should treat our fellow human beings.

Anyway, I dumb myself down to them, and ask for their help. Truth be told, they would have helped me even if I had not dumbed myself down. My action and judgment of them was purely my own. They agreed to keep Tony for the month. A week later I drove seven hours with my foot down, and it was, --

--------- no words. The **"blood attack"** is what I call it. The foot was destroyed in such a way that the blood path no longer existed. The blood would send a brain freeze, is the best comparison I have, to my brain. It felt like a thousand bees stinging my brain, when my foot was not elevated. It was truly hellish. The blood could not circulate through the path it was used to. Thus, it would send a horrible signal back to my brain in a numbing, painful tingling signal. All I could do was hold my head until it subsided, but while driving the seven hours, I could not, I had to just keep driving, and just make it through the journey. I had to survive the trip for my child.

Believe it or not, I started working the next day. It was horrific. By nine thirty a.m. I kid you not, my foot gave out, and I had to drag it along. Pick it up and put it down. By that Friday I was fired. I had four jobs left. Remember, I never gave them an answer. I started the other and it lasted three days. I had three jobs left. I interviewed and added to the three. They would fire me and I would move on to the next.

Two weeks into being in the new city the couple called me. They said they were not comfortable with me being so far away, and they needed me to come that weekend to get Tony. I drove up that Friday after work to get Tony. The next day Saturday, I drove seven hours back to the new city where we stayed with my retired family member. I rested that Sunday and started a new job that Monday. I thank that couple for giving me those two weeks. Those two weeks' paychecks that I earned; afforded me the ability to relocate us. It was the very help I needed, so that I could earn enough to jump start our lives. Think about it all, that two weeks, and here I am today. Please just start, just try living and allow the rest to materialize. **"Please just try living."**

I Forgive You

For you within society, that judged me and cast my soul into the grave, when in reality I was the precious victim, an innocent child that was desperately in need of help, **"I forgive you."** I had no voice, I had no defense, I had nothing to grasp onto. I was looked upon with pure disdain. I lived in fear of many, I had no strength. I tried my best to go unnoticed. I hoped that you would pass me by, because your attention would inflict pain upon me, I lived in fear of society.

I Survived

I survived all of you. I survived sorrow, tremendous pain and heartache, that cripples the mind and stops the lungs from breathing. You turned me into a mentally broken, suicidal human being, with the desire to die, more than to live. You gave me shame, fear, weakness, and horror. I was innocent and yet judged as guilty. The life that I was meant to have was taken from me. I was laughed at, scorned, and despised. Nevertheless, **"This person, once broken in heart and mind, has survived."** The sorrowful now laughs, and the fearful now lives in strength and hope. Whether we are poor in love, poor in finances, poor in family, or in friends, precious soul, if you are poor in health, or in any other circumstances, please be encouraged, and please know that your wealth will find you. No matter the distance traveled, the twists and turns along the way, please rest assured, your blessings, your positive change will find you.

Do not cast your precious soul into the grave I beg of you. Please allow your destiny to find you alive. Do not allow your blessings to show up, and your soul has entered the grave. Do not allow your providence to arrive, and all that is left of you is your ashes.

Embrace the burden of continuity for your life. That way no matter how difficult the path you travel, you will be resolute, in the fact that your life must continue on, no matter how difficult the journey. Call on your undiscovered inner strength for the journey; and commit to the fact that; your blessings, your providence will find you, and not just any you, NO; your blessings, your providence must find the authentic you, the real you, when it arrives.

Do not allow people places and things to erase the authentic you. Do not allow you to erase the genuine you, NO, fight to hold on to the kind and gentle you, the merciful you, the understanding you. Even in our kill or be killed fight, once the battle is over, we must come to the surface, allow the sunlight to shine bright on us, and we must find our peace and we must live. Yes, your blessings will find you. Yes, your destiny, your providence will find you; the heavens have the patience to outlast the earth. **Do not quit, please live.**

To my mother, Miss Yvonne Wilson-Isaacs

I love you mom and I thank you, I am grateful to you. I thank you for believing in the works of my hands. I thank you for believing in my gifts and my talents. Again, I thank you, and I am forever grateful to you. Our relationship has not always been easy, this I readily admit. Nevertheless, it has survived. We have survived the tumult of it all and I am beyond grateful. Having a daughter that lets no one in, and does not have the ability to draw close to others, could not have been easy for you. That wall in my brain, that blocks everyone out, had no ability to differentiate between you my mom, my sister, or the stranger. It just blocked everyone out. Please forgive me. I believe it was a survival mechanism that kicked in, to save my life. To stay alive, I had to let go. I had to leave everything and everyone behind except Tony. Other than Tony, something inside my brain broke the connection between me and others, and that could not have been easy for you.

Miss Yvonne Wilson-Isaacs, please know that you are forever in my heart, I love you. Your children, grandchildren, and your great grandchildren adores you. Your strong work ethics is an example for us all. I inherited it, and so did my son. Generations have followed in your work ethics, and your determination in life. You have set the bar very high for us mom, and we readily admit it. Please give up the weight of the world to your younger bloodline, we will gladly carry its weight for you. Please rest and enjoy your retirement, you mom has earned it. I love you mom.

• • •

To my daughter, Natashia Lawrence

Natashia, you became my precious daughter, when you became Tony's wife. I have never considered you my daughter-in-law, you Natashia are simply my daughter. The value you have brought to our family is so very precious. You are the quiet fixer. Perhaps it is the occupational traits of you being a Human Resource Generalists. You are always seeking out solutions in life, and that is so very special.

I thank you my daughter, I am beyond grateful for how you love Tony. Your care towards him means so very much to me, and I thank you.

You stepping in when you did when it comes to this book was impeccable timing. I was tired, I was so very tired and disappointed with others, and their lackluster attitude towards suicide prevention. The, "just quit," the, "just walk away no one cares," voice was loud. Eight long years in the fight, and watching people die by suicide during these years, have taken its toll. But then you called out of nowhere to talk with me about the book. You stepped in and brought me back to my work and I am so very grateful.

The last-minute final touches were made possible by you, and I thank you my daughter. You Natashia Lawrence, you are a precious gem, and I love you. You enrich the lives of the people you come in contact with, and it is beyond admirable. Some cultures believe we have many lives. My daughter the "FIXER" was a Mafioso in her past life, (smile).

My son, my little baby Tony, that is towards his forties. Mr. Keith Anthony Lawrence; no matter your age, you will always be my little baby Tony.

You are a grown man, a husband and a father. The memory of your first steps you took outside. You were wonderfully happy, running amongst the leaves on the ground. Son, it is as if it happened today, I love you my precious son. To my son, Keith Anthony Lawrence, fondly known as Tony. You Sir are the iron that sharpens the iron. I am beyond proud of you. My son. I was tough on you. I raised you within a disciplined environment. There were times when I knew you were offended that I would make you pull up your shirt, so that I could make certain your pants was on your waist, and not down on your butt. I stood close enough to you to make certain that you had on deodorant, that your perspiration did not smell.

I now realized you must have hated it. My checking your room to make certain it was clean, and asking about your phone calls if I felt they were too long. My harassing you to make certain you floss, that your oral hygiene was good. Yes, I know, I was annoying and I was tough on you, but I had to be. Society would not do to you, what they did to me. I had to ensure you could stand shoulder to shoulder or higher, but certainly not lower. Society would not eat you alive, the way it ate me alive. Thank you, my precious son; you were receptive to my instructions, even if at times, it was grudgingly. You listened, you understood, and you lived out my instructions, to the betterment of your life. You, son, bore the burden of the abuse that society inflicted upon me. Yes, I did my best to shield you, but I was not able to shield you from it all.

You have grown into a GOD fearing, productive member of society, and my son, I am beyond proud of you. Your desire to be a great husband, father, and citizen is evident, and my Tony, I bless you. Your faith in, and your tremendous love for GOD is your foundation, and I see it within you. Your respect towards, and your care that you give to others, is admired son. Your exemplary work ethics are known to those who know you. Keith A. Lawrence, my Tony, I am beyond proud of you. Your love for GOD is your beacon of light, and it goes before you, and it reveals you to others. My son, I love you, I encourage you, and I am proud of you.

On the day of your birth in the month of September, before you were born, I cried out to GOD for help. I had no one else, I understood nothing else, but I knew and understood GOD. You more than most, know the story my son. I fell in love with GOD in the first grade. The neighborhood church van picked us up and took us to a crusade, and there I heard the word and fell hard for GOD at seven tender years old. My son you are now close to forty. The seven-year-old passed on her love for GOD to you son, and you have already passed it on-to your son.

Never forget my son, I gave you to GOD. I made an agreement with GOD on our behalf. If HE allowed us both safe passage through childbirth, I would give you to HIM. I would take care of you for as long as HE allowed. But you will always be HIS. You, my son, are set apart. You belong to GOD, and you must never forget it.

To Every Soul that has Been There for my Tony

In reality, you have been there for me, and I thank you, Sir or Madam. I am beyond, I am so very, very, very beyond grateful to you, and Sir or Madam, I thank you. To Mr. Richard Gordon, Tony's business partner, Sir I bless you and yours. I thank you for trusting the business partnership between you and my precious son. You Mr. Gordon are beyond appreciated; and Sir, again I thank you.

To "<u>EVERYONE</u>" that has my son's products in your stores. Sedanos, Broward Meat, Bravo Supermarket, Key Foods, Dutch Pot, Presidente, Elegant Beauty, and all the additional businesses, you have done this mother's heart good. I bless each and every one of you, and again I thank you, I thank you, Sirs and or Madams, I thank you, I am beyond grateful.

I pray that my son will never disappoint you, and that his products will help to enhance your business. I pray that the blessings that flow from my Tony, will flow to every one of you also. Please know that this mother will forever appreciate you all, and again I thank you and I bless you.

To the dragon lady, **The Dragon Signifies Royalty.** I will not say your name; some things do not need to be spoken. You take special care of my Tony; you purchase in large quantities; which makes a positive financial difference for his business. Madam I thank you so very, very much, I am beyond grateful.

I thank you stranger, wherever you are now, you are forever in my heart

I was employed with a dental practice and they had multiple offices. This was about a year and a half into my injury. I worked between the main dental practice and the satellite office. I would be the only person there, and so everything to do with the patients and the front office was on me at the satellite office. I had to answer phone calls, check in and check out the patients; I scheduled appointments for patients that called in to the office, and for patients in front of me within the office also.

I had to confirm appointments, and fill appointments that had been cancelled, and pull future appointments charts for multiple days. I had to put together the patient treatment plans, and financial arrangements also. On one particular day, once I was done for the day, I headed over to the main office. They had called and instructed me to do so; the main office had late hours. The work I did at the satellite office was a day's work. Which means my foot was done for the day. I had nothing left, the pain and swelling, sigh.

Once I returned to the main office, I was told I had to pull charts for I believe it was five days. It was horrific. This meant being on my foot for additional hours. There were multiple dentist's patient's charts that I needed to pull. The type of pain I was feeling after already putting in a day's work at the satellite office was excruciating. It was so bad that it was ricocheting from one limb to the other. The referred pain I felt was beyond, beyond, beyond brutal. My brain felt numb, my chest felt tight, and my foot had stopped working. My mind came apart after I was told to pull the charts. I went next door to an empty space; I was completely overcome with bitterness and sorrow, while being in excruciating pain.

I dared not complain, complaints were already being filed against me. When I walked away, I passed the manager's office, and they were already complaining because I took the break. Remember, all day at the satellite office. As I mentioned before, the head office stayed open later. I sat down inside that empty room, while the pain was so intense that my heart quivered. I knew I had to quit, but I was behind on my rent. I needed to work; but I was finished. My intention was to walk over to the manager's office and quit on the spot, without giving any notice.

Just then a dentist came over to me, and I promise you, it is as if he knew my secret; that I had a horrific injury, and that I was crashing fast. It is as if that man saw into my soul, and saw the dark billowing sorrow that was there. He just started encouraging me for no reason. I did not know him, he worked in another area, I had never spoken to him before. This man spoke life into me like you would not believe it. He sat there with me and just encouraged me for no reason, other than being a humane person that cared for this stranger. Once he was done encouraging me, he just went about his evening. I went back to work, I grabbed a chair and sat down next to the files. The patient folders that I could reach while sitting down I worked on first. I moved the chair right or left as needed and worked on the charts. Then I took my time to get to the higher charts. His kind words helped me to pay off my back rent and surged ahead. That stranger took time out of his day to encourage me; to breathe life back into me and please hear me when I say, "I am forever grateful."

Those kind words paid my rent, and pushed me ahead where I was able to pay my future rent early. What do I mean when I say his words paid my rent? His precious words of encouragement kept me from quitting. The moment that gentleman spoke those kind words into my soul, those words encouraged me and kept me from quitting, which would have caused a break in my income; and caused me to fall further behind on my rent and other bills.

His kind words kept me on the job, which gave me the ability to catch up on my rent, and to also pay my future rent early. This human being went on about his life never knowing what he had done, but you mark my words when I say, "I will never forget him." Had I quit, I was hurting so bad, and I was so very broken and discouraged in heart, that this was one time when I knew I would not have just moved on-to another job. I had no strength; I needed a lift and there was no one that knew this. I was suffering in silence. That is until that one gentleman, that one person sat down beside me, with respectful space between us, and encouraged my heart and mind, and then went on with his life.

He was a pediatric dentist and I knew him as Dr. Bezos. This man threw me a lifeline like you would not believe it, and it is my hope, my intention to throw you a lifeline also. He did it for me, and I am doing it for you also. Please accept my words of encouragement, I beg you. Please allow my words of encouragement to help you to get back into the fight. This is the cycle of life when it comes to the noble act of us doing our part for our fellow human beings. We receive kindness from others, and we hold it so very dear to our hearts, and some of us pass it on-to others. As we have received, we also give.

When my accident happened, I was betrayed, and I was humiliated. My insurance company abandoned me. Said my car payment went to renters' insurance. I had to move into a filthy dilapidated mobile home, without the ability to help myself and my precious child. In spite of the betrayal of humanity, humanity was also there for me. I was able to stay in a church sister's home for two weeks, and I will be forever grateful. A neighbor in the apartment complex where we had just left, knew Tony. Her nephew and Tony were friends. That young lady rallied for me. It was through her that I found the mobile home.

Yes, roach infested, but it was affordable, and was a roof over our heads. My check was two hundred and seventy-five dollars monthly; my rent was only two hundred dollars. The mobile home had sat empty for years, which is why the roaches felt they had first dibs on it. She spoke with the owner of the mobile home, and the owner agreed to help me. She was taking her nephew to Disney World, and she took Tony also. Do you have any idea what that meant to me? In the middle of this horrific injury, my Tony was able to go to Disney World. He called me from there on her phone, and told me he was going to visit Shaq to say hi. That made me laugh so hard after he hung up the phone. Shaquille O'Neal's home was in Orlando, at that time. To his young mind, he could just go say hello to Shaquille O'Neal, his favorite basketball player. That was so funny to me. **That was a southern, "bless his heart moment."** I am still smiling now thinking about it.

She would pick Tony up so that he could hang out with them. She would bring us food. I could not use the kitchen until I had evicted the roaches. The judge gave them until I ran out of raid spray to leave. She would bring sandwiches. This meant I did not have to be on my foot cooking. She checked in on us. When I set off foggers to get rid of the roaches, we would stay with her. I will never forget her precious, selfless kindness, how could I? She probably thinks that I have forgotten about her, but she is mistaken. I make certain to look for her information, and I save her information every few years. She was in college at the time, now she is employed as an elementary school principal. When I sell my book, I will go back and bless her with a financial gift, in a very special way. Her first name was Lashawn. I am grateful.

My orthopedic surgeon, he was so very young at the time, for his incredible accomplishment on that day.

He had never treated such a horrific injury before. That man fought for me, "dear GOD I pray, I pray, I pray, I pray to GOD, please allow me to go back and pay what the insurance company did not pay, and what I could not pay."

He was the orthopedic doctor with the gap in his anterior. Dr. Edward. D. Y., Sir I will never forget you, and I thank you. To the entire team that did my first surgery, my radiologist, he was an older man, an immigrant from Poland, I still remember you.

A few weeks later, the anesthesiologist at my second surgery. He said, "O my GOD, your foot is still there!" I then asked him, "was it as bad as I thought it was?" He in turn answered, "it was ten times worse than anything you could think of."

The doctor, that team on that day, could have taken off my foot, but they honored my request to not remove it. To instead allow it to die on me, before amputation takes place.

They dug in, and, _____, no words. That incredible team of doctors, and nurses, worked hard to saved my foot. I honor and acknowledge their precious gifts and their talents, the incredible work of their hands, and their hearts. Their hard work and their dedication to my wellbeing, to my recovery, to GOD be the glory; and to them all I say, "I acknowledge you, I thank you, I will never forget you, I am forever grateful. May the flames of the gratitude that I feel, towards the heaven and the earth, never stop burning bright; may the fire grow hotter and hotter within me. I thank you all, I am forever grateful to all of you.

My final words to you

You who are hurting, and you are now experiencing extreme mental stress, mental breakdowns, or you are now suffering from suicidal thoughts and tendencies.

Please accept these words inside this book as my way of giving back; my way of saying thank you, to all those who showed mercy to my son and I. These words to you that are written inside this book, are sincere. These words to you are filled with love, mercy and understanding. This book is filled with words of encouragement. This complete book, each chapter, except for the agency and the government information and biography, and website information; all else are my sincere words from my heart. These words are inspired, by my precious tender love, and an abundance of care that I feel towards you.

They are being given to you with much sincerity of heart and mind, with the intention of encouraging your precious heart and mind, and to save your oh so very precious, precious, precious life. My life was restored back to me, and it is my hope that springs eternal, that your life will be restored back to you also. Please precious soul that you are, **"please make your way to the mountaintop." Many of us have made it here and are waiting for you. This will be your place of peace, your place of redemption, your place of incredible joy and wonderful rest.**

Claw your way to the top of the mountain, precious you. Please fight your way there. Yes, your strength is gone, I get it. Please do not doubt me, I completely without a doubt, understand what you are going through. Yes, repeated words, same meaning. That precious is my way of emphasizing to you that I one hundred percent understand your pain and heartache.

Take your time, go slow, stop and rest, but precious, **"you must not, you cannot give up."** In spite of the kick in your gut, the abuse, the sorrow; in spite of them casting your soul into the grave, precious, **"you must live."** You have distance to travel, and victories that will be won by you. You have some failures and wonderful accomplishments up ahead. Precious you I love you, and precious soul that you are, and always will be, I beg of you, please precious I implore you; I admonish you, and I encourage you, **"Please Live."**

Please head to the mountaintop and join us. We who were turned into ashes; we have now been risen from those very same ashes; like the mythology bird the Phoenix. Please arise from your ashes of pain and sorrow. Please rise from your ashes of heartache and unrelenting pain. Please arise from your ashes of disappointments. I say to you now, "Arise from your ashes of addiction, rise from your ashes of the loss of your loved ones. Arise from the ashes of lack, rise from the ashes of sickness, and crawl your way to your mountaintop of change."

Make your way to your mountaintop of rest, your mountaintop of peace, of joy, and of change. find redemption and live. I say to you now, **"GET UP!"** Face the sun and live again, and again, and again, I implore you. We who were once weak, broken, discarded, wounded and beaten, and cursed at, are waiting here for you; and are cheering you on, while you are traveling to your destination of redemption.

A very long closing statement, yes, I know; I need to make certain there are no words needed, that have gone unspoken. This is my last chance to reach you.

Your faith, "what you believe in." Your fate, "who you are destined to be," is the very essence of who you are. Do not allow ignoble human beings to rob you of your faith, and your fate. Head to the top of the mountain, and claim every bit of who you are, who you are truly meant to be, the authentic you.

Claw back what was taken from you; believe for your precious existence, and for the gifts and the talents that are within you, and yet to be released. Yes, they will block you, yes, they will sneer at you, yes, yes, and yes; they will jeer at you, with the hope that you will quit. But I say to you, you Sir or Madam, you young lady or young man, you will ascend to your mountaintop, **"AND YOU WILL WIN."**

Stay alive! And keep on breathing; keep the oxygen flowing inside your lungs. Live, laugh, and smile. Breathe in, and breathe out, and cry, and cry and cry some more and live. Please allow yourself to recover. Allow the future healthy you to come alive within you. Allow the unforeseen to come alive within you. Please allow the new you to find his or her way to the surface. Please allow the ebb and flow of who you are to manifest itself. The greatness of you will enter in, and the broken you will exit out, and will flow away. Please allow yourself to believe that, that which seemed impossible is now possible. believe that you too will get to the top of the mountain, and you also will find safety, peace, joy and precious rest.

The desperation, the urgency that I feel is profound, in trying to save your precious life. "NFL Phrase," did I leave it all on the field? Is there something else that I need to say to you? Your precious life is on the line, what else do I need to say to you? Yes, there is something else that I need to say to you before I go. I need to tell you that although your life was rerouted, and much has been lost, precious you, you will certainly find you all over again, and your life will be restored back to you. Do not give up on your life, I beg of you, I implore you, and I admonish you.

I lost it all and survived; I lived, and you will also.

"PLEASE PRECIOUS YOU, PLEASE LIVE."

Yes, it does feel and seem as if all is lost. Yes, it is as if your entire life has been wiped out, and all hope is gone. But please hear me, please see me, please listen to me when I say to you; <u>"no matter your age, and no matter your status in life, and in spite of your horrific circumstances, you absolutely can, and will survive this devastating season in life, and your opportunity to rebuild, will come."</u> I too have lost much in life, I too faced the mountain, and I too have had to fight and crawl my way back to the top, and I survived the journey, and you will also. **"Please do not give up."**

Although I was alive, I had already died a thousand deaths. My hope had died, my trust in humanity had died. The road I was meant to travel had died, and the person I was to become had died. The incredible human being that I was to mature into, in my teens, my twenties and thirties had died. The respect I was to receive from others died. My good mental health died. My happiness was no more. My financial possibilities dead. My providence gone. My precious future, dead. The husband I was meant to marry, gone. The friends I was meant to have, gone, and replaced with ignoble human beings, that would pretend to care about me, while behind my back they were helping to burn my life to the ground, and push me closer to the grave. The home I was meant to live in, no more. The desired education, the career that I wanted, Mass Communication, UNESCO had died.

My laughter died, my joy was no more, my gifts and my talents, the work of my hands had died, before they came to fruition. Every road I was meant to travel was now gone. My peace died. My sleep died. A teenager not even on the earth for two decades, and insomnia was my best friend that was to haunt me for years to come. My confidence died. My ability to fight back, dead. My victories, died. My voice, gone. Every bit of me destroyed while they with arrogance, did nothing; except ushered me to the grave, while being filled with malice, self-righteousness, and pure unadulterated traitorous hypocrisy. I died a thousand deaths, while they all looked on, and did nothing; except hasten my precious soul to the grave.

Then the heavens said, "Not So, You Must Live." And incredibly, to the dismay of those who cast my soul into the grave, "I LIVED." And you also "Must Live." Every one of you that are going through these seasons of sorrow, of devastation please listen to me, "The burden of continuity is heavy, yes, I agree, but it is very rewarding also.

You must ascend that mountain that is before you. Assail that mountain as if it were your enemy. Throw everything at it, and then some; in your bid to stay alive; and to make it to the top of your mountain. In your bid to claw back, to get back everything that was stolen from you. In your bid to restore your mental health, or to come back from your mental breakdown, please fight! Please crawl your way to the top of your mountain, all is not lost, your redemption will come. Please do not give up, you precious soul that you are, **"YOU MUST LIVE."**

Please survive your journey! You must improvise and overcome, and someday tell others of your journey, and how you overcame it all. Tell them how you survived, and how you lived through it all.

Do not give in to the depression that tries to keep you as a prisoner in the dark. Do not give in to the mental stress that is causing you to react, by you making irrational decisions. You have nothing to be ashamed of, please get the help that you are in need of. Do not give in to the suicidal thoughts and tendencies that haunts you, and are using the violence of your very own hands, to put you into the grave.

I now say to you, "Precious, precious, precious soul that you are, you must survive, you must live." And incredibly, to the dismay of everyone that had cast your precious souls into the grave, I now say to them all, **"he lived, she lived, they lived."** Yes, they all survived the grave that their enemy dug for them. While their enemy was busy digging their graves; while the enemy hastened their soul to the grave; they were repeating over, and over, and over again,

"I AM GOING TO LIVE; I AM GOING TO LIVE; I AM GOING TO LIVE."

Yes, precious you that are reading this book right now, please say it with me; "No matter the pain, and no matter the horrific heartache, and no matter the utter devastation that I am experiencing in my life; I will not commit suicide. And I will not kill others because of what others have done to me. I will not cast my precious soul into the grave. Instead, I will dig in, and I will rebuild my life, one brick at a time; and I will survive this very, very, very difficult season in my life.

"I AM GOING TO LIVE."

Please say it with me; "It does not matter the devastation, I will do everything in my power including asking for help, running towards help, and begging for help, to keep my soul upon this earth, to make sure I stay alive. My journey, my story is still being written."

"I AM GOING TO LIVE"

"I will use the Suicide & Crisis Lifeline at 988, and I will press (1), or text to 838255, Or I will use the **Crisis Text Line at 741741,** or I will go to the **website at 988lifeline.org.** I will use the options that are available to seek treatment, because I want to stay alive."

"I AM GOING TO LIVE."

Please everyone, never forget that, humanities mercy given, is humanities mercy received, and is the same exact precious mercy within humanity, that is continually passed on by the receivers

Translation? The mercy given to humanity, is mercy received by humanity; and humanity that received that mercy in gratitude, will ensure that this cycle never breaks, by giving back to humanity.

LORD, please I pray, please let the words within this book soar high into the sky. Please let these words swim oceans, and walk throughout valleys. Please cause these words inside this book to travel amongst men and women, and live within their hearts and their minds throughout nations I pray. Please allow nations to embrace these words and invite them over for breakfast, for tea, for lunch, and for brunch and dinner, and for supper I pray. Please allow these precious words to receive invitations from schools, from boardrooms, corporations, unions, and governments, and all others. I pray O GOD. Please allow these words to be invited on vacations, to gatherings and all else.

I pray O GOD; please cause these words to live with children, teens, young adults, adults and seniors alike throughout their journey I pray. Please allow these words from this book, to comfort hearts and minds long after I am no more. Please give these words life I pray, and I thank YOU O GOD. I am grateful, the gratitude I feel towards YOU Most High GOD, is forever cemented in my heart, **i THANK YOU.**

My readers, please give me a smile before
I go.

There is no bigger "I blame YOU" than
GOD. We lie; we blame GOD. We steal;
we blame GOD. We cheat on our wife or
our husband; that's right, it was GOD.

Others harm us, we blame GOD.
It does not matter the perpetrator, we
blame GOD.

We are quick to say,
"GOD DID IT."

"The bank was just robbed. Officer, I am
telling you, I saw HIS getaway car with
wings on it after the bank robbery. I saw
HIS personalized vanity license plate, and
it said,"

"Heaven Is My Home."

"Yes, yes, yes, and yes some more, I
am telling you, I am certain of it,"

"IT WAS GOD, GOD DID IT"

Distributed by: Living Abundantly Inc.

P.O. Box 9438
Coral Springs, FL 33065

Copyright© 2018
All Rights Reserved

ISBN: 978-0-9968965-3-5

Website:
www.TheVJCGROUP.com

E-Mail
VJC@THEVJCGROUP.com

Copyright Agreement:

By having anything to do with this book and or its program, you are agreeing to all rules and or regulations, in keeping with all copyright laws, that is both here and abroad, that is protecting this book and its Suicide Prevention materials used within its program.

You are agreeing to copyright protection formats, in writing, in copying, in recording or verbally speaking, in artificial intelligence also. You are agreeing to non-transference through all social media formats; phone, e-mail, or online mode of transfer, copying, duplicating, publishing, this information or material, that is owned by the author, without their approval or signed release.

Victoria J. Colma

HUMANITY I SAY TO YOU, "YOU MUST LIVE"

"PLEASE I BEG OF YOU" "PRECIOUS SOUL THAT YOU ARE" "PLEASE LIVE"

LORD, I pray, O GOD I pray, please LORD I pray, please let it never be said when I die, "She served no purpose upon the earth."

I know very well that; this book is a very, very small pebble, that is being thrown into the great oceans of the world. Nevertheless, it is my hope, it is my desire that; I will create a great magnificent wave of change, in love, in compassion, in hope, and in understanding and patience for humanity. Please survive, and never, ever, ever stop saying,

"I Am Going to Live." "Please I beg of You, "Please Live."

Made in United States
Cleveland, OH
25 August 2025